THE TAPESTRY OF EARLY CHRISTIAN DISCOURSE

In this original study, Vernon K. Robbins expounds and develops his system of socio-rhetorical criticism, bringing together social-scientific and literary-critical approaches to explore early Christianity. Denying that there is only one valid way of interpretation, this book investigates Christianity as a cultural phenomenon, and treats its canonical texts as ideological constructs.

The Tapestry of Early Christian Discourse first establishes a concept of culture and then combines it with Geertz's anthropological concept of 'thick description'. Subsequently, it explores the relation of texts to society and culture. In this manner, the approach uses multiple methods of interpretation in an organized and programmatic way, allowing the reader distinctly new insights into the development of early Christianity.

Robbins' approach opens new doors not only for students of the Bible, but also for those interested in new theories and applications of textual interpretation.·

Vernon K. Robbins is Professor of Religion at the Department and Graduate Division of Religion, Emory University. He has published widely in the field of biblical interpretation. Among his works are *Jesus the Teacher: A Socio-Rhetorical Interpretation of Mark* (1984) and *New Boundaries in Old Territory* (1994).

THE TAPESTRY OF EARLY CHRISTIAN DISCOURSE

Rhetoric, society and ideology

Vernon K. Robbins

London and New York

First published 1996
by Routledge
11 New Fetter Lane, London EC4P 4EE

Simultaneously published in the USA and Canada
by Routledge
a division of Routledge, Chapman and Hall, Inc.
29 West 35th Street, New York, NY 10001

Routledge is an International Thomson Publishing Company

© 1996 Vernon K. Robbins

Typeset in Garamond by BC Typesetting, Bristol

Printed and bound in Great Britain by
Mackays of Chatham PLC, Chatham, Kent

British Library Cataloguing in Publication Data
A catalogue record for this book is available from the British Library

Library of Congress Cataloging in Publication Data
Robbins, Vernon K. (Vernon Kay), 1939–
    The tapestry of early Christian discourse: rhetoric, society, and
ideology/Vernon K. Robbins.
        p.   cm.
    Includes bibliographical references and index.
    ISBN 0-415-13997-X (hb.) – ISBN 0-415-13998-8 (pbk.)
        1. Bible. N.T.–Socio-rhetorical criticism.   2. Bible. N.T.
Corinthians, 1st, IX–Criticism, interpretation, etc.   I. Title.
BS2380.R63 1996   95-42837
225.6–dc20   CIP

ISBN 0-415-13997-X
0-415-13998-8 (pbk.)

To Deanna
My special partner and friend
from the conception and birth of this approach
through its growth to maturity

CONTENTS

List of illustrations   ix
List of abbreviations   x
Preface   xi

1 THE CHALLENGE OF SOCIO-RHETORICAL
  CRITICISM   1
  The relation of Christianity to culture   4
  The relation of texts to society, culture and history   6
  The relation of New Testament interpretation to theology   10
  *The relation of disciplinary methods to an interpretive
  analytics*   11
  Conclusion   13

2 REDRAWING THE BOUNDARIES WITH
  SOCIO-RHETORICAL CRITICISM   18
  The interpreter's location and ideology   24
  Inner texture   27
  Intertexture   30
  Social and cultural texture   33
  Ideological texture   36
  Conclusion   40

3 INNER TEXTURE: EVERY READING HAS
  A SUBTEXT   44
  Repetitive–progressive texture   46
  Opening–middle–closing texture   50
  Narrational texture   53
  Argumentative texture   58
  Sensory–aesthetic texture   64

CONTENTS

Inner texture in 1 Corinthians 9   65
Conclusion   91

4   INTERTEXTURE: EVERY COMPARISON
    HAS BOUNDARIES   96
Intertexture in socio-rhetorical criticism   96
Oral–scribal intertexture   97
Cultural intertexure   108
Social intertexture   115
Historical intertexture   118
Intertexture in 1 Corinthians 9   120
Conclusion   143

5   SOCIAL AND CULTURAL TEXTURE:
    EVERY MEANING HAS A CONTEXT   144
Specific social topics in religious literature   147
Common social and cultural topics   159
Final cultural categories   167
Summary   174
Social and cultural texture in 1 Corinthians 9   176
Conclusion   189

6   IDEOLOGICAL TEXTURE: EVERY THEOLOGY
    HAS A POLITICS   192
Ideology in texts   193
Ideology in authoritative traditions of interpretation   200
Ideology in intellectual discourse   207
Ideology in individuals and groups   215
Ideological texture in 1 Corinthians 9   220
Conclusion   235

7   THE PROMISE OF SOCIO-RHETORICAL
    CRITICISM   237
Multiple textures in texts   238
Rewriting the historiography of first-century Christianity   240
Socio-rhetorical criticism and other fields of study   243

Bibliography   245
Index of scriptures and ancient texts   266
Index of modern authors   271
Index of subjects   274

LIST OF ILLUSTRATIONS

FIGURES

2.1	Socio-rhetorical model of textual communication	21
2.2	Inner texture	29
2.3	Intertexture	31
2.4	Social and cultural texture	35
2.5	Ideological texture	37

TABLES

3.1	Narrative agents in Luke 1.26–56	49
3.2	Repetition of personal pronouns in 1 Corinthians 9	68
3.3	Conjunctions and 'have the right to'	70

LIST OF
ABBREVIATIONS

BETL	*Bibliotheca ephemeridum theologicarum lovaniensium*
Bib	*Biblica*
BTB	*Biblical Theology Bulletin*
CBQ	*Catholic Biblical Quarterly*
HTR	*Harvard Theological Review*
Int	*Interpretation*
JAAR	*Journal of the American Academy of Religion*
JBL	*Journal of Biblical Literature*
JSNT	*Journal for the Society of the New Testament*
JSOT	*Journal for the Society of the Old Testament*
LXX	*Septuagint Greek Bible*
MT	*Masoretic Hebrew Bible*
Neot	*Neotestamentica*
NovT	*Novum Testamentum*
NTS	*New Testament Studies*
RelSRev	*Religious Studies Review*
RevExp	*Review and Expositor*
Rhet. ad Alex.	*Rhetorica ad Alexandrum*
SBL	*Society of Biblical Literature*
SBLDS	Society of Biblical Literature Dissertation Series
SBLSP	*Society of Biblical Literature Seminar Papers*
SCHNT	Studia ad corpus hellenisticum novi testamenti
SNTS	*Society for New Testament Studies*
SNTSMS	Society for New Testament Monograph Series

PREFACE

This volume is the result of the enthusiasm, diligence, trust and encouragement of many people. My remarks will fail, without doubt, to mention some who made substantial contributions to the development of the socio-rhetorical approach in it. To the students in the College, the Graduate Division of Religion, and the Institute for the Liberal Arts at Emory University who wrote socio-rhetorical papers of various kinds during the past decade, I express my deep gratitude. Special mention is due to Wesley H. Wachob and Russell B. Sisson, who wrote programmatic socio-rhetorical dissertations under my guidance. Their courage, persistence and insight have made substantive contributions to the approach. The faculty of the Department of Religion, with special mention of our Chair Paul Courtright, have been exceptionally supportive, and my colleagues in the New Testament Department of the Graduate Division of Religion have been essential conversation partners in the formulation of this project. The energetic support of John G. Cook during two years of post-doctoral work with me was a special gift at an important time, and the enthusiasm and insights of David B. Gowler have contributed in special ways to the volume. Support through the years from Dr Tore Meistad and Roald Kristiansen of Finnmark College, Alta Norway, have been significant as well.

To Robert Detweiler, with whom I co-taught three Ph.D. seminars before his tragic strokes, I owe a debt that can never be repaid. Many of the broader reaches into literary theory come from our work together in this context. Special thanks to John Gager, Jeff Stout, Lorraine Fuhrman, and other faculty and staff of the Department of Religion at Princeton University for an invigorating year as Visiting Research Professor during 1993–4. Their support in many ways, including e-mail and the remarkable resources of the Harvey

S. Firestone and Speer Libraries, have brought many additional features to this volume. Mutual gratitude goes to Dean David F. Bright and Emory College for providing a research leave to write this book.

In addition, heartfelt gratitude goes to international colleagues and their families who opened their homes and institutions for lectures, seminars and discussions that contributed centrally to this volume. The first series occurred during Fall 1993. The opportunity to deliver the Exegetiska dagen New Testament lecture at Uppsala University, Sweden, in September 1993, with the kind invitation and hosting of Professor René Kieffer and Dr Tord Fordberg, created a special context for development of the cultural analysis. Professor Peder Borgen and Dagfinn Rian hosted a twenty-year reunion at the University of Trondheim, Norway, that provided a stimulating seminar and an opportunity to lecture on the intertextual analysis. Professor Petr Pokorny sponsored a lecture and seminar at the Biblical Institute of Charles University in Prague, and Professor Zdenek Sazava offered special hospitality. Professor Birger Olsson and Dr Walter Übelacker hosted a special lecture and seminar at Lund University.

The second series of international lectures occurred during Spring 1994, with seminars and discussions at the University of Glasgow hosted by Professors John Riches and David Jasper, and Dr Joel Marcus, and at the University of Edinburgh hosted by Professor John O'Neill. Professor Sjef Van Tilborg sponsored a lecture and seminar at the University of Nijmegen and Heerlen, Netherlands, and Bas Van Iersel offered special hospitality and discussion. Professor H. J. de Jonge, Rijks University at Leiden, generously hosted a lecture for the department of New Testament and Early Jewish Studies of the Netherlands Network for Advanced Studies in Theology at the University of Utrecht. Since a significant number of issues were unresolved when I began to write in the Fall of 1993, patterns of issues that emerged in discussions at these institutions had a profound effect on the final manuscript.

My thanks to members of the Context Group, who have welcomed me and watched the development of socio-rhetorical interpretation with interest. Special gratitude to Thomas Olbricht for his sponsorship of international conferences on rhetorical interpretation of the Bible at Heidelberg in 1992 and London in 1995. His graciousness and insight in the planning of these conferences has contributed decisively to my own development of rhetorical analysis and the opportunity to meet and work with others engaged in similar analysis. I am grateful to the Steering Committee of the Society of Biblical Literature Rhetoric and the New Testament Section during the last six years, and to all who have contributed by reading papers and attending the sessions. I express my gratitude to Sarah Melcher for her work on the indexes. Deanna, the one to whom I dedicate this volume, I thank for her love, care and continual encouragement.

Vernon K. Robbins
Emory University
April 1996

1

THE CHALLENGE OF SOCIO-RHETORICAL CRITICISM

The appearance of the New Hermeneutic during the 1960s was simply the beginning of a succession of challenges for biblical studies during the last half of this century. Liberation theology, feminist criticism and African-American interpretation have followed on its heels with exceptional vitality and persistence. In the midst of these vigorous movements, biblical interpreters have been applying new literary, rhetorical, structuralist, linguistic, sociological, materialist and ideological methods to biblical texts (Detweiler and Robbins 1991). It is no surprise that these movements and methods have given rise to an environment fragmented by individual interests and insights rather than an environment unified by issues they have in common with one another. The emergence of so many movements and methods in such a short span of time has produced a scientific revolution in biblical studies, and revolutions are times of disunity rather than widespread co-operation (Kuhn 1970). For both personal and professional reasons, I have viewed this situation as a challenge to integrate major strategies of the new movements and methods through a rhetorical approach that focuses on literary, social, cultural and ideological issues in texts. From my perspective, the issues exhibit the common ground among these movements and methods – namely, a growing perception that texts are performances of language, and language is a part of the inner fabric of society, culture, ideology and religion.

Amos N. Wilder's views have had a profound influence on me as I have analyzed these issues and brought strategies together for an integrated mode of analysis and interpretation of texts. Already in 1955, Wilder presented an embryonic form of my approach in his presidential address to the Society of Biblical Literature. In his address entitled 'Scholars, Theologians, and Ancient Rhetoric', he discussed the nature of religious symbol and symbolic discourse, referred to New Testament eschatology as 'a tremendous expression of the religious imagination, an extraordinary rhetoric of faith', and encouraged the use of insights from the fields of cultural anthropology and folklore to interpret biblical literature (1956: 1–3).

It has taken nearly forty years for systematic strategies of analysis and interpretation to emerge that can reach the goal envisioned by Wilder's address. His focus on both ancient rhetoric and symbolic discourse was a way of merging the project of proponents of the *Religionsgeschichtliche Schule* (Räisänen 1990: 13–31; Riches 1993: 14–49) with analysis that was grounded in and attentive to the rhetorical, literary and linguistic dimensions of early Christian texts. New Testament texts are, from this perspective, products of a living religion. They contain 'expressions of a common developing religious and cultural heritage' (Boers 1979: 50). Wilder's appeal to cultural anthropology and folklore, therefore, is based on a perception that language itself is a rich and thickly configured historical, social, cultural and ideological phenomenon. The inner workings of language presuppose that words, phrases, clauses and sentences stand in an interactive relation not only with thoughts, convictions, attitudes and values but also with trees, rocks, buildings, people, institutions and events.

During the years since Wilder's address, biblical interpreters have worked diligently to fulfil many of the challenges he set before them. Interpreters have developed many new strategies for exploring the inner nature of New Testament texts and for exhibiting social, cultural and ideological aspects of New Testament discourse. But the years have also brought intense struggle. There is no agreement on an approach that would reach the goals evoked by Wilder's assertions. Some interpreters, it appears, are unsure that such an approach can be scientific; others, perhaps the same ones, question whether such an approach will stay in touch with issues they consider to be central to New Testament interpretation. Nevertheless, there is a growing number of interpreters who are calling for serious dialogue among interpreters who focus on literary and rhetorical phenomena and interpreters who focus on historical, social, cultural, ideological and theological phenomena.

In 1984, I introduced the term 'socio-rhetorical' in *Jesus the Teacher* to describe a set of integrated strategies that would move coherently through inner literary and rhetorical features of the Gospel of Mark into a social and cultural interpretation of its discourse in the context of the Mediterranean world. With the publication of the paperback edition, I introduced a four-arena approach to socio-rhetorical criticism that programmatically addresses inner texture, intertexture, social and cultural texture and ideological texture in exegetical interpretation (1992a: xix–xliv; 1992c; 1994b). This systematic approach asks the interpreter to develop a conscious strategy of reading and rereading a text from different angles. When certain strategies prove to be exceptionally fruitful, the interpreter should programmatically develop them to produce a richly textured and deeply reconfigured interpretation for this moment in time and space in the known inhabited world. The approach in this manuscript is to display a wide range of strategies programmatically with 1 Corinthians 9. Few studies will, and perhaps few should, set a goal of explicitly displaying with any one text the full range of strategies displayed in this manuscript. Focusing programmatically on such an extensive range of strategies runs the risk of burying the text in a morass of theory and method. The purpose for displaying such a wide range of strategies with 1 Corinthians 9 is to give an initial perception of the manner in which a socio-rhetorical approach generates multiple strategies for reading and rereading texts in an integrated environment of interpretation. Since this chapter of Paul's letter to the Corinthians contains such richly textured discourse, it is hoped that the text itself will not only maintain its own prominence in the discussion but will, in the end, begin to give the reader a glimpse of its incredible far-reaching horizons of meaning.

One of the goals of a socio-rhetorical approach is to set specialized areas of analysis in conversation with one another. While this may clarify certain issues, it will continually raise others. The goal is not so much to attain agreement among interpreters as to nurture cooperation in the gathering, analysis and interpretation of data, even among people who disagree with one another. In order to understand what some of these areas and projects might be, it will be helpful to identify some of the places where it has been difficult, if not impossible, for us to reach some mutual understanding during the last quarter of a century.

THE RELATION OF CHRISTIANITY
TO CULTURE

First of all, Wilder's appeal to cultural anthropology implied that New Testament texts have something to do with culture. But it has been, and remains, a highly challenging task to describe the relation of Christianity to culture. H. Richard Niebuhr's classic work *Christ and Culture* articulated important insights for us when it described good Christianity as *against* culture, *above* culture, *paradoxically* related to culture, or as a *transformer* of culture (1951). Yet the underlying implication of this approach is that culture is something bad. Since culture is at least implicitly bad, 'good' Christianity separates from culture – hopefully, as oil separates from water. In our best moments, we have known that this underlying dualism is not entirely true. 'Good' Christianity creates a particular kind of culture with the hope that its adherents will steadfastly choose this mode of conviction, belief, attitude, feeling, action and thought as their 'primary' culture. But what kind of terminology can we use to describe the kinds of culture we would consider to be positive forms of Christianity?

The initial step in activating a cultural analysis of Christianity must be a working definition of 'culture'. From my perspective, culture is 'a system of patterned values, meanings, and beliefs that give cognitive structure to the world, provide a basis for coordinating and controlling human interactions, and constitute a link as the system is transmitted from one generation to the next' (Smelser 1992: 11; based on Berger and Luckmann 1967). Another insight into the nature of culture can be gained from describing it as 'simultaneously a product of and a guide to actors searching for organized categories and interpretations that provide a meaningful experiential link to their rounds of social life' (Smelser 1992: 11; based on Geertz 1973).

Still another angle can be to perceive culture as a system that arises in 'the game of social control, social conflict, and social change' (Smelser 1992: 25). Culture is a product of a human game, and religion is an ingredient of that game. It is most helpful, however, not to use the concept of culture simply as a 'global entity' – a concept that covers all things. Rather, culture has 'discrete parts (values, beliefs, ideologies, preferences)' that can help us to investigate and display a range of different 'cultural' manifestations of Christianity throughout all periods of its existence (Smelser 1992: 24). The particular range represented by New Testament texts can appropriately be referred to as the 'cultures' of 'New Testament Christianity'. The symbiosis and tension among these cultures, in turn, represent the 'culture' of New Testament Christianity as it may be contrasted with the 'culture' of Christianity in other times, places and manifestations.

Fortunately, a number of anthropologists and sociologists have been helping us to find the terminology with which to investigate and describe Christianity as a cultural phenomenon. The work of an anthropologist like Clifford Geertz helps us to understand that some form of Christianity is 'the primary culture' in which many people live (1973). Also, his work helps us to understand the function of 'local cultures' and their relation to national and international cultures (1983). Thus, concerning early Christianity we must ask questions like the following:

(a) What kinds of local cultures did Christianity create during the first century?
(b) What kinds of coalition cultures, groups working together in temporary alliances for limited purposes (Elliott 1993: 127), emerged during first-century Christianity?
(c) What kind of culture is 'New Testament culture', the culture transmitted by canonical New Testament literature? What is it that characterizes 'New Testament Christianity' as a culture in the midst of other cultures?

In addition, the work of the Norwegian anthropologist Fredrik Barth raises the possibility that Christianity nurtures 'attitudinal boundaries' in ways that create distinctive forms of 'ethnic identity' (1969). This means that group members in the first century nurtured strong convictions about one, two or three major values or behaviors that defined them over against other groups with whom they had close contact (Østergård 1992: 36–8; Gourdriaan 1992: 75–7). In other words, they did not emphasize, or even regularly admit, the things they had in common with these other groups. Rather, their attitudes were deeply informed by a few basic convictions and behaviours that set them apart from other groups with whom they shared many things in common. These differences in attitude and behavior created clear boundaries that separated them

5

from other groups and gave them a special identity (Barth 1969: 9–10). Perhaps this insight into the manner in which a group can form a distinct boundary between itself and other groups on the basis of a few deeply felt convictions can help us to describe the boundaries that Christianity persistently creates between itself and other cultures and between 'local cultures' in Christianity itself. The challenge lies before New Testament interpreters to describe the kinds of local and extended cultures that are visible in the discourse available to us in New Testament texts, and many resources now are available to meet this challenge (Robbins 1993c, 1994d).

THE RELATION OF TEXTS TO SOCIETY, CULTURE AND HISTORY

Second, as we face the challenge of describing the relation of first-century Christianity to culture, how do we deal with integrity with the inner nature of New Testament texts themselves? In the midst of his address, Wilder asserted that '[o]ur task must be to get behind the words to what semanticists call their "referents"' (1956: 3). This means that he presupposed that words in texts are always in some way interacting with phenomena outside of texts as they interact with words in that particular text. This, as it turns out, is another thorny issue for us (Lategan and Vorster 1985). In order to drive home the insight that a text creates its own world with its own words, many interpreters have taken the position that written discourse has no clearly definable relation to cultural, social and historical phenomena outside itself. Perhaps, then, the 'referents' are simply firmly held values, beliefs and convictions that an individual creates out of emotional and psychological needs and desires. Maybe, in other words, the referents are primarily psychological phenomena related to biologically driven desires to survive, feel secure and procreate in an environment that, if left unencountered, naturally produces starvation, loss of physical strength and death within humans.

The relation of texts to phenomena outside themselves is an especially pertinent issue in New Testament study, since this is the arena in which many interpreters enact their most deeply held convictions about the nature of humans, God and the world. Is it the 'true nature' of humans that they are not 'actually' an internal part of this world we see, feel, touch, hear and smell each day? Are humans really 'foreign' to this world? Do New Testament texts show a person 'another world' – a world in which our true nature 'lives', rather than the world in which we dwell on earth for the purpose of dying? Are New Testament texts a kind of literature that creates a world in which no one, in the final analysis, truly can 'live' as an earthly human being? Could it be, therefore, that no one ever really enacted the historical, social and cultural assertions we encounter in the New Testament, since all of these are reconfigured in terms of a world other than this earthly world? To put it still another way, is it possible that the all-encompassing nature and function of New Testament texts is to introduce the Word of God as a reality that can exist only outside any earthly human reality? Is it possible, then, that New Testament texts are not at all reliable as a resource for understanding the cultural, social and historical nature of first-century Christianity? Is it possible that New Testament texts are completely a 'world unto themselves' – a world in but not of the world?

Amos Wilder himself began to tackle this issue in his remarkable book *Early Christian Rhetoric*, which appeared less than a decade after his presidential address (1964). After discussing New Testament language as 'The New Utterance' in the first chapter, he programmatically explored the rhetorical nature of dialogue, story, parable and poem, and he ended the book with a chapter on 'Image, Symbol, Myth'. Yet Wilder's aesthetic conceptualization of literature evoked a limited ability to work with the manner in which language persistently interacts with phenomena outside itself. Aesthetics concerns beauty, pleasure, fulfilment and creativity – the imaginative resources of humans. Yet interpreters activate aesthetic analysis in ideologically different ways in interpretation (Eagleton 1990, 1991). Most biblical interpreters who responded to Wilder's call considered the goal to be an explanation of the imaginative resources of the mind at work in the writing and reading of the text. Many of these interpreters have included in their purview the concrete circumstances of the body that are embedded in these texts. Many of these same interpreters, however, have approached the workings of the mind as though they existed outside the body and its functions. Particular social and historical aspects of the body, they have reasoned, are 'outside the text' rather then 'inside the language', because they are outside rather than inside the mind. This is a result of approaching literature as a product of the mind alone rather than the product of interaction between the body and the mind (M. Johnson 1987).

Researchers in various fields have shown both that the concrete circumstances of the body are 'inside' language itself and that language is 'inside' the concrete circumstances of the body (Geertz 1973: 55–83; M. Johnson 1987; R. H. Brown 1987). Biblical scholars, in turn, are bringing these insights into analysis and interpretation of biblical literature (Meeks 1986a; Krondorfer 1992). Language always emerges out of particular locations of the body in social, cultural and historical circumstances. Yet language is also an ingredient that 'makes' these circumstances social, cultural and historical. In other words, language is an integral, constitutive and cognitive feature of human society, culture and history. This means that language is always simultaneously interrelated to speech, writing and actions of particular people, to social and cultural meanings and meaning effects that concern groups of people, and to particular phenomena that people see, feel, touch, smell, fear and desire in particular regions of the world (Roger Fowler 1986: 85–101).

But how do we enact these insights in exegesis, the central practice of New Testament interpretation in which we read meanings 'out of' texts (ex-egesis) rather than simply read our meanings 'into' them (eis-egesis)? The multiple methods of historical–critical exegesis are subdisciplines of historical method. Therefore, they emphasize historical and theological referents in biblical texts rather than symbolic, rhetorical and narratorial referents. Historical–critical methods create the context for biblical interpretation to be a liberating venture in Western culture. These are the methods that make the biblical text available to us with its variant wording in different manuscripts and invite us to the challenges this variation communicates to us about Christianity in the world. But historical methods have their limitations (L. T. Johnson 1986: 8–11). They were not designed to explore the inner nature of texts as written discourse. Their role was, and still is, to answer a comprehensive range of historical and theological questions about people who can be identified as Christians and about events, institutions and beliefs that exhibit the history of the growth and expansion of the phenomenon we call Christianity. The goal is always to draw some conclusion about phenomena outside the New Testament texts themselves, even when there is significant focus on the internal wording of the text. On the other hand, formalist literary and rhetorical methods and the New Criticism were designed specifically to explore the relation of words to one another in texts. Interpreters did not generate these methods for the purpose of exploring the manner in which texts referred to phenomena that exist outside of texts. The purpose was to gain a clear understanding of the nature of written discourse in contrast to spoken discourse and in contrast to other kinds of visual communication.

Fortunately, a number of interpreters have been working both from texts to society and culture and from society and culture to texts. The earlier interests of proponents of the *Religionsgeschichtliche Schule* are being supplemented by the work of a number of sociolinguists and literary interpreters who have been analyzing the social and cultural nature of language in texts at the same time that a number of cultural anthropologists, sociologists of culture and social philosophers have been analyzing the nature of society and culture as text (Lentricchia and McLaughlin 1990). Society, culture and texts are all environments in which meanings and meaning effects interact with one another. The challenge, then, is to develop strategies of analysis and interpretation that exhibit the multiple networks of meanings and meaning effects that the words in our texts represent, engage, evoke and invite.

The question stands before us, then, whether we are able to develop a systematic approach that brings specialized arenas of biblical interpretation into a productive working relation with one another. Can we find a way, without violating the nature of texts as particular kinds of written discourse, to investigate the phenomena with which texts interact as they participate in multiple networks of meanings and meaning effects? Can we develop practices of exegesis that explore multiple contexts of meanings and meaning effects without establishing insurmountable boundaries between them? Socio-rhetorical criticism has evolved as a systematic approach that sets multiple contexts of interpretation in dialogue with one another. Both literary and rhetorical interpreters have begun to explore social and cultural aspects of New Testament texts. In turn, social science critics are engaging in conversation with literary and rhetorical critics to find ways to join ranks wherever possible in the exegesis of New Testament texts (Robbins 1995). The challenge is to use these dialogues and activities to explore the relation of texts to society, culture and history at the same time as we are negotiating our understanding of the relation of Christianity and Christian belief to society, culture and history. We need the best efforts of many people to meet these challenges.

THE RELATION OF NEW TESTAMENT INTERPRETATION TO THEOLOGY

Third, most New Testament interpreters have wrestled mightily with dogmatic theology, but can we engage in a kind of exploratory theology that contributes to constructive or systematic theology? Despite the all-pervasive use of the terms 'theology' and 'Christ-ology' in New Testament interpretation, most theologians pay little attention to the specific results of New Testament exegesis. Many, perhaps most, New Testament methods of exegesis produce specialized results that theologians consider to be of interest only to people inside the boundaries of biblical interpretation. In fact, the boundaries are so noticeable that specialists in Old Testament interpretation regularly have nothing to do with specialists in New Testament interpretation, and even within the two major fields many interpreters either ignore or avoid one another.

During the last four decades, many biblical interpreters have been developing methods of interpretation they think should contribute to constructive and systematic theology. Redaction criticism was designed to explore the theology of biblical texts in the settings in which they were produced. This paved the way for various kinds of structural, literary and rhetorical methods that were designed to explore coherence, consistency and tension in texts; and interpreters considered these approaches to be much more congenial to the articulation of constructive and systematic theology.

The challenge of bringing theologians and biblical interpreters into a cooperative relation, however, appears to be very difficult. A growing number of interpreters are seeking ways to explore deep theological and ideological issues in biblical scholarship. Yet theology itself is a wideranging and changing field with its own interests and concerns. For many theologians the Bible is an essential but minor phenomenon in a large arena of concerns. Biblical interpretation, therefore, is informative only if it engages this larger arena in a manner that challenges it and contributes further insight and information to its projects.

Socio-rhetorical criticism is grounded in a pragmatic approach to language and interpretation that functions in a manner related to the theological project of the feminist theologian Rebecca Chopp. The goal is to weave a discourse of judgment and transformation that shows 'the relation of language, politics, and subjectivity in the dominant social–symbolic order and, standing on the margins and in the breaks of that order, to glimpse and whisper possibilities of transformation' (Chopp 1989: 102–3). One of the goals of socio-rhetorical criticism is to bring the margins and boundaries into view, to invite the interpreter into the discourses that dwell in those marginal spaces, to criticize the dominating interpretive practices that exclude these marginal discourses and to seek discourses of emancipation for marginalized, embodied voices and actions in the text.

A major goal, then, is for socio-rhetorical criticism to function as a prolegomenon to a constructive theology guided by discourses of emancipatory transformation (Chopp 1989: 107–15). As it enacts this role, it regularly takes the form of exploratory rather than constructive theology. In accord with this, the method moves from highly intricate and detailed analysis of language in texts to broad, complex and controversial issues concerning subjectivity and politics (Chopp 1989: 101–7). The final goal is to explore not the private and political arenas of life in and of themselves but the religious dimensions of life in a world constituted by language, subjectivity and politics. In the end, then, socio-rhetorical criticism as it is presented in this book focuses on language about God and Christ, subjectivity in the context of both private and public religious practice and speech, and politics both among and within different religious groups and between and among religious people and various kinds of historical, social, cultural and ideological phenomena in the world they inhabit.

THE RELATION OF DISCIPLINARY METHODS TO AN INTERPRETIVE ANALYTICS

As a guild of interpreters, our forebears and we ourselves have been good at creating specialized disciplines of study. Are we capable now of using the tools of 'a "grand theory", a broad-based interpretive analysis that moves across discursive and nondiscursive practices of the present' (Chopp 1989: 103) to bring our different kinds of specialized knowledge into dialogue and to create a context for generating new insights, new areas of research and new specialties that lead to a new account of first-century Christianity? To fulfill this task, the field of biblical studies needs an interpretive analytics rather than a method or theory in the usual sense. An interpretive analytics approaches texts as discourse and 'sees discourse as part of a larger field of power and practice whose relations are articulated in different ways by different paradigms' (Dreyfus and Rabinow 1983: 199). The rigorous establishment of the relations of power and practice is the analytic dimension. The courageous writing of a story of the emergence of these relations is the interpretive dimension. The interpretive task moves through these steps:

1) the interpreter must take up a pragmatic stance on the basis of some socially shared sense of how things are going; ...
2) the investigator must produce a disciplined diagnosis of what has gone on and is going on in the social body to account for the shared sense of distress or well-being; ...
3) the investigator owes the reader an account of why the practices he [or she] describes should produce the shared malaise or contentment which gave rise to the investigation.

(Dreyfus and Rabinow 1983: 200)

Socio-rhetorical criticism does not present a program for a full-scale interpretive analytics, but it is a step toward it. Among other things, resources from the discipline of psychology are noticeably absent from the socio-rhetorical practices of exegesis in this book. I began to incorporate social and developmental psychology in socio-rhetorical exegesis during the 1980s (1992a), but so many other challenges lie at the interface between the historical–critical methods and social, rhetorical and modern literary methods that it has been necessary to exclude psychology from this presentation. Other resources as well will steadily emerge for interpreters of religious texts. One of the goals of socio-rhetorical criticism is to provide a beginning place for inviting these resources into an environment of systematic exegesis of texts.

A beginning place for psychological analysis and interpretation in a new mode has already begun in the context of social, cultural, ideological and theological dimensions of New Testament texts (e.g. Theissen 1987). But significantly new work will be necessary to bring the resources of cultural and cognitive psychology into analysis and interpretation of the psychological texture of the literary, historical, social, cultural and ideological phenomena in New Testament texts (e.g. Lawson and McCauley 1990). Some initial explorations of Pauline texts with the aid of insights from the work of Wilhelm Dilthey hold promise for analysis of the psychological texture of texts in a socio-rhetorical mode (Na 1995). A reason for mentioning this here is to emphasize that one of the goals of socio-rhetorical criticism is to nurture a broad-based interpretive analytics rather than simply to introduce another specialty into New Testament interpretation. An interpretive analytics invites the development of specialties that will programmatically explore aspects of human reality that have heretofore been unexplored. Of special concern during this era in our history is the relation of power, practice and self-perspective. Since socio-rhetorical criticism is a textually based method, the goal is to explore the inner phenomena and nature of power, practice and self-perspective in the context of exegetical practices with texts.

CONCLUSION

Socio-rhetorical criticism challenges interpreters to explore human reality and religious belief and practice through multiple approaches to written discourse in texts. As an interpretive program that moves toward a broad-based interpretive analytics, it invites investigations that enact integrated interdisciplinary analysis and interpretation. At present, interpreters are practicing many multiple approaches, but they are often practicing them either without knowledge of one another or in contexts where animosity is articulated with an absence of an understanding of the profound interrelation between the respective projects and their results. The specific texts under discussion in this book are in the New Testament. The approach, however, is applicable to any texts anywhere. Since my own specialty is New Testament literature, I have accepted this task in the context of the challenges that currently face interpreters of New Testament texts.

As I began the task, I had hoped that historical–critical methods could simply be reformed to meet the challenges that lie before us. My experiences during the past quarter of a century in the field, however, suggest that historical–critical methods in the form in which they have developed during the last fifty years are not well equipped to perform all the tasks that face us as we look toward the beginning of the twenty-first century. A number of current historical–critical methods still do not seriously incorporate literary, rhetorical and semiotic modes of analysis. To the extent that these methods avoid these new modes of criticism, they regularly reduce New Testament texts to forms of historical and theological discourse that exclude meanings and meaning effects that are highly pertinent for addressing the issues of our day. Methods that overemphasize a single dimension of a biblical text, like structuralism or linguistics, have also not been sufficient for the task. New Testament texts are not simply historical, theological or linguistic treatises. Rather, their written discourse is a highly interactive and complex environment. Interpreting a biblical text is an act of entering a world where body and mind, interacting with one another, create and evoke highly complex patterns and con-figurations of meanings in historical, social, cultural and ideological contexts of religious belief. Rhetorical argument, social act and religious belief intertwine in them like threads and yarn in a richly textured tapestry. By renewing many of the interests of proponents of the *Religionsgeschichtliche Schule* with insights from literary, rhetorical and semiotic practices of interpretation during this last decade of the twentieth century, it is possible to explore in quite new ways the nature of New Testament texts as religious discourse. In this new context, a well-tuned interdisciplinary approach that explores the relation between rhetorical argument and social location and action can merge programmatic, systematic investiga-tion with multiple insights into language, subjectivity, politics, belief and practice in a more satisfactory manner than methods limited to the practices of a single discipline of investigation.

Socio-rhetorical criticism is part of a context at the end of the twentieth century where people in every area of life face the challenge of relating 'specialized' knowledge to larger contexts than those to which the specialists who produce that knowledge regularly relate it. On the one hand, it behooves anyone who is engaged in such an enterprise to build on previous knowledge rather than to discard it. It would be a mistake, therefore, for a socio-rhetorical approach to bypass insights attained by the wide range of historical–critical approaches that currently exist. Historical–critical methods have yielded treasured insights into biblical literature, and they will continue to do so. The methods of text, source, form and redaction criticism bring the details of ancient manuscripts into view in a manner that deserves, and must continue to receive, support and respect. In addition, history of religions, tradition criticism and canon criticism each add additional data and understanding. On the other hand, each method limits its interest in texts as written discourse, because its focus is first and foremost on 'historical' interests. This means that the texts themselves do not, in the final analysis, receive primary attention. Rather, the focus lies on 'the historical world' to which the texts, in the mind of the interpreter, point. The common practice of referring to New Testament texts as 'documents' exhibits this focus. In the context of much historical–critical interpretation, the value of New Testament writings lies in what they 'document' in the world outside the text, not in what they contain as texts, as written discourse that has its own inner nature and meanings. The second interest lies in 'theology', the 'beliefs' that arise out of the historical world in which people produced these texts. Socio-rhetorical criticism accepts the challenge to move beyond modes of historical and theological analysis that limit the resources of the text. It brings dynamics of religious belief into view by establishing a dialogical environment for analytical strategies from widely different arenas of investigation. The dialogue invites a wide range of historical, social, cultural, ideological and psychological phenomena into the project of theological reflection and construction. Again, the possibilities for this lie in the merger of new modes of textual analysis with broad interests in religion that were characteristic of proponents of the *Religionsgeschichtliche Schule* (Boers 1979; Räisänen 1990; Riches 1993).

Amos Wilder, who died after a long and full life in the year in which this manuscript began to emerge (1993), introduced a vision already in 1955 that can inform us as we attempt to move toward a new interpretive analytics. Yet Wilder's focus itself caused him to limit the resources for new insights into the nature and function of image, myth and symbol in biblical texts. As a result, it has taken New Testament interpreters nearly four decades to begin to integrate analysis of the inner imaginative and argumentative nature of early Christian texts with analysis of the social, cultural and historical nature of their discourse. Beginning around 1970, many biblical interpreters began to read the works of scholars outside the field of biblical studies whom they had never read before, and they began to include references to these scholars in footnotes and comments as they wrote their articles and books on the Bible. The scholars to whom they referred were not simply philosophers or theologians about whom people had not yet heard. They were literary critics who read novels, structuralists who made detailed diagrams, linguists and sociolinguists who created difficult words in order to study language, anthropologists who studied a wide variety of people and sociologists who developed long lists of different types of groups, alternative kinds of activities for producing goods and services, and multiple systems for distributing and trading items that people valued. The new roll call was bewildering, but the new names and the new diagrams just kept coming. The purpose was to expand the field of biblical studies so it included the rich resources available from the fields of literary study and the social sciences as well as history, philosophy and theology.

Socio-rhetorical criticism was born in this new environment, and it uses the works of many people outside the field of biblical studies, various kinds of diagrams, and many strategies and techniques to invite the reader into its practices, purposes and goals. The chapter after this introduction is a case in point. Socio-rhetorical criticism identifies four arenas of texture in a text. These arenas have appeared gradually as I have gathered strategies of analysts and interpreters both outside and inside the field of biblical studies to create an approach that brings new aspects of interpretation into a form that not only my scholarly colleagues but also college, seminary and doctoral students as well as lay people and clergy can regularly use as they interpret the Bible. The task is not especially easy, since the new names and the new words can be bewildering for the most eager reader. But within time the new names become familiar, even if a person has not read the writings of the people, and with a little care the new words can acquire meanings that are helpful as a person interprets a biblical text. The purpose, in any case, is to bring biblical studies forthrightly into the world of thought, activity and belief at the end of the twentieth century so it can meet the challenges of the twenty-first century as they come quickly and relentlessly into our lives.

At this point in New Testament study, interpreters who responded to Wilder's call but at first resisted the insights of social scientists into myth, the social construction of reality and the ideological nature of culture now have new resources at their disposal. Socio-rhetorical criticism has been designed to help interpreters to use these new resources. The purpose of the strategies and techniques in the approach is to move us into new forms of dialogue, exploration and cooperation that will fulfil the potential that lies in the robust field of biblical study today. Socio-rhetorical criticism does this by bringing insights from literary critics, linguists, sociologists and anthropologists into an organized frame of understanding and activity. The works of about twenty people outside the field of biblical studies contribute significantly to the diagrams and discussion in the next chapter. In the interest of communicating as clearly as possible to the reader, however, only a few of their names appear in the references in parentheses.

2

REDRAWING THE BOUNDARIES WITH SOCIO-RHETORICAL CRITICISM

When we look at a thick tapestry from different angles, we see different configurations, patterns and images. Likewise, when we explore a text from different angles, we see multiple textures of meanings, convictions, beliefs, values, emotions and actions. These textures within texts are a result of webs or networks of meanings and meaning effects that humans create. One person has explained in the following manner how the term 'text' itself signifies these networks or webs:

> Writing and the texts produced by writing are, from the first, expressions of a metaphor of figuration as 'weaving'. The word 'text' itself derives from Latin *texere* ('to weave') and we still speak of weaving or 'stitching together' (cf. *rhapsode*, 'stitch together') a discourse in which the 'seams' are not obvious, or one that makes a 'seamless web'. This weaving metaphor occurs in story after story as a symbol of order, and order itself is another weaving metaphor, derived from Latin *ōrdō*, a technical term for the arrangement of threads in the warp and woof of a fabric. And, do we not still speak of the 'fabric' of a tale, the 'thread of discourse', or words as the 'clothing of thought', of the 'network' of ideas in a text, and of 'spinning a yarn', which others may 'unravel'?
>
> (Tyler 1987: 35)

With socio-rhetorical criticism, the metaphor of texts as a thick tapestry replaces the traditional metaphor of texts as windows and mirrors (Krieger 1964; Petersen 1978: 24; cf. Abrams 1953). The idea has been that the interpreter who is truly interested in literature as literature treats all the characters, actions and episodes in a text as mirrors that reflect back and forth on one another. All of the reflections create the world 'inside the text'. Historians in contrast to literary interpreters, so the understanding goes, use the text as a window either to look briefly in at the text or to look out at the outside world, rather than as a set of mirrors, to find out what is inside the text. They look in or out of the windows of texts for the purpose of creating a story, namely a 'history', outside of texts.

This metaphor of mirrors and windows has served a very useful purpose, but it is my opinion that it is now causing us problems. The problem is that it separates the 'internal' mind of a text from the 'external' body of the world in a manner that is not true either to the texts we read or to the lives we live. The metaphor of windows and mirrors reflects a polarity between literature and history that is part of the dualism between mind and body in modern thought and philosophy. This approach overlooks the nature of language as a social product, possession and tool. Language is at all times interacting with myriads of networks of meanings and meaning effects in the world. Texts exist in the world, and we exist in the world. Interpreters who talk about reading texts from the perspective of a text's own internal mirrors actually bring their own view of social reality to the language in the text. Every reader does this. On the one hand, it is appropriate for an interpreter to place a text in a laboratory that temporarily seals the outer edges of the text with a 'poetic' boundary for special kinds of systematic analysis. The term 'poetic' comes from a Greek word meaning 'to make', and the idea is that writing is such a special activity that language is made to function in a special way in a text. This special function of language creates a 'language border' between itself and other language that calls for special attention. On the other hand, it is an exaggeration to approach a text as a language object 'unto itself'. The problem is that a text is not simply a 'thing unto itself' but is also a 'message which is read'. As a message, it is a communication. To be what it truly is, a text must be read, which may mean 'read aloud'. Social, cultural and ideological meanings at work in the environment of reading – whether aloud or privately to oneself – are the medium through which the text becomes communication. There is no way, then, for a text to be what it is and to be outside the world.

19

The boundaries some literary critics have established around a text for the purpose of sustained analysis of language in a text are not the only boundaries interpreters should use and reconfigure in the act of interpretation. Interpretation is more like a ritual than a single act (Robbins 1994c). Exploring phenomena within one set of boundaries should be understood as one phase of an extended process. At any one particular time in history, the perception of the beginning, middle and end of the process will differ, much as the laboratories scientists create today look significantly different from the laboratories of the nineteenth century. The creation of boundaries in and around texts is a necessary step if an interpreter is interested in systematic analysis. It is improper to think, however, that the text itself contains these boundaries. The socio-rhetorical approach in the following pages invites interpreters to explore a wide range of textures of text through a process of creating and dismantling various boundaries to create arenas of understanding that interact dynamically with one another. A text is a thick matrix of interwoven networks of meanings and meaning effects. These networks extend far beyond the boundaries we construct to analyze and interpret phenomena; they interconnect phenomena inside and outside of texts in ways quite difficult for us even to imagine. Therefore, no interpreter should allow one arena of texture to be an environment for creating boundaries that separate this arena permanently from other arenas of texture. We must learn both how to create boundaries and how to take boundaries away. At the outset, then, we should admit that it is impossible for us to think without boundaries. Even the most simple use of language creates them. In addition, however, we should see that language continually moves boundaries it initially evokes for the purpose of communicating 'beyond itself'. This approach to language and boundaries within language provides the context for socio-rhetorical criticism.

Figure 2.1 represents a diagram for socio-rhetorical analysis and interpretation as it currently exists. The outside rectangle represents boundaries around the world of the interpreter. Every interpreter has a limited experience of and relationship with the world, even though many interpreters consciously attempt to take a large part of the world into account as they approach a text. No matter how large the world of an interpreter may be, there are limits to the interpreter's knowledge of that world.

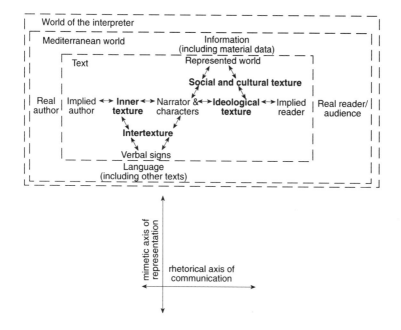

Figure 2.1 Socio-rhetorical model of textual communication

The rectangle inside the world of the interpreter represents the boundaries to the world of the author who wrote the text. For the New Testament, this is the ancient Mediterranean world. The innermost rectangle represents boundaries around a text. The real author, language, information and the real reader/audience are phenomena inside the Mediterranean world. Real authors are historical persons. The texts they make somehow are extensions of themselves. Literary critics use the term 'implied author' for authors as they can be known through manifestations of their expressions in texts (Powell 1990: 19–29). Words in texts 'imply' authors, and the kind of author a reader constructs on the basis of words in a text is the implied author of the text. Thus, 'real author' is in the rectangle representing the Mediterranean world and 'implied author' is in the rectangle representing the text. Likewise, the language of New Testament texts is a phenomenon in the Mediterranean world. Texts contain signs that imply language. Instead of using the phrase 'implied language', which would be appropriate, the diagram uses the term 'verbal signs'. Verbal signs stand in relation to language in the Mediterranean world in a manner similar to the relation of implied authors to real authors. This relation continues around the rectangle that represents the text. The diagram uses the phrase 'represented world' for the 'implied information' in the text that stands in relation to information in the Mediterranean world. Again, the phrase that designates information as it is manifest in texts signals that a particular manifestation of the world, a distinctive configuration, is implied by the verbal signs in the text and inferred by readers in particular ways. Finally, the phrase 'implied reader' designates the reader the text implies and the interpreter infers in relation to real readers and audiences both in the Mediterranean world and in the world of the interpreter today.

All the boundaries in the diagram are broken lines, because they are human-made boundaries for the purpose of focusing analysis on a text. All kinds of meanings and meaning effects travel through the gaps in the boundaries. Meanings and meaning effects travelled between the Mediterranean world and the text when the author wrote the text, and they travel through the boundaries from the world of the interpreter through the Mediterranean world when a person reads these texts today. Language and other texts travel through the boundaries just as information and material data travel through the boundaries. Many, though not all, interpreters build boundaries to keep various things from their own world out of the ancient Mediterranean world and to put certain things 'foreign' to their own world into the Mediterranean world in which they embed New Testament texts. Since New Testament texts were written in the Mediterranean world of late antiquity and are also located in our world, both the ancient Mediterranean world as we infer it and our own world, conscious and unconscious to us, flow into the text. Texts are in the world and of it. Nevertheless, interpreters can focus on an inner world of the text that calls for special attention on its own terms.

Literary interpreters have concluded that the inner texture of a narrative text contains a narrator who tells the story and characters who think, act and have their being in the story. The narrator and characters exist in a context of 'images' of the real author, language, information and the real reader/audience. In other words, the inside of a text is a combination of 'show' and 'tell'. The narrator tells the story. The reader hears the narrator and sees the characters, who may themselves speak and 'look'. In this context the image of the author of the text, the 'implied author', appears. The implied author is the image created by everything the reader sees in the text. Also, readers give 'voice' to verbal signs as they see them. That is, readers turn the signs into sounds that are 'language' among people. This is the means by which the verbal signs in a text become 'implied language'. In addition, readers hear and see phenomena in the context of the action and thought that are 'implied' information and material data. Finally, readers of texts create an image of a reader who can read a particular text with understanding. This is the 'implied reader'. If they themselves cannot understand the text, they create an image of a reader who the implied author imagined could read and understand the text. Whether or not all of this is clear to the real reader who is now reading this, literary interpreters have drawn these conclusions about the inner texture of texts. These conclusions guide socio-rhetorical criticism as it approaches the inner texture of a text, and the goal is to create activities for an interpreter that will make it possible to investigate these and other inner phenomena in texts.

At the bottom of the diagram are horizontal and vertical arrows. The horizontal arrow represents what literary interpreters call the rhetorical axis. An axis is an imaginary line through the center of something, like the imaginary line through the center of the earth as it spins, as we say, 'on its axis'. Through the center of a text is an imaginary 'rhetorical' line between the author and the reader. The term *rhetorical* is related to the word *orator*, a person who speaks a message to people. The rhetorical axis in a text represents 'speaking' or 'communicating' both from the author to the reader and from the reader to the author, since the author creates 'implied' voice in the text and the reader actually 'gives' voice to the text. The text speaks or communicates, then, through reciprocal action between author and reader. In addition to the horizontal arrow there is a vertical arrow at the bottom of the diagram. The vertical arrow indicates a 'mimetic' axis. The word *mimetic* comes from the Greek word *mimesis*, meaning 'imitation'. As indicated above, the written signs in the text 'imitate' the sounds of language, and the narrator, actors and things in the 'textual world' imitate information and material data in the world. Thus, the vertical lines represent an axis of 'imitation'. This axis exists in angles in the diagram, rather than straight up through the center, since the horizontal movement of the communication from the author to the reader and from the reader to the author causes the vertical axis to run up and down at angles. In other words, the diagram is meant to exhibit action. In the dynamic movement from author to reader and from reader to author, words, characters, represented world, implied author and implied reader all 'imitate' the world.

In the midst of all of these phenomena in the text are four arenas of texture printed in bold print: (a) inner texture; (b) intertexture; (c) social and cultural texture; and (d) ideological texture. One of the special features of socio-rhetorical criticism is its identification of these four arenas in a text. Pointing to these arenas, the approach gathers practices of interpretation for each arena to enable a person to investigate each arena both on its own terms and in relation to other arenas. The remainder of this book works carefully through each part of the diagram displayed above, using various New Testament texts to illustrate how socio-rhetorical criticism works with each part of it, then focusing specifically on 1 Corinthians 9 at the end of each chapter. Each arena is given a name for its own particular 'text-ure'. In order to explain more about each arena, the remainder of this chapter dismantles the model for the reader and rebuilds it in four steps after it focuses for a moment on the world of the interpreter.

THE INTERPRETER'S LOCATION AND IDEOLOGY

The outside rectangle in Figure 2.1 calls for attention to the world of the interpreter. Interpreters construct this 'world' interactively with phenomena in their own personal lives and with the historical, social, cultural, ideological and religious worlds in their world. I will begin, therefore, with some open reflection about my own 'theological ideology'. My own ideology includes feelings, convictions, beliefs and points of view that were formulated in the context of the circumstances into which I was born, raised, schooled, married and employed. I have engaged seriously with 'traditional' biblical interpretation and theology, both North American and international. In the end, it has been necessary to develop strategies of analysis and interpretation that would carry out my own view of reality and truth in the world. I was born and raised on a small farm on a sandhill outside a village with a population of 139 people, not of my own choosing. We did not have electricity until I was in the second grade, again not of my own choosing. I did not choose to milk cows by hand morning and evening until I was in high school when we milked cows on Treptow's hill where we could use milking machines and sell grade A milk. I did not choose to grow up in an agonistic, rural culture. I did not choose not to have a political voice of any kind because I had no daily newspaper, radio or television that would give up-to-date, firsthand news about what was happening in Washington, DC and New York City. I did not choose to be born and raised as a WASP who is supposed to hate and suppress blacks, Jews, women, native Americans and all kinds of other people. I did not choose these things.

So what am I supposed to do about these things now? Should I join in an academic project that was envisioned, launched and nurtured to maturity by city dwellers who know how to use the power structures of the university, the large metropolitan areas and the national and international scholarly organizations and book publishers? Even if I join these things, should I contribute to strategies of New Testament interpretation that only see the big power plays as the significant parts of early Christian history? Should I pretend that I do not hear the voices and see the plights of the 'little people' who cry out in biblical texts? Should I pretend that I do not know what it is like to live in a family where the father and mother are tenant farmers? Should I pretend that I do not know what it is like to live in a family so indebted that the father has to sell out and go to work in a city in the humiliating job of a school janitor? Should I pretend that I do not know what it is like not to have honor?

But there is also another part to the story. Should I pretend that I did not have the opportunity to achieve a college and seminary degree, yet another master's degree and a Ph.D.? Should I pretend that I have not been gradually inducted both into cosmopolitan urban life and into the central power structures of professional biblical interpretation? The truth is that most stages of my life have involved me in at least two worlds, or two 'cultures', at the same time. As a rural farm boy I also lived in an evangelical Christian culture. As a college student I worked during the summers in a job that combined dairy and agriculture farming with a union construction job in urban areas. As a married seminary student I rode a large motorcycle, which I personally repaired, around the cosmopolitan urban city in which we lived, simply because it was inexpensive transportation like that to which I had been accustomed on the farm. As a doctoral student I repaired cars and drove a bus to deal with the onslaught of inflated living expenses in a cosmopolitan center of urban America. As an assistant professor, I repaired bicycles to keep in touch with my 'working body' as I pursued the 'inner recesses of the scholarly mind'. As an associate and full professor, I have rather fully taken my 'working body' into my teaching and publication of articles and books.

So the truth is that the experiences of my life, body and mind are now coming to expression in socio-rhetorical criticism. This approach is not somehow based in 'objective' reality, except insofar as my life is based in objective reality. This approach is based in the realities of my life. I have regularly experienced being an insider and outsider at the same time: in relation to some people I have regularly been an 'insider', in relation to others regularly an 'outsider'. And this is the principle that lies at the foundation of socio-rhetorical criticism – namely the dialogical relations between inside and outside, center and margins, power and weakness, influence and exclusion, success and failure.

Therefore, when faced with the question of what kind of biblical interpretation I myself should enact and teach, the situation is like when Camden Gowler, at 2 years old, was playing with the bubble solution his mother Rita had mixed for him, and spilled some of it on the floor of their storage shed. When Rita told him he wasn't supposed to do that, he said, 'What am I 'posed to do?' That is the question. Just what are some of us white male Protestants supposed to do when we hear the voices, sight the boundaries and see both the plights of the people on the margins and the flaws of people at the center of the New Testament texts we read?

Socio-rhetorical criticism is my answer to what I think I must do to perform biblical interpretation in a manner that embodies who I am. As I do this, the image of my father looms before me – that tenant farmer turned janitor who died while I was writing this book. Many people, including me, tried to persuade him to be less pessimistic about his own life and less critical of those whom he loved, in a context where he did so many good things for so many people every day. But he did the best he could. He let his voice be heard in the best way he knew how. And this view of the world was no crazier than the views of many highly sophisticated philosophers and theologians. He did not have all the words they have. But he had plenty of the experiences, most of the visions, many of the insights and various ways to communicate most of them. He was a philosopher and a theologian in his own right, but he never wrote a book, never ran for public office and was always afraid he would bring shame on himself if he asserted himself too strongly in public. He was one of the 'little people'. His voice is still around in many places. The only question is whether anyone can hear it.

I happen to think that we *can* hear the voices of the little people throughout history. But we must also realize that most people regularly live in two, three or more worlds at the same time. I am thankful that I have many colleagues who have been showing me and others how to hear the voices and see the worlds in which people live. I feared for many years that I could not be a truly academic professor of the New Testament and remain true to those voices and worlds at the same time. But little by little – with the help of John F. Kennedy, Martin Luther King, Jr., Bobby Kennedy, Jimmy Carter, Garrison Keillor, Desmond Tutu, Mikhail Gorbachev, Bill Clinton, Nelson Mandela, Toni Morrison, Cornell West and many others – I have begun to find a way. We simply have to find ways to be true to ourselves as we are being true to both the little people and the great traditions of the past, and to the many worlds in which people, both powerful and weak, live in the present. I cannot change myself to a woman, a person of color, or a fascinating mixture of Catho-Ortho-Prote-Asio-Native-Christian. I must be what I am, and one of the ways is to bring to consciousness and evoke the interactive body and mind that continually take me into many different worlds at the same time. Socio-rhetorical criticism, then, is my way of finding and exhibiting a way of living responsibly in the 'worlds of our time' as we rush toward the third millennium CE.

INNER TEXTURE

The first arena in the text to which I turn is the inner texture of the text. When a person first looks at a text, one only sees signs on a flat surface. A reader or interpreter knows that these signs represent what an author, or someone writing for an author, has written on the page. If the text is written in a language one understands, a process of reading can begin. Since this is a very complex process (Grimes 1975; de Beaugrande and Dressler 1981), it is necessary to give an extremely abbreviated account here. In very brief terms, with the act of reading, a person may begin to explore the 'inner texture' of a text. This means that the inner texture of a text concerns communication. What is in a text is 'part of a communication transaction' (Vorster 1989: 22). For a text to 'be itself', it must have a

27

reader who activates it – a reader who 'receives' the message. In other words, inner texture is only one part of the communication transaction. Because a reader must engage a text in this way for it to communicate, it is very difficult to determine what is actually in a text itself in contrast to what a reader 'puts into' a text. At the very least, readers put their own ability to speak, hear, see, think, act, smell, taste and feel – their nature as 'subjects' – into texts. Only in this way can a 'nonhuman' object become a 'human object'. Or would it be better to say that a nonhuman 'subject' becomes a 'human subject'? The concept of object versus subject raises a major issue. A subject is a person, and a text is not a person. A text has an inner nature that is somehow different from a person but which somehow 'comes to life' when persons read it. In turn, however, a person can be treated by an interpreter either as a subject or as an object. One of the special issues, then, is whether an interpreter treats narrators, characters, authors and readers as 'objects' or as 'subjects' when he or she 'brings them to life' in a text. Since this is a lifelong commitment one way or another, we will not try to solve this issue at this point. Some interpreters prefer to treat all people as objects while others prefer to treat them as subjects. And there is much to be gained by both approaches, just as there has been incredible gain by medical investigation of people as 'objects' and there has been incredible gain also by investigating them as 'subjects'. The goal of socio-rhetorical criticism is to approach people as interactive subjects–objects. Not only do people treat other people as both objects and subjects, but we treat ourselves interactively as objects and subjects. We have the ability to think about our own bodies and minds both as objects and as subjects, and we alternate between our ways of thinking about them. Socio-rhetorical criticism attempts to nurture such interactive subject–object, body–mind interpretation of texts.

The inner texture of a text appears primarily among the implied author, the narrator and the characters, who work together to communicate a message. Various literary critics have displayed a horizontal diagram to exhibit this communication process, 'the whole narrative-communication situation' (Chatman 1978: 151; Rimmon-Kenan 1983: 86), and this is the beginning point for building a socio-rhetorical model for interpretation. Adapting the diagram so it includes the concept of inner texture creates Figure 2.2.

At this stage of analysis, interpreters were identifying the real author and real reader/audience outside the text, but not language

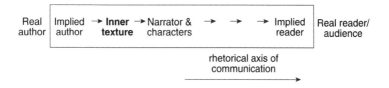

Figure 2.2 Inner texture

and information. The reason was that only the rhetorical axis of communication, the movement of the message from the author to the reader, was the focus of attention. Inside the box, thus inside the text, interpreters identified and defined the implied author and the implied reader – the images of the real author who caused everything to be as it is in the text and the real reader who is able to read and understand the text – and the narrator and the characters – who are the agents and voices in the text who tell the story. Socio-rhetorical criticism identifies the environment among the implied author, the narrator and the characters as the arena where interpreters investigate the inner texture of a text. In other words, analysis of inner texture regularly does not concern itself with language or information outside the text. Literary and narrative critics who have contributed significantly to this kind of analysis have focused on the text, with both the author as producer of the text and the represented world evoked by the text in the background of the analysis. Anglo-American New Criticism, Russian Formalism and French Structuralism have represented special attempts to maintain a completely 'intrinsic' or 'text-immanent' approach to texts in this manner. With important exceptions that cannot be discussed here, representatives of these approaches considered an intrinsic focus to be a disciplinary activity that set literary interpretation in opposition to historical criticism and its subdisciplines, either because the latter impose 'extrinsic' data on texts or because they simply use texts as treasure houses of data that can be used to construct a story extrinsic to texts.

Socio-rhetorical criticism does two things with intrinsic or text-immanent analysis. First, it sets these 'disciplinary' results in dialogue with other disciplinary results that are the product of exploring other textures of a text. Second, it adds the real reader/ audience as an interactive counterpart of the real author in the construction of the inner texture of the text. In the diagrams throughout the rest of the chapter, therefore, arrows point not only from the author to the reader, but from the reader to the author. As mentioned above, a text does not truly become a text until someone reads it. Prior to its being read, it is a written artifact with webs of signification buried in it as if it were a tomb. Only readers can bring the webs of signification into the world of meanings and meaning effects. As soon as readers do this, however, their own world of meanings and meaning effects works interactively with meanings and meaning effects from the ancient Mediterranean world to create the meanings and meaning effects of the text. Thus, socio-rhetorical criticism approaches the inner texture of a text as an interactive environment of authors and readers. Authors create texts in their world; readers create a world of the text in their own world. Socio-rhetorical criticism interactively explores the world of the author, the world of the text and the world of the interpreter to interpret the inner texture of a New Testament text.

INTERTEXTURE

In a context where interpreters were focusing on the inner texture of texts, the concept of 'intertextuality' arose when some interpreters observed that not only are author and reader involved in the writing and reading of texts, but other texts play a decisive role. Every text is a rewriting of other texts, an 'intertextual' activity. To display the dialogue that occurs between texts in the context of the communication from the author to the reader, a vertical axis has to be added to the horizontal axis. With the addition of a vertical axis that represents the dialogue between the text itself and other texts (Kristeva 1969: 145; Hutcheon 1986: 231), an interpreter sees the 'intertexture' of a text. To investigate this aspect of a text thoroughly calls for comparison between the text under investigation and other texts. Analysis of a number of texts brings into view language outside of texts, because the interpreter sees language 'between' texts in addition to 'inside' one text. Therefore, the vertical axis features language itself, and other texts are a specific manifestation of language outside the particular text under investigation. Again, the reason the vertical axis becomes angled lines is that the text evokes language and information only in the context of a communication transaction, which the diagram depicts as dialogical interaction that moves back and forth from author to reader and reader to author.

Adding 'intertexture', then, produces Figure 2.3. Language stands at the bottom of the vertical axis, outside the boundaries of the text itself, and other texts represent a manifestation of language that plays a special role in authors' writing of texts. When the intertextuality of the text comes into view, the boundary around the text becomes a broken line. It becomes obvious to the interpreter at this point that the boundary is a human-made boundary for the purpose of focusing analysis on a text, since all kinds of meanings and

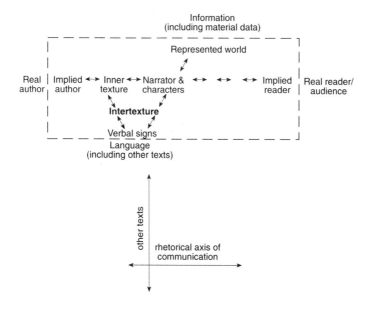

Figure 2.3 Intertexture

31

meaning effects travel through gaps in the boundary. At this stage of analysis, the interpreter focuses special attention on the relation of the verbal signs inside the text to verbal signs in other texts. In addition, the interpreter compares the represented world evoked by the text with the represented world evoked by other texts. One of the results is that the interpreter 'textualizes' not only the 'represented' world in the text but also all language and information outside the text. For the intertextual interpreter, 'the world' is limited and structured by 'textual' communication; 'the world is a text'. The arena of intertexture as it is defined in socio-rhetorical criticism, then, emphasizes the author as producer of the text over the reader as constructor of the meaning of the text. The interpreter investigates the act of production by comparing verbal signs in the text under investigation with verbal signs in other texts. In other words, the interpreter begins with verbal signs in the text that explicitly evoke verbal signs in other texts. Thus, analysis of intertexture begins in an environment among the inner texture, the verbal signs, the narrator and the characters. This analysis reaches out into language through the verbal signs in the text, and it reaches into information in the world through the narrator, the characters and the represented world in the text. The implied reader and the real reader stand at a distance from the analysis. At this stage, the interpreter presupposes their presence but pays more attention to the language in texts than to authors and readers of this language.

For intertextual interpreters, then, while real authors, real readers, language and social, historical and material information lie outside of texts, texts intrinsically incorporate these phenomena within themselves through language. This is immediately noticeable when a text contains fragments of other texts in the form of explicit quotations and allusions. But cultural, social and historical phenomena are also in texts, and intertextual interpreters perceive them to be present in a 'textualized' form – that is, in an ordered, patterned and structured form related to language. This nature of a text is its intertexture. Texts stand in a dynamic relation to phenomena outside them. Language, which is the medium for texts to be what they are, comes from outside any particular text and is embedded in them, indeed shaped in them, bearing the data that language carries with it.

Analysis and interpretation of intertexture in a socio-rhetorical mode, then, appropriates and refigures source, form and redaction criticism in biblical studies. Source and redaction criticism become environments for investigation of the dialogue between structures, codes and genres in a particular configuration. Intertextual investigation analyzes and interprets the dynamics of recitation, recontextualization and reconfiguration when different sources, traditions, redaction and amplification stand in relation to one another.

It is generally recognized that intertextuality emerged in the context of 'cross-fertilization among several major European intellectual movements during the 1960s and 1970s, including Russian formalism, structural linguistics, psychoanalysis, Marxism, and deconstruction, at the least' (Morgan 1989: 240). My analysis suggests that the current terminology of 'intertextuality' collapses three arenas of analysis and interpretation together in a manner that is confusing. For this reason, socio-rhetorical analysis separates the three arenas out and uses different terminology to refer to them. Intertexture in socio-rhetorical criticism represents the arena of intertextual analysis that maintains a close relation to verbal signs in the text. Socio-rhetorical criticism identifies two other arenas of intertextuality – social and cultural texture and ideological texture – on which it focuses separately. In the arenas of intertexture as defined by socio-rhetorical criticism the goal is to analyze the manner in which signs and codes evoke a textual form of cultural, social and historical reality. Since this mode of analysis approaches all literature within a closed system of signs, it is a disciplinary practice of interpretation with its own data, strategies and goals. Socio-rhetorical criticism puts this disciplinary mode in dialogue with the disciplinary practice of analysis of inner texture, social and cultural texture and ideological texture. This dialogue interactively deconstructs and reconfigures insights from other arenas as the analysis proceeds. The interpreter faces a challenge to allow the tension and conflict that emerge from the different approaches to inform the overall process of analysis and interpretation rather than to allow one arena substantially to close down information from the other. The tensions and conflicts are to remain significant data for analysis and interpretation even as the interpreter draws final conclusions.

SOCIAL AND CULTURAL TEXTURE

Mikhail Bakhtin, Kenneth Burke and Roland Barthes have been most responsible for the appearance of the social and cultural texture of texts. Bakhtin contributed to it by exploring the social and ideological location of the voices in texts (Reed 1993). Burke contributed by developing a method of interpretation that uses the resources of philosophy, literature and sociology to understand language as symbolic action (Burke 1966). Barthes contributed by interpreting a text as a product of various cultural discourses, 'a tissue of quotations drawn from innumerable centers of culture' (Barthes 1977: 146).

Approaching a text from the perspective of symbolic action that puts many socially, culturally and ideologically located voices in dialogue with one another calls special attention to the arena in the text between the represented world and the narrator and characters. The voices in the text are 'mimetic' in relation to the action and speech of people in the world. When Paul Hernadi assessed both axes of the diagram that arose when intertextuality emerged, he called the horizontal axis the rhetorical axis of communication and the vertical axis the mimetic axis of representation (Hernadi 1976). In other words, the vertical axis exhibits a text's 'representation' or imitation of the world through language. When the emphasis on the vertical axis is the 'mimetic' nature of language in a text, the social and cultural nature of the arena between represented world and the narrator and characters becomes a special focus of attention. Adaptation of Hernadi's diagram so it includes the arena of the social and cultural texture of a text produces Figure 2.4.

The social and cultural texture of a text concerns the dynamics of 'voice' as they function among the narrator and the characters in texts. Socio-rhetorical criticism views voice in text as the medium for the 'consciousness' or 'vision' of the characters and the narrator, who are 'concretizations drawn from a represented world' (Frow 1986: 159). In addition, analysis of the social and cultural texture of texts focuses on the full range of rhetorical topics in the text rather than only the four topics of traditional literary criticism – metaphor, metonymy, synecdoche and irony (Vickers 1988: 435–79). Rhetorical topics – which ancient rhetoricians divided into material (specific) topics, common topics and final (strategic) categories – are manifestations of social responses to the world, enactments of social and cultural systems and institutions, and performances of cultural alliances and conflicts. Investigation of the social and cultural texture of texts moves beyond the mimetic environment of the verbal signs to the mimetic environment of the action and speech of the narrator and the characters that evoke the represented

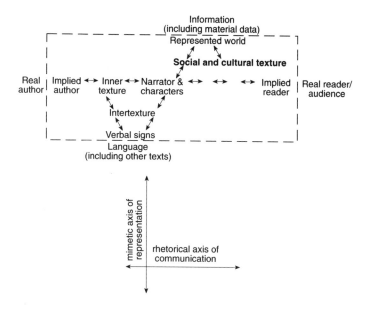

Figure 2.4 Social and cultural texture

world. In contrast to the kind of intertextual analysis that textualizes culture, society and history, social and cultural analysis invites the full resources of the social sciences into the environment of exegetical interpretation.

Extensive resources are available for analyzing the social and cultural texture of texts with greater detail than literary critics have yet achieved. Agents and actors in the text interact in discursive modes that evoke a wide variety of social, cultural and ideological vocabularies, dialects, attitudes and dispositions. As these voices dialogue with one another in the context of the represented world of a text, the work of Clifford Geertz on 'local cultures' and the work of sociologists of culture furnish insight into dominant culture, subculture, counterculture, contraculture and liminal culture (Robbins 1993c, 1994b). In addition, Bryan Wilson's social typology for religious responses to the world furnishes specific resources for analysis of texts (Wilson 1969, 1973). Social-scientific critics of the Bible have gathered extensive data that can enrich analysis of the social and cultural texture of texts with insights into honor and shame culture, patronage, hospitality, health systems, relation of countryside to cities, purity systems, etc. (Malina 1993; Neyrey 1991; Elliott 1993). Both biblical and literary studies are poised to engage in a fully interdisciplinary analysis of the social and cultural texture of texts if interpreters bring insights from the social sciences into a dynamic environment of textual analysis and interpretation.

IDEOLOGICAL TEXTURE

Investigation of social and cultural texture takes the analyst to the doorstep of ideological texture. The term 'ideology' has meant, and still does mean, different things to different people. From a socio-rhetorical perspective, ideology is

> the ways in which what we say and believe connects with the power-structure and power-relations of the society we live in . . . those modes of feeling, valuing, perceiving and believing which have some kind of relation to the maintenance and reproduction of social power.
>
> (Eagleton 1983: 15)

Ideology concerns the particular ways in which our speech and action, in their social and cultural location, relate to and interconnect with resources, structures and institutions of power. Kenneth Burke, who almost singlehandedly brought the social, cultural and ideological texture of texts into view (cf. Jameson 1981, 1988), and Roland Barthes, who introduced the concept of readers as 'writers' of the texts they read, opened the ideological texture of texts to view for interpreters (1967, 1972, 1974, 1981). Clifford Geertz adapted Burke's work to reconfigure sociology of knowledge as sociology of meaning. Michel Foucault analyzed discourse as a 'relationship between truth, theory, and values and the social institutions and practices in which they emerge', which brought 'increased attention to power and the body' (Dreyfus and Rabinow 1983: xxv). Mieke Bal, in turn, has reworked narratology to bring special attention to the ideological nature of texts (1985, 1991). The ideological texture of texts features the arena between the implied reader and the narrator and characters. The particular way in which the narrator and characters evoke the message and the particular way in which the implied reader and real reader/audience receive it concerns ideology. Thus, adding ideological texture to the diagram produces Figure 2.5.

Reciprocity between the empowerment of the narrator and characters, the verbal signs and the represented world by the implied author and the implied reader represents the ideology *in* the text. In turn, reciprocity between meanings and meaning effects of the text in its world and meanings and meaning effects in the world of the real reader represents the ideology *of* the text. In other words, now the emphasis lies on the arena of the text where the implied reader and the real reader/audience receive and empower the message of the text.

Analysis and interpretation of the ideological texture of texts raises, in the end, the issue of spheres of truth and how we attempt to approach them. It has been traditional to think that truth can be

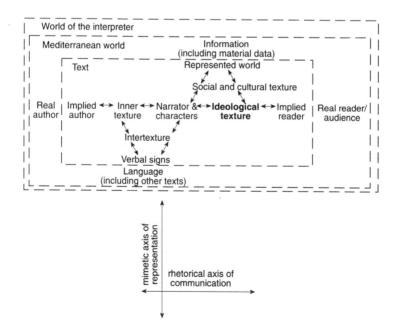

Figure 2.5 Ideological texture

'captured' in ideas or concepts. In other words, truth can be captured in frames of understanding. It has now become obvious that this is an illusion. Truth always escapes us. Our best chance for getting insights into the nature of truth is to understand the relationships things can and do have to one another. Things stand in relation to one another. There are different kinds of relationships. Some relationships are close enough that we can rather successfully talk about them in terms of sequence in time. In other words, some things stand in relations of quite direct 'influence' one way or another on each other. But other things stand in relations that will have 'influence' only if someone 'brings them into a particular sphere of influence'. These other things were there before they were brought into this sphere of influence, but traditional historians and scientists may not include these other things in their analysis. Socio-rhetorical criticism focuses on the relation of things to one another. In the context of relationships, some things stand in a relation of 'influence', of cause and effect. In interpretation, these phenomena are regularly perceived to be 'historical', and the historian includes them in the 'correct interpretation' of a text and excludes phenomena that do not have this 'relation of influence'. Socio-rhetorical criticism includes data in the Mediterranean world that stand in various kinds of relation besides a directly perceivable 'relation of influence' to a biblical text and uses comparison to analyze the nature of the 'relation' in terms of difference and similarity.

The issue of ideology comes into full prominence with the focus on readers of texts. Prior to the twentieth century, methods focused on some combination of a text and its author. Rarely did interpreters include readers in the analysis. During the twentieth century, the inclusion of an author in analysis of a text became more and more problematic. Many texts exist for which there is no certainty concerning the author, in certain instances authors write in the names of other authors and in other instances the only information about an author comes from the text which is the focus of interpretation. In this context, formalist literary critics, structuralists and linguists began to focus entirely on phenomena in the text itself. The author either completely disappeared from the context of interpretation, receded far into the background as an 'implied' author or simply existed as a way of referring to phenomena in the text itself, like 'Mark' says (meaning 'the text of Mark' says). Even if significant information was available about the author, interpreters regularly perceived their task as ascertaining the nature of the text. If interpreters said anything about the author, they were simply referring to the 'implied' author evoked by the text itself. In this context, something of a division of the house arose among historical critics. Some historical critics retain an interest in the authors of texts as historical figures, even if it was uncertain exactly who the person was. Some 'sceptical' historians focused their interests on the activity and location of the author of a text in a historical and geographical location, even if they were working with an unnamed or falsely named author, or perceived the author to be an editor of data produced by a 'community' of people. Whether the focus was somehow on the author or somehow on the text, however, rarely did this focus seriously include the reader.

During the twentieth century interpreters began to include the reader in the context of interpretation, and ideology began to appear in the context of this emphasis. From the perspective of socio-rhetorical criticism, a 'complete' interpretation includes the interrelation among the author, the text and the reader. This vision comes from rhetorical analysis, which traditionally focuses on a speaker, a speech and an audience. In the context of analysis of a text, interpretation includes presuppositions, implicit or explicit, about the author, the text and the reader. Socio-rhetorical criticism brings all three into the arena of textual interpretation. The reason is that language is produced out of social interaction among people: there is not simply a speaker or writer; the speaking and writing presuppose the presence of a hearer or reader. There is not simply a text; texts were produced by authors and they are meaningless without readers. There are not simply readers; readers are meaningless without texts to read and authors who write texts. All three presuppose historical, social, cultural and ideological relations among people and the texts they write and read.

Analysis and interpretation of ideological texture raise the issue of readers in the twentieth century and authors and readers in the first century. What is the relation of our reading of a New Testament text to the way in which a first-century person might have written or read a text? The answer is that all people choose ways to write and to read a text. For this reason, socio-rhetorical criticism interprets not only the text under consideration but ways people read texts in late antiquity and ways people have interpreted New Testament texts both in the past and in different contexts in our modern world. Each interpretation of a text is a text on its own terms, inviting socio-rhetorical analysis and interpretation as much as each New Testament text invites analysis and interpretation. This produces the two rectangles outside the boundary of the text which complete the diagram of socio-rhetorical criticism. Between the text and the world of the interpreter lies the world of the author who wrote the text. Especially with ancient texts, the world of the author calls for special attention since it clearly is a foreign world to the interpreter. Interaction among the world created by the text, the world of the author and the world of the interpreter represents the environment in which socio-rhetorical criticism explores and interprets a text.

CONCLUSION

A text intrinsically contains textures of meaning that cover a spectrum from the most intricate details about discourse itself to extensive details about historical, social, cultural and ideological phenomena. Socio-rhetorical criticism provides an intricate environment for analysis and interpretation in the context of interaction between rhetoric and mimesis, communication and representation, in texts. There are, of course, many implications that come with this model. I will introduce a few of these to bring this chapter to a close.

First, this model presents a 'system' approach to interpretation. This means that presuppositions and strategies in one arena reverberate throughout the entire system. For example, if interpreters emphasize 'opposition' in the inner texture of a text, they are likely to investigate intertexture which features texts that this text opposes, social and cultural groups against which this text pits itself and an ideology of separation from other people in the world. In contrast, if interpreters emphasize 'dialogue' in the inner texture of the text, they are likely to investigate intertexture which features texts that this text reconfigures, social and cultural groups with which this text is in conversation and an ideology of interaction with other people in the world. When interpreters are at work in any one arena of a text, therefore, implicit if not explicit presuppositions about the other arenas are at work in the analysis and interpretation.

Second, socio-rhetorical criticism uses a strategy of reading and rereading a text from different angles to produce a 'revalued' or 'revisited' rhetorical interpretation. This means that the mode of interpretation is explicitly interdisciplinary. The goal is to use the resources of other disciplines 'on their own terms' and to allow these resources to deconstruct and reconfigure the results of a particular focus and set of strategies in a particular discipline. In this deconstructive and reconfiguring environment, no particular discipline should be allowed to achieve a position of hierarchical authority. The rule of the game is that various disciplines engage in conversation with one another on equal terms, rather than dismiss one another through their power structures. The final result is at least as conflictual as intradisciplinary debate, and in some instances more so. The difference is the range of insight brought to the conclusions the interpreter draws. Socio-rhetorical criticism presupposes that the skills of specialization are well enough in hand in textual interpretation that much is to be gained by bringing 'specialized' conclusions of various kinds into active dialogue with one another.

Third, socio-rhetorical interpretation uses the same strategies of analysis on other people's interpretations of the text under consideration as the strategies for analyzing the biblical text itself. The reason is that both texts and interpretations of texts are symbolic actions that create history, society, culture and ideology. If the interpreter does not subject interpretations of the text to the same kind of interpretation as the text itself, some interpretation somewhere will hold the trump cards and dictate the final conclusions without yielding to the responsibility to give audience to its presuppositions, strategies and conclusions.

In conclusion, a four-texture approach was not explicit in the earliest socio-rhetorical interpretations, including my own. Rather, I began to use strategies of one kind and another designed to explore social and discursive aspects of texts, and only within time have the four arenas of texture emerged. While multiple textures of interpretation were becoming evident in New Testament interpretation during the 1970s and 1980s, it was difficult to discern the relation of these textures to one another. It has become common in certain circles, as a result, to present one's analysis as a 'fragment' of interpretation and to leave unattended the relation of one's analysis to other analyses. Socio-rhetorical criticism is the result of a concerted effort to integrate new practices of interpretation. The four arenas of textures, each with its own range of strategies and data, represent a significant refiguration of historical criticism and theological criticism (Montrose 1992: 397–8, 412). The impulses underlying the refiguration are an embedding of disciplinary research and interpretation in an interdisciplinary mode, an embedding of literary modes of interpretation in rhetorical modes and an embedding of historical modes of analysis and interpretation in social, cultural and ideological modes.

A tendency within much historical and theological criticism is to make every new specialization a subdiscipline of historical and theological reasoning. This means that additional disciplines are not allowed into the exegetical arena as equal partners. The disciplines of history and theology maintain the role of judge and jury, issuing restraining orders, establishing laws that govern 'accurate' exegesis and deciding when an interpretation has gone beyond the bounds of acceptability. One of the strategies has been to declare various kinds of interpretation 'unrelated' to historical and theological interpretation.

The goal with socio-rhetorical criticism is to bring disciplines into interpretation on their own terms and engage those disciplines in dialogue on an equal basis. No discipline stands in a privileged position that allows it to disqualify the observations of another discipline. Each discipline exhibits its data with its own particular strategies and point of view. This creates a somewhat different experience in biblical interpretation. The traditional environment presupposes that certain historical and theological approaches stand in an authoritative position over other disciplines. A truly interdisciplinary environment presupposes that intensive dialogue and debate occur in contexts where interpreters with specialties in other disciplines show interest and respect for data gleaned by interpreters using other methods and presuppositions. This creates a context of deconstruction and reconfiguration of each other's data which is more characteristic of conversation and conflict in a global world than conversation and conflict in the context of multiple cultures 'colonized' by another culture. The overall goal, therefore, is to create an approach that can serve us well as we live in the global world of the third millennium CE.

To enable this dialogue, socio-rhetorical criticism creates spaces among and around arenas of specialty that normally function in a strictly disciplinary manner: historical, social, linguistic, literary, theological, aesthetic and ideological. The next four chapters discuss the appearance in biblical interpretation during the 1970s and 1980s of the four arenas socio-rhetorical criticism uses for analysis and interpretation, and apply these arenas in succession to 1 Corinthians 9. A concluding chapter assesses the promise of socio-rhetorical criticism for the field of New Testament study in particular, but also for interpretation in other fields of study.

3

INNER TEXTURE
Every reading has a subtext

One of the first arenas to emerge in the new climate of interpretation was the inner texture of a text. Before we begin to discuss this, however, it will be helpful to think for a moment about different ways of approaching texts for analysis and interpretation. This moment may help us as we proceed through the next four chapters, which analyze major arenas of texture in a text. Any broad-based interpretive approach contains at least two to three hundred strategies and techniques for analysis and interpretation. Socio-rhetorical criticism is no exception. Some are strategies that any human uses to investigate any kind of phenomenon in the world. Others are strategies humans use specifically to investigate written phenomena. Still others are strategies humans use to investigate religious phenomena. The list could continue with social, historical, cultural, aesthetic, ideological, psychological and still other phenomena. A major point in all of this is that no interpretive approach is entirely different from all others; no interpretive approach is entirely new. Every mode of analysis and interpretation is related somehow to others.

Socio-rhetorical interpreters use many strategies and techniques similar if not identical to those that other interpreters use. Some interpreters, however, use similar strategies toward such different goals that it is difficult, if not misleading, to include their work in this book. In the chapters that follow, I discuss interpreters who have applied some kind of strategy or technique that has contributed in some way to the development of socio-rhetorical criticism.

This does not mean that these people themselves are, or would ever want to be considered, socio-rhetorical interpreters. Sometimes the work of certain people has been formative simply because it came at a time when I was developing the approach. At other times, the work of certain people has such similar goals that the relation is obvious, but these interpreters may not use any term for their approach. The reason for discussing other people's work is that much needs yet to be learned about the application of socio-rhetorical criticism to texts. If interpreters return to studies that have somehow been formative for this approach, it is quite possible that they may improve the strategies recommended and applied in this book. But if readers are to read works that are not clearly socio-rhetorical, questions may arise concerning just what socio-rhetorical criticism is. In what ways is socio-rhetorical criticism different from other interpretive approaches currently being used in New Testament studies?

First, the chapters that follow show a gathering and organizing of strategies and techniques of analysis and interpretation in a manner that no other interpretive approach currently follows from beginning to end. I have been pleased to discover some studies that move through a fourfold procedure of analysis with similarities to the approach of socio-rhetorical criticism (Robbins 1992a: xix–xliv), but the particular organization, description and application of the strategies in the following chapters are distinctive to socio-rhetorical criticism.

Second, socio-rhetorical criticism differs from current literary and social approaches by using rhetorical theory for its principle of organization and application. Basic to rhetorical theory is the presupposition that speaker, speech and audience are primary constituents of a situation of communication. This threefold emphasis calls for significant attention to all three, in contrast to the kind of singular focus characteristic of one or another literary method. One of the most common mistakes has been to consider socio-rhetorical criticism to be a reader-response method. Socio-rhetorical criticism does not limit its attention to readers and the manner in which they construct the text, the story, the implied author, the narrator and the characters. Reader-response theorists, in turn, do not use a comprehensive range of rhetorical figures in their analysis (Vickers 1988: 491–8) nor do they study all the components, including the implied author of the text, rhetorically. I will discuss this at some length later in this chapter.

It is my hope, then, that the reader will not be confused by discussions of works written by interpreters who are not themselves socio-rhetorical critics. Socio-rhetorical criticism integrates strategies and techniques used among various literary, social, cultural and ideological interpreters in an integrated, rhetorical system of analysis and interpretation.

Let us turn, then, to the inner texture of texts. Modern literary critics have a special interest in the nature of texts as discourse. Therefore, they initially led the way in analysis of the inner texture of texts. Literary critics who work with poetic boundaries rather than rhetorical boundaries in texts, however, decisively limit the historical, social and cultural nature of their investigations. Socio-rhetorical critics explore textual discourse in the context of all kinds of discourse, since they perceive language to be a symbolic act that creates history, society, culture and ideology as people know it, presuppose it and live concretely in it.

Inner texture concerns relationships among word–phrase and narrational patterns that produce argumentative and aesthetic patterns in texts. These intermingling patterns are the context for the 'networks of signification' in a text. Socio-rhetorical criticism challenges interpreters to use rhetorical resources as they analyze and interpret five kinds of inner texture in texts: (1) repetitive–progressive; (2) opening–middle–closing; (3) narrational; (4) argumentative; and (5) aesthetic. This section identifies key moments in the emergence of each of these types of inner texture in New Testament interpretation.

REPETITIVE–PROGRESSIVE TEXTURE

Repetitive–progressive texture began clearly to appear when Robert Tannehill (1975), Phyllis Trible (1978, 1984) and Robert Alter (1981) published literary–rhetorical interpretations that displayed integrated patterns of repetition and progression in biblical texts. Tannehill's presentation and discussion of Luke 6.37–8 exhibit well how this first appeared. In *The Sword of His Mouth*, he displayed the text for his reader, but he did not add italics and bold print to aid the reader in identifying the repetition and progression in the unit:

[37](a) *Judge not*, and **you** will *not* be *judged*;
Condemn not, and **you** will *not* be *condemned*;
(b) *Forgive*, and **you** will be *forgiven*;
[38]*Give*, and it will be *given* **to you**;

    (c) A *measure* good,
        pressed down,
            shaken together,
                running over,
                    will be put into the lap **of you**.
(d) For by the *measure* with which **you** *measure*
    it will be measured back **to you**.

(Tannehill 1975: 107)

These four sayings have repetitive–progressive texture based on various kinds of restatement and sequence. The first two lines establish a repetitive pattern in three basic ways: (1) the first and second parts of each line repeat the word 'not'; (2) a verb that occurs in the first part in active voice ('judge') occurs in the second part in passive voice ('will be judged'); and (3) each line addresses 'you' (plural in Greek). This repetitive pattern creates a context for repetition and progression throughout the verses. Sayings (a), (b) and (d) all contain a sequence in which the same verb occurs first in active voice and then in passive voice (italicized words). In the context of this repetitive pattern, a progressive pattern unfolds that builds to a dramatic conclusion. Saying (b) removes the 'not', so that the prohibitions 'judge not' and 'condemn not' in saying (a) become positive exhortations to 'forgive' and 'give'. In this context of positive exhortation, saying (c) introduces the concept of a measure. But instead of repeating the pattern of the first two sayings precisely, it builds on the progressive pattern that introduces a new verb in each new line: judge, condemn, forgive, give. Four new verbal concepts occur in saying (c): pressed down, shaken together, running over, will be put. A passive verb occurs at the end of the sequence, continuing the last part of the repetitive pattern in the first two sayings. Progression builds new expectations as the saying starts with a noun rather than a verb ('measure') and introduces four new verbs. What will follow after this repetitive–progressive sequence? The fourth saying starts with the conjunction 'for', which signals a conclusion, and with the noun which appeared at the beginning of the third saying ('measure'). Then the active verb 'measure' (repeating letters and sounds in 'measure') occurs in the first part of the saying followed by the passive 'will be measured back' in the second part. The concluding saying, then, presents the repetitive pattern of the first two sayings in a context of the progressive pattern that has emerged from the beginning to the end.

In the midst of this progressive–repetitive texture, 'you' (plural) occurs in every saying throughout the unit. In the first three and next to last lines, 'you' is the implied subject of each verb. In Greek this subject is part of the verb form itself rather than a separate pronoun as it is in English. In English translation, 'you' is implied with the active form and stated with the passive form of the verb. In the fourth line, the saying (c) and the last line of the unit, either 'to you' or 'of you' occurs as the very last word of the line (in Greek). This means that address to 'you' is a repetitive feature that gives a unified focus throughout the unit. Tannehill, working closely with the repetition and progression throughout the unit, observed that its special meaning effects emerge from the manner in which it 'brings together situations which we may normally keep apart' (1975: 107).

While Tannehill was using this approach to produce commentaries on Luke and Acts (1986/9), others were bringing additional rhetorical and exegetical resources into analysis and interpretation of repetitive–progressive texture. I produced a series of articles and a book during the 1980s (1981; 1982: 224, 232; 1984; 1987) that merged Tannehill's insights with Frans Neirynck's display of duality and tripartite expressions in the Gospel of Mark (1972), Kenneth Burke's rhetorical insights on repetitive and progressive form (1931) and Robert Alter's exploration of repetitive 'type scenes' in biblical literature (1981). Neirynck's work grounded the observations in the rich philological context of traditional New Testament criticism, Burke's work called attention to the difference between logical and qualitative progression in extended portions of texts and Alter's work exhibited the manner in which biblical narrative is truly literary in nature and function.

More recently, I have begun to locate and display repetitive–progressive patterns in word diagrams. At this stage, the interpreter assigns only basic lexical meanings to the words in the text. This procedure withholds fuller meanings to allow sign and sound patterns to emerge (Scott and Dean 1993). In other words, the emphasis is on relations of the signs and sounds rather than content and meanings. At this stage, the interpreter is exploring primary process and form, structured movement that produces meaning process and meaning effect (Wuthnow 1992: 165). Interpreters can begin with a span of text that they perceive intuitionally to be a rhetorical unit. The occurrence of a word more than once in this unit represents a repetitive feature. The interpreter may display the repeated words and phrases in vertical columns. It works best to display words that have some kind of systematic relation throughout the unit. In a recent study of the scenes featuring Mary, Elizabeth and the Magnificat in Luke 1.26–56, for example, I displayed basic narrative agents as in Table 3.1 (1994b). This display brings an initial view of God and the angel Gabriel as agents of activity. The angel who comes to Zechariah and Mary is a character who arrives, speaks and leaves. God, 'the Lord' and 'Holy Spirit' are agents who never speak. Mary and Elizabeth, in addition to the angels, both act and speak in this unit.

Two, three or more displays of systematic patterns may work best for a unit with complex repetitive–progressive sign patterns. This new practice is part of a concerted effort to take repetition and progression seriously on their own terms. The inner features of the text itself are important for understanding the nature of the discourse in it. Some of the questions evoked by rhetorical analysis of

Table 3.1 Narrative agents in Luke 1.26–56

26:	God	angel			
27:					Mary
28:			the Lord		
30:	God	angel			Mary
32:	God		the Lord		
34:		angel			Mary
35:	God	angel		Holy Spirit	
36:						Elizabeth
37:	God				
38:		angel	the Lord		Mary
39:					Mary
40:						Elizabeth
41:				Holy Spirit	Mary	Elizabeth
						Elizabeth
43:			my Lord		
45:			the Lord		
46:					Mary
47:	God		the Lord		
56:					Mary

repetitive–progressive texture are as follows: What patterns emerge from the repetition of certain topics in the text? What topics replace other topics in the progression of the text? Is there continual repetition of the same word throughout the unit, or is there slight modification at almost every progressive stage? Does the progression bring certain kinds of words together but not others? Is there repetition that occurs in steps that create a context for a new word in the progression?

OPENING–MIDDLE–CLOSING TEXTURE

In the context of explorations of repetitive–progressive texture in biblical texts, *opening–middle–closing* texture began to appear. Literary analysis of the opening and closure of New Testament texts raised the issue of the beginning and ending of plotted time in relation to story time (Petersen 1978). In Mark, plotted time opens with John in the wilderness, to whom Jesus comes to be baptized, and it ends with an empty tomb, which four women discover and from which they flee with fear and trembling. Story time, in contrast, begins 'with the indeterminate time when Isaiah prophesied and ends with the equally indeterminate time of the coming of the kingdom predicted by Jesus' (Petersen 1978: 52). Interaction between plotted time and story time creates the narrative world of Mark. This world is significantly distinct from the real world of Mark's time of writing, yet the manner in which the narrative focuses on the future return of the Son of Man provides some clues to the nature of that world (Petersen 1978: 78–80). Subsequently, Norman Petersen wrote an article on the nature of the ending of Mark (1980), and a group of scholars wrote a series of essays on the nature of the beginnings of the gospels (D. E. Smith 1991).

Meanwhile, rhetorical analysis was emphasizing the integral relation among opening, middle and closure. Opening and closure (*inclusio*: Kennedy 1984: 34) exhibit the span of a rhetorical unit – whether that unit be the entire work or a section in it. A discernible beginning and ending are part of an overall arrangement of units and subunits. '[T]he rhetoric of large units often has to be built up from an understanding of the rhetoric of smaller units' (Kennedy 1984: 33). An interpreter must correlate analysis of subunits with analysis of the overall unit to define their function in relation to one another. The goal is to discern the persuasive effect of the parts, how they work together, in relation to the persuasive nature of the entire text.

In Luke 6.37–8 displayed at the beginning of the last section, for example, the final saying (d) contains the pattern of active verb ('you measure') followed by passive verb ('it will be measured back'), which is a pattern that appears in the first four lines. The repetition of this pattern in the opening and closing creates a strong outer frame for the unit. A fascinating challenge then exists for determining the middle of the unit. Do sayings (b) and (c) both constitute the middle, or is only saying (c) the middle? The two sayings in (b) continue the pattern of active verb followed by passive verb, so they could be the final part of the opening of the unit. I would propose, however, that both sayings (b) and (c) are the middle of the unit. The sayings in (a) use the negative 'not' throughout; they open the unit. The sayings in (b) have made a transition from negative to positive, and the saying in (c) continues with positive formulations. The sayings in (b) and (c), then, constitute the middle of the unit. The middle contains two sayings in (b) followed by saying (c) which ends with a positive formulation of a passive verb ('will be put') like the two verbs in the second part of the two sayings in (b). This creates a very interesting middle portion that builds concept upon concept to the significant conclusion 'will be put into your lap'. Now one can see the full effect of the conclusion in (d). This final saying starts with 'for', which provides a rationale for everything that has been said previously in the unit. It uses positive rather than negative formulation, like the initial sayings in the middle. The topic of 'measure' which it uses throughout is the same topic with which the saying (c) in the middle began. Then saying (d) ends with a sequence of active and passive verb, which the opening two sayings introduced to the reader. The final saying, then, embeds a topic ('measure') and positive formulation – achievements of the middle part – in a pattern of active verb followed by passive verb, which was present in the first two sayings. Repetitive–progressive patterns, then, create a strong, tensive opening, middle and closing for this unit.

A quick glance at the word diagram for Luke 1.26–56 (Table 3.1) shows that the beginning of the unit features special activity by the angel Gabriel (Luke 1.26–38). Something special occurs between Mary and Elizabeth in the middle of the unit (Luke 1.36–41). Then, the ending of the unit (Luke 1.43–56) does not mention Elizabeth or the angel. Only a close analysis of the text will reveal with precision the beginning, middle and ending of the unit. Already in a word diagram, however, basic aspects of opening–middle–closing texture begin to appear.

At the level of the entire text of the Gospel of Mark, Bas Van Iersel has exhibited a most interesting opening, middle and closing that interpreters had missed until his close analysis in recent years. For some years, interpreters have known that the Second Gospel opens with thirteen verses depicting John the Baptist, Jesus' baptism and Jesus' testing in the wilderness, followed by a transitional unit (Mark 1.14–15) that both closes the introduction and opens the activity of Jesus in Galilee (Robbins 1981, 1984: 25–31; Van Iersel 1989: 21–2; Stock 1989: 58–71). The transitional unit looks forward and backward in the same context: backward to the 'gospel' which occurs in the title of the book and forward to the activity of Jesus in Galilee. Van Iersel has shown that a corresponding transitional unit, or 'hinge', occurs in Mark 15.40–1. At this point, immediately after the centurion's confession of Jesus as Son of God, the narrative looks backward and forward at women's participation in the story. Suddenly the reader is asked to refigure the activity of Jesus in terms of the presence of women who 'followed him and ministered to him' from Galilee to Jerusalem. This, of course, takes the reader back to the calls to discipleship that begin with Mark 1.16 and do not end until the unsuccessful calling of the rich man in Mark 10.21. But also the reader is asked to revalue the scenes in which the angels ministered to Jesus in the wilderness (1.13), Peter's mother-in-law ministered to all after he removed her fever (1.31) and Jesus inverts this activity in his assertion that 'the Son of Man came not to be ministered to but to minister, and to give his life as a ransom for many' (10.45). This same unit looks forward to the burial and empty tomb. In other words, not only does it integrate women in the activity of Jesus prior to his death but it places them at the center of his burial and resurrection. Women who had followed and ministered to Jesus see Jesus die on the cross, see Joseph of Arimathea bury him, go to the tomb to anoint his body and find a tomb occupied by a young man in a white robe who tells them about Jesus' resurrection and future appearance in Galilee. The story ends with an abruptness related to the abruptness with which it begins. Many interpreters have noted the abrupt ending of Mark. Careful attention to the opening–middle–closing texture of the story enriches the insights of interpreters as they ponder the meaning effects of this remarkable act of composition sometime during the early decades of the Jesus movement.

Close analysis of repetitive–progressive texture and opening–middle–closing texture can be the initial steps in close reading that prepare the interpreter for detailed analysis of narrational, argumentative and aesthetic texture. The implication is that these analytical practices should precede the traditional practice of underlining the words in common among the Gospels or finding the related passages among the letters of Paul. Source, form and redaction criticism presuppose analytical comparison among texts before close wholistic analysis of one text on its own terms. Socio-rhetorical criticism reverses this process. The initial analytical practices, it presupposes, should be with the text itself. It also presupposes that the interpreter will work with a critical text, in dialogue with variants among different manuscripts. This approach can be highly instructive for analysis of a particular pre-printing press manuscript on its own terms.

Literary and rhetorical analysis of opening-and-closing texture in relation to sequential texture has been introducing a new era of scholarship. Some of the questions evoked by this analysis are as follows: What is the nature of the opening of a unit in relation to its closure, whether the unit is an entire text or a subdivision in it? What is the nature of the topics with which the text begins in relation to the topics with which it ends? What is the nature of the topics that replace the topics at the beginning? Is there repetition that interconnects the beginning, middle and end; or is repetition of a particular kind limited to one or two of the three regions of the discourse? What is the function of the parts of a text in relation to the entire text?

NARRATIONAL TEXTURE

While literary interpreters were analyzing narrational aspects of opening, middle and closing, rhetorical interpreters were analyzing argumentative features in them. While literary interpreters were discussing point of view and the reliability of narrators and characters, rhetorical interpreters were discussing enthymemes and arguments from contrary, example, analogy and written testimony. Literary and rhetorical interpreters were bringing new aspects of the inner nature of texts to light in biblical scholarship.

Narrational texture appeared in the work of Rhoads and Michie on the Gospel of Mark (1982), followed quickly by the work of Alan Culpepper on the Gospel of John (1983). Both of these studies used Seymour Chatman's *Story and Discourse* (1978) to distinguish between real author, implied author, narrator, characters, narratee, implied reader and real reader. One of the issues these studies raised was the level of narration for any statement; another was point of view in the narration. This work moved beyond poetics as Rhoads and Michie discussed the narrator, point of view, style, narrative patterns and other features like riddle, quotations, prophecies and irony as rhetorical techniques in the text (Rhoads and Michie 1982: 35–62). Culpepper continued this trend by describing the narrator as the 'rhetorical device' of 'the voice that tells the story and speaks to the reader' (1983: 16). Jeffrey Staley's *The Print's First Kiss* (1988) took narrational analysis yet further into a rhetorical mode in the name of reader-response criticism. Since real readers lie outside the text, he stated, his study looked at what the narrator does rhetorically with the narratee and the implied author does rhetorically with the implied reader. To do this, Staley addressed four intratextual elements of narrative discourse: (a) levels of discourse and their relationships; (b) focalization; (c) discourse order and story order; and (d) the reading process. He observed (Staley 1988: 31) that Wayne Booth pays tribute to the influence of rhetorical studies on narratology (Booth 1983: 123–41) and that Seymour Chatman makes explicit reference to Chaim Perelman in his analysis of intratextual readers (Chatman 1978: 261–2). Then he analyzed the formation of the implied reader by the implied author in the prologue and John 1.19–3.36 followed by the victimization of the implied reader in John 4–21. While subsequent interpreters have been reluctant to adopt Staley's conclusion wholesale that the implied author of the Fourth Gospel continually misleads the implied reader, his analysis is playing a significant role in current narratological analyses (cf. Van Tilborg 1993: 5) and he has advanced this work further in a recent book (Staley 1995).

David B. Gowler advanced the analysis and interpretation of narrational texture in yet a different way. His book *Host, Guest, Enemy, and Friend: Portraits of the Pharisees in Luke and Acts* moved analysis of characterization beyond narrational analysis into narratological analysis and interpretation (1991). No other study to date has achieved the level of analysis of characterization in a narratological mode, nor has any achieved a greater integration of narratological analysis with social scientific analysis (also 1989, 1993). His approach is built on highly advanced narratological theory that uses the comprehensive system developed by Baruch Hochman (1985) for understanding both narration and character-ization. Gowler applies his narratological system to portions of eleven texts outside the New Testament: Aeschylus's *Agamemnon*, Sophocles's *Antigone*, Euripides's *Medea*, 1–2 Samuel and 1 Kings, Plutarch's *Alcibiades*, Suetonius's *The Deified Augustus*, Tacitus's *Annals*, Josephus's *Jewish War*, 1 Maccabees, *Chaereas and Callirhoe* and Lucius's *The Golden Ass* (Gowler 1991: 333–58). This analysis displays the manner in which direct definition functions in contexts of indirect presentation that occur through speech, through descriptions of action, external appearance and environment, and through comparison and contrast in a broad spectrum of Mediter-ranean literature. Then he uses the insights he has gained from this analysis to analyze the characterization of the Pharisees in Luke and Acts. We will return to this landmark study in the chapter on social and cultural texture, since its integration of social scientific criticism with narratology represents its outstanding achievement in the field of New Testament studies.

From the perspective of socio-rhetorical criticism, the limitation of narrational and narratological analyses by literary critics has been the narrator's seduction of the interpreter. The one major exception has been Staley's study discussed above. Literary critics have not used rhetorical resources to analyze and interpret the nar-rator as a rhetorical device in the text. In the words of Culpepper, 'As the narrator tells the story, and because of the way he tells it, we soon accept him as a reliable guide to the meaning of Jesus' life and death' (1983: 17). Although Culpepper identified narrational voice as a rhetorical device within the text, he and most literary critics have ignored this rhetorical aspect of New Testament texts. As a result, literary critics regularly re-enact the rhetoric of the narrator rather than exhibit the nature of that rhetoric to their readers. Instead of using a form of analysis that looks at the text both in the world of its language and the world of its culture, interpreters adopt strategies of exclusion they think the implied author embodies. For example, if the author does not talk about Homer, neither does the inter-preter; if the author does not mention adultery, neither does the interpreter; if the author wants to be understood as against society, the interpreter adopts a position against society. In other words, instead of using a method that explores the distinctive nature of the text in its Mediterranean context, many interpreters use a method that stays within the confines of the discourse and the approach to the world that the interpreter presupposes for the text as the interpretation begins.

One of the most recent attempts to analyze the rhetorical devices of the narrator rather than to be seduced by them is Robert Fowler's *Let the Reader Understand* (1991). Since this is an analysis and interpretation from the perspective of reader-response criticism and many interpreters have misconstrued socio-rhetorical criticism as a form of reader-response criticism, I will discuss Fowler's analysis at some length. Fowler's interest lies in the experience of reading a text itself and in the text's narrational techniques to seduce and entangle the reader in its own view of the world. The book masterfully and programmatically displays rhetorical devices in the Gospel of Mark designed to lure the reader into its point of view; to position the reader in relation to people, place and time; and to motivate the reader to participate in certain beliefs, attitudes and actions. At the end of the book, Fowler discusses two tendencies in the history of interpretation of Mark: (a) to read Mark through the Gospel of Matthew, bringing Markan narration to fuller, clearer expression with statements from Matthew; and/or (b) to read Mark through a Diatessaron created out of all four Gospels. In response to this, Fowler presents a skillful account of Matthew's 'creative and powerful misreading of Mark' (p. 237) and discusses the dynamics of reading Mark as 'one Gospel through four' (p. 265).

Fowler's creative and informative study participates in the new metaphor of texts as a product of weaving (pp. 62, 147–54), it exhibits narration as rhetorical technique throughout the Gospel of Mark and it introduces a perception of 'meaning' as a dynamic, dialectical process rather than as 'content that fills cognitive, emotive and convictional space' (pp. 47–58). There are, however, three dimensions that keep Fowler's work from becoming a fully rhetorical form of analysis and interpretation.

First, Fowler's perception of the cultural context for first-century texts is based on the dichotomy between oral culture and literate culture (i.e. print culture) perpetuated by Walter Ong and Werner Kelber (Fowler 1991: 51–2). The problem with this approach, as I perceive it, is that early Christianity did not emerge either in an oral or in a literature culture, but in a rhetorical culture (Robbins 1991b, 1993b, 1994e; cf. Scott and Dean 1993). A rhetorical culture is aware of written texts, uses written and oral language interactively and composes both orally and scribally in a rhetorical manner. Mark did not write, as Fowler following Kelber asserts, 'to bring the spoken word under control, to domesticate it and replace it with his own written version of *euangelion*' (Fowler 1991: 51). Rather, in his rhetorical culture, Mark sought to give word its *full rhetorical power by embodying it in both speaking and writing.* In antiquity a written text did not imprison words. Written texts were simply an additional tool to give language power (Tompkins 1980). Powerful speaking referred to authoritative writing and authoritative writing referred to powerful speaking. The Gospel of Mark contains significant references to both powerful speaking and authoritative writing, and it dynamically interrelates them in its presentation of its overall story world and in its characterization of Jesus, the disciples and other characters.

Second, at times Fowler interprets the text through a romantic personification of the text. The issue is important to clarify the difference between reader-response criticism and socio-rhetorical criticism. Fowler's own words exhibit his most blatant personification:

> This narrative pulls (and entices) the reader so vigorously (and seductively) in different directions simultaneously that it is ultimately an ambivalent narrative. This narrative seems not quite able to make up its mind about what it wants to do to us.
>
> (1991: 261)

I suggest that in this statement Fowler has transferred romanticism's glorification of the individual creative mind to a glorification both of the creative mind of oral speech and of written text. Since, for Fowler, the creativity of the mind of the oral speaker works differently from the creativity of the mind of the writer, these two minds fight one another throughout the Gospel of Mark. The 'divided mind' of the narrative is located in the division between spontaneous orality and calculating literality upon which Fowler's project is founded. This is a remnant of the traditional dichotomies which nineteenth- and twentieth-century 'modern disciplines' bring to investigation of texts written in the rhetorical culture of Late Antiquity. This dimension in Fowler's work exhibits the complexity of moving from an old paradigm to a new one. In many ways, Fowler has written a book on the frontiers of formalist and romantic literary criticism. Yet it contains decisive remnants of the traditional polarizations which are ingredient to the body–mind dualism that pervades so much of Western thought and practice. As a critical theory of rhetoric, socio-rhetorical criticism calls upon interpreters to assess the presuppositions in their own discourse as they personify the narrational functions of the text.

A final issue concerning Fowler's book is the absence of rhetorical resources for analyzing argumentation in the Gospel of Mark. In the context of a rich display of rhetorical techniques within Markan narration, there is no rhetorical analysis of the argumentation itself either in the narration or in speech attributed to characters. As a result, there is also no rhetorical analysis of the entire enterprise of the implied author. In the end, Fowler is seduced both by the implied author and by the narrator, virtually as much as the rest of his literary critical colleagues. He looks at what 'the narrator' is doing and how 'he' does it, but he does not ask what 'the implied author' is doing and how the narrator advances the goals of the implied author. When Fowler omits the rhetorical nature of the overall selection and presentation of the story from his analysis, he remains, unwittingly perhaps, within the boundaries of the New Criticism. The traditional polarity between literary analysis (inside the text) and historical analysis (outside the text) remains, as does the traditional dichotomy between oral and literature cultures, and the dichotomy between meaning as signification and meaning as event. In other words, Fowler has not thoroughly enacted a perception that language functions simultaneously in interactive contexts of utterance, reference and culture. Ultimately this excellent study is grounded in the traditional practice of separating contexts for the function of language in the manner in which traditional Western disciplines establish boundaries for scientific investigation which they do not deconstruct and reconfigure. Fowler, among all his literary colleagues, introduces a significant heuristic dimension in his approach (1991: 36–40). Yet the project primarily enacts the traditional practice in historical and literary scholarship of setting 'disciplines' of study against one another rather than using them interdisciplinarily to inform one another.

ARGUMENTATIVE TEXTURE

Argumentative texture appears when interpreters use rhetorical resources of analysis in the context of repetitive–progressive, opening–middle–closing and narrational texture. One of the most obvious forms of argumentative texture is logical or syllogistic reasoning, which produces what Kenneth Burke has called logical progressive form (1931: 124; cf. Robbins 1984: 9–12). Logical reasoning regularly occurs in contexts where narrators attribute speech or action to specific people; thus discussions of the rhetorical chreia provide special insights for this kind of analysis (Hock and O'Neil 1986; Robbins 1983, 1985a, 1985b, 1988a, 1988b, 1993a; Mack and Robbins 1989; Mack 1990: 25–92). One of the most characteristic aspects of logical argumentation is the function of unstated premises in the discourse. Identifying and articulating these premises reveals aspects of the argumentative texture in its social and cultural environment that the narrator may never state.

An interesting instance of syllogistic reasoning in a narrative context occurs in the Matthean version of the woman who touched Jesus' garment (Matthew 9.20–2). As the woman approaches Jesus, she reasons in her mind: 'If I only touch his garment, I shall be made well'. Rhetoricians contemporary with early Christianity called this kind of statement an 'enthymeme':

> a statement with a supporting reason introduced by *for,*
> *because* or *since* or an *if . . . then* statement. In contrast to a
> logical syllogism, the premises and conclusion are ordinarily
> probable, not necessarily logically valid. A premise may be
> omitted if it will be easily assumed by the audience.
> (Kennedy 1991: 315; Aristotle, *Rhetoric* 1.2.8–22, 2.22)

Obviously the narrator presents the enthymeme in the form of 'if . . . then' in the mind of the woman. A major problem, however, is that only some people in Mediterranean society may consider the reasoning to be 'ordinarily probable'. Two chains of reasoning appear to underlie the statement by the woman. One chain leads to the conclusion that Jesus possesses special healing powers. Different cultures have different presuppositions about the manner in which healers receive such powers. Perhaps they are born with such powers, perhaps they are given these powers some time during their life without any choice of their own or perhaps they do something extraordinary to receive such powers. In Matthew, Mark and Luke, the narrators appear to presuppose that Jesus received these powers from heaven at his baptism, where the Holy Spirit entered into him (Matthew 3.16; Mark 1.10; Luke 3.22). Perhaps the woman's point of view is the same as that of the narrator in each Gospel. Another chain of reasoning leads to the conclusion that touching Jesus, who possesses exceptional powers, will make her well. It is difficult to know precisely what the accompanying presuppositions might be concerning such touching. Would people think there was a possibility that touching a person with such power could cause the one who touches to die? Such a view existed in biblical tradition about the Ark of the Covenant, where Uzzah touched the Ark of God and died (2 Samuel 6.6–7). If so, some people may consider the woman either to be foolish or to be courageous. In any case, underlying reasoning focuses attention on the exceptional powers of Jesus, and perhaps there would be some presupposition that this woman's approaching of Jesus from behind and touching him could lead to her death. The particular drama of the story occurs when Jesus' statement breaks into these chains of reasoning and introduces a new chain. Jesus' response in the Matthean version pays no attention to his own possession of healing powers, while the Lukan version (Luke 8.46) does. Jesus' comment in the Gospel tradition turns the attention away from himself toward the woman: 'Your faith has made you well'. Jesus' response is a perfect deflection of excessive praise in a traditional culture, like Epameinondas's comment: 'But it is *your doing*, men of Thebes; with *your help alone* I overthrew the Spartan empire in a day' (Plutarch, *On Praising Oneself* 542c; Robbins 1987: 512–13/1994a: 197–200). Not his power but theirs was the cause of their victory; likewise, not Jesus' power but the woman's faith was the cause of her healing. There are two aspects of the story that have special interest from a socio-rhetorical perspective. First is the selection of the term 'faith', *pistis*, among a number of possibilities. Her action could have been considered to be a result of foolishness, simplemindedness, silliness or despair if it had been unsuccessful or disastrous. Or her action could have been understood to be the result of boldness, hope or courage (which would mean 'manliness'; Robbins 1987: 506/1994a: 191). At the moment the story features Jesus' selection of 'faith', 'trust' or 'belief' – however *pistis* should be translated – it creates a particular logic that nurtures 'Christian' culture. To be Christian is to believe that faith heals. But, second, the story does more than this. When Jesus' statement in the Matthean version performs the healing and creates the wellness (Held 1963: 217; Robbins 1987: 507/1994a: 192), it creates the concept of 'faith' within her. In other words, 'faith' does not exist apart from specific attitudes, dispositions and perceptions among a particular group of people. When Jesus names the woman's action faith, and the simultaneous result is the healing of the woman, the story creates a particular 'culture of belief'. Language, then, does not simply 'represent' things, it creates 'reality' for people.

As insights from Greco-Roman rhetorical treatises (re)appeared in biblical studies during the 1970s (Watson and Hauser 1994), some interpreters began to use Chaim Perelman and L. Olbrechts-Tyteca's *The New Rhetoric: A Treatise on Argumentation* (1969; cf. Perelman 1982) as an additional resource for investigating the argumentative texture of New Testament texts. This book places rhetoric at the center of a social theory of language by defining all rhetorical strategies as argumentation (Mack 1990: 14–17). Wilhelm H. Wuellner has been one of the most persistent explorers of argumentative texture from the 1970s into the 1990s (1976, 1978, 1979, 1986, 1987, 1988, 1991, 1993), and Burton L. Mack's *Rhetoric and the New Testament* (1990) has brought analysis of argumentative texture clearly and programmatically before interpreters of the New Testament. These resources have introduced 'reinvented' or 'revalued' rhetoric that investigates biblical texts as 'social discourse' and biblical hermeneutics as 'political discourse' (Wuellner 1987: 453, 456, 462–3).

The roots of analysis of argumentative texture in narrative texts in the New Testament lie in rhetorical analysis of the chreia, the term rhetoricians used for the anecdote in which a narrator attributes speech and/or action to a specific personage. Burton Mack made a remarkable discovery for New Testament scholarship when he observed the relevance of rhetorical elaboration of the chreia for analysis and interpretation of major portions of the New Testament. Jewish scholarship has shown that much of the overall argumentation in the Gospels would not persuade people who were specialists in rabbinic argumentation (Daube 1956). Perhaps especially for this reason it has been informative to discover that many of the basic rhetorical techniques in the Gospels and the Epistles were common in the transmission and amplification of anecdotes and stories in Mediterranean society (Robbins 1989). Of special importance is the manner in which people learned how to develop a chreia (or anecdote) into a speech or essay. Beginning with a chreia, they would provide a rationale for the action and speech in the chreia, clarify their assertion with a statement of what the opposite would mean, then add an analogy, an example, a citation of written authority and some kind of conclusion (Mack 1987,

1990: 41–8; Mack and Robbins 1989: 51–67; Robbins 1993a: 111–31). Once people knew these basic steps for building an argument, they could use enough of the insights from it as were necessary to make a saying or story effective and interesting.

Extensive portions of the New Testament contain this kind of reasoning in the context of speech and action attributed to Jesus, Paul and others in early Christian tradition (Mack and Robbins 1989: 69–193; Mack 1990: 49–92; Robbins 1993b). This means the early followers of Jesus did not transmit Jewish tradition through a 'primarily foreign and strange' form of argumentation but in 'a generally understandable' form widely known in Mediterranean society. Their manner of elaborating a saying or action attributed to John the Baptist, Jesus or Pilate is commonly discussed and recommended in the Greco-Roman rhetorical treatises of the time.

Mack's analysis of the woman who anointed Jesus is an especially interesting example of the manner in which rhetorical elaboration works in the context of a story in early Christian tradition (Mack and Robbins 1989: 85–106). From the perspective of narrational analysis, every account of the story in the gospels features someone introducing an initial topic which is the item to which Jesus responds. In each instance where disciples respond, the topic is the waste of expensive ointment. In the Lukan account where a Pharisee responds, he calls attention to the nature of the woman as a sinner. From a rhetorical perspective, it is noticeable that in the accounts where disciples set the agenda there is complete avoidance of topics that raise socially embarrassing issues like the sinfulness of the woman. The disciples raise conventional issues which Jesus turns into distinctive Christian discourse.

Using insights gleaned from discussions of the chreia in rhetorical treatises from Late Antiquity, Mack observes that the narrational strategy of the story is to feature Jesus responding in a manner that embodies a central topic of Christian belief. From a rhetorical perspective, this central topic comes in 'artificially'. The two most likely functions of anointing in a setting of dining would be either to 'cool the head' after drinking wine or for intimate purposes with sexual connotations. The Lukan version of the story addresses the sexual connotations, but puts them on the lips of an antagonist whom Jesus can teach a 'Christian' lesson of love and forgiveness. The other versions avoid the social functions altogether to address Jesus' burial, which is a central topic in early Christian discourse after the emergence of Pauline discourse.

From a rhetorical perspective, all of the versions of this story are setups to allow Jesus to argue basic topics of Christian discourse during the last quarter of the first century. The social settings do not evoke a 'realism' in a first-century Mediterranean context. They evoke discourse that creates 'Christian culture'. The discourse features Jesus embodying topics that have become central to Christian identity. Instead of Jesus creating the discourse, then, the discourse is creating the image of Jesus in Christian tradition.

Since most literary critics have not incorporated insights from study of the chreia into their narrational analysis, they do not investigate the creative effects of various discourses in early Christianity. Early Christian chreiai attribute certain kinds of speech and action to specific people to 'authorize' them – to establish their authority. This was a common procedure in Mediterranean Antiquity. Plutarch's fifty lives of Greeks and Romans, written in Greek at the end of the first century CE, transmits the values, attitudes, dispositions and presuppositions of Greco-Roman culture by embedding them in 'authoritative' leaders of the past (Robbins 1989). Chreiai were a major medium for transmitting tradition and culture in Late Antiquity. Expansion and addition in chreiai may take the form either of interchange between characters or of commentary, dispute or affirmation after the narration of the speech and action. Insights from analysis of the chreia in the New Testament, Jewish and Greco-Roman literature bring into view the entire enterprise of assigning voice to specific people and groups in Mediterranean society and culture. In this context, it becomes obvious that the biographical discourse in the Gospels, Acts of the Apostles and Epistles, which attributes specific actions and speech to specific people, played a decisive role in the success of Christianity in the Mediterranean world.

Stanley K. Stowers's interpretation of Romans 7.7–25 as speech-in-character is an additional example of the manner in which rhetorical resources can contribute to analysis of the argumentative texture of New Testament discourse (1995). Stowers analyzes the manner in which *prosopopoiia*, writing in such a manner that one 'creates character', plays a decisive role in Paul's letter to the Romans and elsewhere. Recently, literary critics have shown an interest in characterization in literature (Malbon and Berlin 1993). Unfortunately, they have not used the insights gained from rhetorical analysis of the chreia in Mediterranean antiquity. Therefore, most interpretations and analyses thus far have not exhibited the fundamental significance of attribution of certain kinds of speech and action to specific people in the context of Mediterranean society and culture.

One of the most important results of these insights into the argumentative texture of texts has been the awareness of social and cultural presuppositions and networks of reasoning that interpreters can investigate in New Testament literature. In other words, analysis and interpretation of the argumentative nature of New Testament texts is revealing significantly new insights about the participation of early Christian discourse in Mediterranean society and culture.

SENSORY–AESTHETIC TEXTURE

Aesthetic texture began to appear in the works of Amos N. Wilder (1956, 1964). Dan O. Via used the concept of aesthetic literature to explore the parables in the New Testament (1967), Robert Tannehill explored this dimension of gospel texts extensively in *The Sword of His Mouth* (1975), and aesthetic issues have played a decisive role in the work of John Dominic Crossan throughout the past two decades (1973, 1976, 1979, 1980).

Robert Tannehill's interpretation of the four sayings which were discussed at the beginning of this chapter exhibits the additional dimension that aesthetics brings into the context of repetitive–progressive, opening–middle–closing, narrational and argumentative texture. Tannehill interprets the meanings of the sayings as follows:

[O]ur text does not merely instruct; it attacks with full force.... [T]he [initial] sayings link man's condemnation or forgiveness to God's condemnation or forgiveness.... These words neatly turn our concern for ourselves against us.... These commands wish to reorder radically the way in which we understand our relations to others. This web of relations, which we order according to rights and debts, must now be seen in terms of God's demand for forgiveness.... [T]he sentence concerning 'good measure' ... serves as a bridge to the final sentence of the verse by introducing the concept of 'measure'.... Here the giving which is promised in response to our giving shows itself as a true gift, for it overflows the expected measure.... It is a measure not used to measure, that is, not used to limit what is given. . . . This vivid metaphor for God's giving and forgiving fills the whole passage with power and reacts upon our understanding of what it must mean for us to give. The final sentence of vs. 38 . . . now serves . . . to apply this vivid picture of an overflowing, unmeasured measure to our actions also, suggesting that we must give in this way, since this is how God desires to give. Thus the passage attacks strongly our vision of life as a network of rights and debts which must be upheld by condemning the wrongdoing of others and substitutes a vision of an order imposed by God's forgiveness.

(1975: 108–12)

Perhaps the best description of this mode of interpretation is 'aesthetic theological texture'. Tannehill observes the tensions in the language that call for reassessment and self-criticism, and evoke new convictions, dispositions and actions. The inner texture of the passage, he suggests, contains webs and networks of signification that evoke and realign the networks of meaning we conventionally and unconsciously espouse and promulgate. The images in the passage, then, concern people's imagination. How do humans imagine new possibilities for their lives? How do they imagine the present concrete realities of their lives? How do they imagine the past and link their imagination of the past with their imagination of the present?

INNER TEXTURE IN 1 CORINTHIANS 9

Having now discussed the manner in which strategies for analyzing and interpreting the inner texture of texts have emerged in New Testament studies since the 1970s, I will now display a socio-rhetorical analysis and interpretation of inner texture in 1 Corinthians 9. This analysis takes us to a letter attributed to the apostle Paul, a leader of a sector of first-century Christianity who himself never saw and traveled as a disciple with the historical Jesus of Nazareth. The inner nature of most parts of Paul's letters is argumentative. This means that the words are designed to persuade the reader to think, do or feel in a certain way, and they regularly give reasons why a person should respond in this manner. Because the letters of Paul are argumentative, Hans Dieter Betz and Wilhelm Wuellner interpreted letters of Paul to reintroduce rhetorical analysis and interpretation to New Testament interpreters. A letter features a narrator who speaks in first-person singular 'I', and it contains explicit assertions that the narrator supports with reasons and confirms with additional reasons. While rhetorical analyses of 1 Corinthians 9 have been informative, most of them have explored only a small spectrum of the meaning effects in the text. Our socio-rhetorical investigation exhibits the manner in which a programmatic changing of boundaries for interpretation brings significantly new questions to guide the investigation and uncovers a range of meanings that can bring quite new insights into New Testament interpretation.

This first set of readings draws boundaries around the text itself. Theoretically, the text for our inner textual analysis is all of 1 Corinthians. For practical purposes, this chapter will focus only on chapter 9 of 1 Corinthians. As the strategies of analysis and interpretation change for the purpose of looking at multiple arenas of meaning and meaning effects, new aspects of 1 Corinthians will continually come into view. The present study falls decisively short of an investigation of all of 1 Corinthians. The following analysis is only meant to be suggestive of an interdisciplinary way to integrate interpretive activities in the field of biblical studies today.

An interpreter draws a boundary around the text itself to create an environment for analysis and interpretation of the inner texture of a text. Socio-rhetorical criticism uses six sets of strategies within this boundary to analyze and interpret inner texture: (1) repetitive texture; (2) progressive texture; (3) opening–middle–closing texture; (4) narrational texture; (5) argumentative texture; and (6) sensory–aesthetic texture. Every section of this study could be expanded, simply using analyses available to us in current interpretation. The purpose of the analysis is not to be exhaustive, however, but to display basic techniques that can be used to analyze the inner texture of discourse an interpreter finds in a New Testament letter.

Repetitive texture in 1 Corinthians 9

One of the most striking repetitive features of 1 Corinthians 9 emerges in its use of personal pronouns. There are only two verses in the chapter in which a first- or second-person pronoun does not occur:

(a) 9.7: Who serves as a soldier at his own expense? Who plants a vineyard without eating any of its fruit? Who tends a flock without getting some of the milk?

(b) 9.14: In the same way, the Lord commanded that those who proclaim the gospel should get a living by the gospel.

Verse 7, referring to people who have common social roles, uses interrogative rather than personal pronouns. Verse 14, attributing a command to the Lord Jesus, refers to people with nouns and a participle rather than personal pronouns. Every one of the other twenty-five verses contains at least one first- or second-person pronoun.

By far the most frequent personal pronouns throughout the chapter are 'I', 'me', 'my', and 'myself'. Either as an explicit pronoun or as a pronoun embedded in a verb, a first-person singular reference occurs forty-six times. In addition, 'we' used with reference to the speaker himself and Barnabas, rather than the *common* 'we' (e.g. *our* Lord), occurs nine times. In total, then, in twenty-seven verses of text there are fifty-five references to the speaker himself, either individually or together with another person like him.

The next most frequent pronouns are plural 'you' and 'your', occurring eleven times. Last of all, there are four occurrences of common 'we', 'us' or 'our'. The pattern of occurrences (based on the Greek text) can be seen in Table 3.2, which brings to light a number of important features of the chapter. First, it is noticeable that nine first-person singular references are present in the opening three verses, twenty-eight are present in a middle section (9.15–23) and seven occur in the final two verses. In other words, first-person singular references dominate the opening three verses, a span of nine verses in the middle and the final verses of the chapter. Second, reference to a partner who stands in a close alliance to the first-person singular speaker occurs immediately after the opening verses (9.4–6) and in the beginning of the middle section (9.11–12). Third, references to plural 'you' or 'your' occur in a constellation in the opening two verses (9.1–2), four verses at the beginning of the middle section (9.9, 9.11–13), and one verse (9.24) in the closing statements in the chapter. Fourth, a reference to common or generic 'our' occurs in the opening verse (9.1) and a verse near the beginning of the middle (9.10), and a reference to common or generic 'we' occurs in the context of the closing verses (9.25). Fifth, while the first two verses corre-

Table 3.2 Repetition of personal pronouns in 1 Corinthians 9

	I, me, my, to me, myself (individual)	we (Paul and Barnabas)	you, your (plural)	we, us, our (common)
1:	4		1	1
2:	3		2	
3:	2			
4:		1		
5:		1		
6:	1	1		
[7]				
8:	1			
9:			1	
10:				2
11:		2	2	
12:		4	1	
13:			1	
[14]				
15–23:	28			
24:			3	
25:				1
26–27:	7			

late references to 'I', 'you' and 'our', the final two verses focus entirely on the first-person speaker with 'I' and 'myself'.

The overall pattern of personal pronouns in the chapter indicates that some kind of verbal transaction occurs in a discursive movement from a singular person to a group addressed as 'you'. The discourse teams another person with the first-person singular speaker, and it strategically incorporates the people in the group in a sphere defined by personal relationship to the speaker and his associate. In the very final statements, the speaker focuses entirely on himself. Whatever this discourse is doing, it is doing it through concrete personal agency and confrontation.

Another striking feature of the discourse in 1 Corinthians 9 is the frequent occurrence of forms of the negative – 'not'. Eighteen of the twenty-seven verses contain at least one occurrence of a form of the word 'not' in Greek. Three additional verses contain words built on negation:

9.17: not of my own will (*akōn*)
9.22: weak = 'not strong' (*asthenēs*)
9.25: imperishable (*aphtharton*)

This means that only six verses do not contain either a form of 'not' or a word built on negation:

9.3: This is my defense to those who would examine me.
9.10–11: [10]Or does he speak entirely for our sake? It was written for our sake, because the plowman should plow in hope and the thresher thresh in hope of a share in the crop.
[11]If we have sown spiritual good among you, is it too much if we reap your material benefits?
9.14: In the same way, the Lord commanded that those who proclaim the gospel should get their living by the gospel.
9.19: For though I am free from all men, I made myself a slave to all, that I might win the more.
9.23: I do it all for the sake of the gospel, that I may share in its blessings.

For some reason, every verse except these six throughout the chapter contain negative statements or concepts. The word 'not' (*ou, ouk, ouchi, mē*) occurs five times in the first two verses and four times in the last four verses. This means that repetitive negation occurs prominently in both the opening and closing as well as in the middle of the chapter. An important aspect of the repetitive texture of the discourse in this chapter, then, is the convergence of first-person singular 'I', 'my' and 'myself' with the 'not' in its opening and closing verses.

Progressive texture in 1 Corinthians 9

The verses in 1 Corinthians 9 that contain no negative words refer to 'defense', 'those who would examine me', 'it was written for our sake', 'the Lord commanded', 'though I am free, I made myself a slave' and 'I do it all for the sake of the gospel'. These statements function prominently in the progressive texture of the discourse, articulating a defense 'against' something which uses an appeal both to written text and to a 'command of the Lord' and which adopts a technique of saying that the speaker does things one way although he 'could' do them another. The remaining discourse asserts that things are 'not' being done in one way 'but' in another. What could

Table 3.3 Conjunctions and 'have the right to'

2:	because		
4:		have the right to	
5:		have the right to	
6:		have no right to	
9:	because		
10:	because		
12:			but
			but
15:			but
	because		but
16:	because		
	because		
17:	because		but
19:	because		
20:			in order that
			in order that
21:			in order that
22:			in order that
			in order that
23:			in order that
24:		but	in order that
25:		but	in order that
27:		but	

be the purpose of such action? The final part of the body of the chapter explains the purposes and goals. If we display the references to 'because', 'have the right to', 'but' and 'in order that' throughout the chapter, we see in Table 3.3 the progressive pattern that moves from the initial statements to the purposes and goals that establish the context for the concluding remarks in the chapter. This display of progressive texture reveals that the discourse of 1 Corinthians 9 is openly argumentative: it provides a series of reasons ('because') in support of a series of assertions ('have the right to'). Moreover, the argumentation concerns a claim to some kind of right that is not being exercised (the right to, 'but' . . .), for a particular purpose ('in order that').

Opening–middle–closing texture

Repetitive and progressive texture begin to reveal important insights into the opening, middle and closing of 1 Corinthians 9.

Let us assess the insights we can attain into opening–middle–closing texture on the basis of repetitive and progressive texture alone.

How far does the opening seem to extend? It is not possible to tell with precision until we analyze both narrational and argumentative texture. At this point we see an opening (9.1–2) that introduces the narrator himself with first-person pronouns, that uses 'not' to evoke certain meanings and meaning effects and that provides at least one reason for understanding certain things in certain ways. Verse 4 introduces the topic of having 'the right to' food and drink. Is this the beginning of the middle part of the discourse? Only analysis of other aspects of the inner texture can provide an answer to this.

What are the basic sections of the middle part? The movement from 'have the right to' to 'but' then to 'in order that' suggests that there are three basic parts in the middle section. Correlating this sequence with the shift in pronouns suggests that a transition from the first part to the second occurs at verse 11, where the discourse begins to juxtapose 'we' and 'you' and introduces the adversative 'but'. A transition from the second part to the third clearly occurs by verse 20, which begins a repetitive occurrence of 'in order that'. Perhaps verse 19 begins the second part with the introduction of a rationale ('because') that calls forth the series of statements of purposes and goals ('in order that'). At this point, however, we cannot tell for sure. But the middle section contains a first part in 9.4–10 that discusses rights, a second part in 9.11–18 or 19 that begins with 'we' and 'you' and continues with 'but' and 'because', and a third part in 9.19 or 20–25 that explains the goals and purposes of having certain rights but not using them.

By verse 26, then, the discourse is ending. We have to hold open the possibility that the reintroduction of the adversative 'but' in verse 24 actually signals the start of the ending, since it is the nature of a conclusion to summarize what has gone before.

On the basis of major aspects of repetitive and progressive texture in 1 Corinthians 9 a basic opening, middle and closing begins clearly to appear, as well as basic movement in the middle part. This discourse starts by setting the stage and asserting a case for the speaker's right to do certain things in certain ways. Then the speaker argues that he does not do these things he has the right to do, and he gives reasons for not doing them. Finally, the speaker explains the purpose that underlies the choice not to do the things he has a right to do. To sum up, repetitive patterns of personal pronouns, negative words, conjunctions and the phrase 'have the right to' reveal movement from opening statements to a series of arguments that create a bridge to final statements that purport to explain the goals and purposes of the speaker as he refrains from exercising certain rights which he, by the nature of his status, has the right to exercise.

Narrational texture

Now let us explore *narrational texture* to see what additional insights it can add to the inner texture of this discourse. Among Chatman's choices between a 'narrative' voice, a 'narrating' voice and a 'narrator's' voice (1978), this discourse presents the last – a *narrator's* voice. The use of 'I' for the narrational voice calls attention to the emergence of the voice from the body of one individual person. In other words, narrational voice embodies the discourse in the speech, action, decisions, emotions and convictions of a person named Paul. In the end, therefore, the authority or force of the voice creates a particular image of a particular person during the early years of the Christian movement.

In the midst of the patterns observed in the previous section, one of the most distinctive features of the narrator's voice is nineteen questions in the chapter. The questions exhibit the following sequence:

> 1: Am I not free?
> Am I not an apostle?
> Have I not seen Jesus our Lord?
> Are you not my workmanship in the Lord?

* * * * * * * * * *

> 4: Do we not have the right to our food and drink?
> 5: Do we not have the right to be accompanied by a wife, as the other apostles and the brothers of the Lord and Cephas?
> 6: Is it only Barnabas and I who have no right to refrain from working for a living?

* * * * * * * * * *

7: Who serves as a soldier at his own expense?
Who plants a vineyard without eating any of its fruit?
Who tends a flock without getting some of the milk?

* * * * * * * * * * *

8: Do I say this on human authority?
Does not the law say the same?
9: Is it for oxen that God is concerned?
10: Does not God speak entirely for our sake?
11: If we have sown spiritual good among you,
is it too much if we reap your spiritual benefits?
12: If others share this rightful claim upon you,
do not we still more?

* * * * * * * * * * *

13: Do you not know that those who are employed in the temple service get their food from the temple, and those who serve at the altar share in the sacrificial offerings?
18: What then is my reward?

* * * * * * * * * * *

24: Do you not know that in a race all the runners compete, but only one receives the prize?

Wuellner suggests that these questions function as part of 'Paul's pastoral guidance for a maturing, stabilizing church' (1986: 52). The implied author of the discourse speaks as a narrator to implied readers whom the discourse 'pastors'. The questions invite the implied hearer to participate in the discourse in an active way, producing answers as the discourse proceeds.

The interesting thing from a narrational perspective is that all the questions provide the information the implied hearer needs to answer them. In other words, all of them are what we commonly call 'rhetorical' questions: implied hearers do not have to answer the questions; the speaker will answer them. There is an interesting sequence in the nature of the rhetorical questions, however.

The first four questions (9.1) invite the implied hearer to say 'Yes'. Yes, Paul is free and an apostle, he has seen Jesus our Lord, and we are his workmanship in the Lord. The sequence, however, may actually evoke somewhat different responses. The first three questions focus directly on Paul. To the first question, an implied hearer may be inclined to say, 'I hear you saying you are free, but in what way are you free?' To the second question, the response may be, 'Well, you call yourself an apostle'. To the third question, the response may be, 'Well, you say that you saw Jesus our Lord'. The first three questions concern attributes of Paul, and only the second and third questions finally have to be answered only yes or no: either Paul is or is not an apostle, and he either has or has not seen Jesus our Lord. But the first question actually calls for qualification: 'In what way are you free?'. 'To what kind of freedom are you referring, Paul?'

After the first three questions focus on attributes of Paul, the fourth question focuses on an attribute of the implied hearers: 'Are you not my workmanship in the Lord?' No matter what the answer of the implied hearers might be, Paul immediately answers it for them: 'If to others I am not an apostle, at least I am to you; for you are the seal of my apostleship in the Lord.' The sequence of four questions, which ends with Paul's answer in 9.2, draws the implied hearers into the discourse, defining not only who Paul is but also who they are. In fact, the discourse asserts that Paul is who he is on the basis of who they are. Their identities are bound to one another, no matter what anyone says about their identities (including the hearers). The first three verses of the chapter, then, embed the identity of Paul and the identity of the hearers in each other. Whatever the hearers do, think or say concerns the speaker, and whatever the discourse says concerns the hearers.

The next three questions in 9.4–6 presuppose the result of the first three verses in the chapter, and they evoke something quite different from the opening questions. Initially, the sequence itself is noticeable. The first question moves abruptly to 'we', meaning Paul and at least one other person alongside him. The second question evokes 'other apostles', 'the brothers of the Lord' and 'Cephas'. The third question refers specifically to 'Barnabas and I'. This sequence defines Paul in relation to prestigious third-person people ('others') then narrows the focus to Paul and Barnabas alongside him. In other words, while the first sequence of questions defined Paul by embedding his identity in the identity of the implied hearers themselves, the next sequence defines Paul on the basis of his relationship to 'other' people with authoritative standing. 'Other' apostles refers to disciples of Jesus while Jesus was on earth; 'brothers' of the Lord would include James; Cephas refers to the disciple Peter, whom Paul says elsewhere was the first disciple to whom Jesus appeared after his resurrection (1 Corinthians 15.5); and Barnabas was probably recognized as a person in good standing with the Jerusalem church. After drawing the circle tight around Paul and the Corinthians, then, the discourse draws a circle around Paul and prestigious leaders in early Christian circles.

Another aspect of the second set of questions is their forceful use of negatives. Instead of proceeding in the straightforward manner of the first questions, these questions intensify their emphasis by using two negatives that reinforce each other (*mē . . . ou*). The meaning effect is something like 'None of you think we don't have the right, do you?' Thus, this set of questions communicates a tone of defensiveness or, perhaps, aggressiveness.

Yet another aspect of the second set of questions is that they address the very first question of the chapter which is the only one that calls for qualification. The questions achieve two things in relation to that initial question. First, they change the concept of freedom to the concept of 'right' or 'authority' (*exousia*). Second, they limit the concept of right or authority to the support of apostles by the people among whom they work. Thus, the second set of questions uses aggressive, negative interrogations as it sets Paul firmly in the midst of prestigious leaders in early Christianity and narrows the focus of 'freedom' to the rights all of them have to live off food and drink provided by the people among whom they work.

The aggressive tone of the second set of questions continues through a third set which presents three examples of people who receive pay or produce for their work: soldiers, vineyard planters and shepherds (9.7). Each question, which asks who does a certain kind of work without receiving pay or produce for it, is meant to evoke a resounding 'No one!' As the questions unfold, they set the rights of Paul and Barnabas solidly in the context of conventional social practice. In other words, after embedding Paul's identity in the identity of his hearers and gathering prestigious leaders in early Christianity alongside Paul, the discourse undergirds the rights of Paul and Barnabas with common practice throughout all society.

At this point the strategy in the questions changes. In 9.8–10 the questions introduce polarities with a rhythm of no . . . yes: 'No, I do not say this on human authority; yes, he speaks entirely for our sake' (9.9b–10). These questions, in other words, differentiate things from one another rather than bring them together (Perelman and Olbrechts-Tyteca 1969: 411–59). God is preoccupied not with oxen but with humans; Paul is on the side not of human authority but of God's law.

This strategy of polarization continues in the questions in 9.11–12. But now the strategy evokes 'us' against 'them'. The distinction between 'spiritual' benefits and 'material' benefits defines the work of Paul and Barnabas as spiritual. Then the question 'if them, not us still more' (9.12) implies that 'others' do not offer as many spiritual benefits as Paul and Barnabas. In this set of questions, then, polarities associate the work of Paul and Barnabas with God's law (9.9), with God's concern for people (9.10) and with spiritual benefits. The other side of the implication is that 'others' are a bit more on the side of human authority, of eating like oxen and of material benefits. Not entirely, of course, but partially.

Next, a single question moves the conventional practice of supporting people into a 'spiritual' space: temples (9.13). While the answer to the question is 'Of course, we know this', the next verse supplements the implied hearers' answer with a command of the Lord Jesus which associates this space with 'doing the work of the gospel' (9.14). At this point, then, the strategy moves away from 'differentiation' to 'association'. Paul and Barnabas, as they do spiritual work associated with God's law and concerns, are doing something more like 'temple' work than work on a battlefield, in a vineyard, or at a place where animals graze.

After the questions have placed Paul and Barnabas alongside one another to differentiate them from 'others' and put them on the side of God, the Lord Jesus, and the gospel, the next question leaves Barnabas aside to focus entirely on Paul: 'What then is *my* reward?' The section below will discuss the intricate argumentation involved at this point in the discourse. The purpose here is to observe the narrational shift from 'we' to 'I'. The question in 9.18 about Paul's reward is the result of a shift to first-person singular in 9.15. After the shift, Barnabas is no longer a matter of concern for the discourse. Beginning with 9.15, Paul's work, identity, goals and reward stand at the center.

One more question appears in the chapter, and this feature in the narrational texture of the discourse seems to solve the issue concerning where the conclusion of this chapter begins. The question in 9.24 starts the conclusion: 'Do you not know that in a race all the runners compete, but only one receives the prize?' The section below will discuss the argumentative force of this question. At this point, we observe that a question shifts the social analogy to a runner after a previous question had shifted it to workers in a temple. This is a remarkable shift indeed. One might have thought that once the discourse had shifted to spiritual work in a spiritual space it would have maintained this field of analogy to the end. Some reasons for this shift will emerge as the analysis moves to other textures of the discourse.

In summary, one of the most obvious narrational aspects of 1 Corinthians 9 is the presence of nineteen questions that extend from the opening verse to the opening statement of the conclusion. The initial questions focus on Paul, then broaden out to the implied hearers, to 'other' apostles which include Barnabas and to social convention. After this, the questions appeal to the Torah, Moses, God and the Lord Jesus. A little more than half way through the chapter the questions turn to Paul himself – his work and his reward. This focus on Paul remains to the conclusion, where athletic imagery provides the language for describing the challenge for endurance and the prize that Paul, and perhaps others, may receive.

Argumentative texture

The analysis of repetitive and progressive texture revealed that the discourse was argumentative, and analysis of opening–middle–closing texture uncovered a basic beginning, middle and ending to the discourse. This analysis suggests that 1 Corinthians 9 represents some kind of basic unit of discourse. The analysis of narrational texture began to reveal special rhetorical features in the text, including shifts from one field of reasoning to another. Analysis of argumentative texture, using insights from Greco-Roman rhetoric as well as literary rhetoric and the New Rhetoric, reveals that the chapter unfolds in the manner of a rhetorical elaboration (Mack 1990; Robbins 1993a). A display of this elaboration, using insights from the work of Russell Sisson (1994), reveals the rhetorical function of each section as it unfolds in the chapter:

(1) *Thesis* (9.1a)
   Am I not free?
(2) *Rationale* (9.1b)
   Am I not an apostle?
(3) *Confirmation of the rationale* (9.1c–2)
   (a) [1c]Have I not seen Jesus our Lord?
   (b) Are not you my workmanship in the Lord?

(c) [2]If to others I am not an apostle, at least I am to you; for you are the seal of my apostleship in the Lord.

(4) *Restatement of the thesis (9.3–6)*
[3]This is my defense to those who would examine me. [4]Do we not have the right to our food and drink? [5]Do we not have the right to be accompanied by a wife, as the other apostles and the brother of the Lord and Cephas? [6]Or is it only Barnabas and I who have no right to refrain from working for a living?

(5) *Argument from analogy (9.7)*
[7]Who serves as a soldier at his own expense? Who plants a vineyard without eating any of its fruit? Who tends a flock without getting some of the milk?

(6) *Argument from written testimony (previous judgment)(9.8–12a)*
  (a) Introduction: [8]Do I say this on human authority? Does not the law say the same?
  (b) Rationale: [9]For it is written in the law of Moses: 'You shall not muzzle an ox when it is treading out grain.'
  (c) Embellishment: Is it for oxen that God is concerned? [10]Does he not speak entirely for our sake? It was written for our sake, because the plowman should plow in hope and the thresher thresh in hope of a share in the crop.
  (d) Conclusion: [11]If we have sown spiritual good among you, is it too much if we reap your material benefits? [12a]If others share this rightful claim upon you, do not we still more?

(7) *Argument from the contrary, with digression and reasons (9.12b–18)*
  (a) Introduction: [12b]Nevertheless, we have not made use of this right, but we endure anything rather than put an obstacle in the way of the gospel of Christ.
  (b) Repositioning of the argument from analogy and previous judgment: [13]Do you not know that those who are employed in the temple service get their food from the temple, and those who serve at the altar share in the sacrificial offerings? [14]In the same way, the Lord commanded that those who proclaim the gospel should get their living by the gospel.
  (c) Restatement: [15a]But I have made no use of any of these rights, nor am I writing this to secure any such provision.
  (d) Rationale: [15b]For I would rather die than have any one deprive me of my ground for boasting.

(e) Confirmation of the rationale: [16]For if I preach the gospel, that gives me no ground for boasting. For necessity is laid upon me. Woe to me if I do not preach the gospel! [17]For if I do this of my own will, I have a reward; but if not of my own will I am entrusted with a commission.

(f) Conclusion: [18]What then is my reward? Just this: that in my preaching I may make the gospel free of charge, not making full use of my right in the gospel.

(8) *Argument from example* (9.19–23)

(a) Introduction: [19]For though I am free from all men, I have made myself a slave to all, that I might win the more.

(b) Embellishment: [20]To the Jews I became as a Jew, in order to win Jews; to those under the law I became as one under the law – though not being myself under the law – that I might win those under the law. [21]To those outside the law I became as one outside the law – not being without law toward God but under the law of Christ – that I might win those outside the law. [22]To the weak I became weak, that I might win the weak.

(c) Conclusion: [23]I do it all for the sake of the gospel, that I may share in its blessings.

(9) *Conclusion* (9.24–7)

(a) Introduction: [24]Do you not know that in a race all the runners compete, but only one receives the prize?

(b) Exhortation: So run that you may obtain it.

(c) Embellishment: [25]Every athlete exercises self-control in all things. They do it to receive a perishable wreath, but we an imperishable.

(d) Conclusion: [26]Well, I do not run aimlessly, I do not box as one beating the air; [27]but I pommel my body and subdue it, lest after preaching to others I myself should be disqualified.

The key to the argumentative nature of the opening of the chapter is the rhetorical force of *interrogatio*, asking a question as an emphatic way of making an assertion. In Greek, the form of the negative in the first four verses calls for an affirmative answer: 'I am free, am I not?', etc. The rhetorical force of these questions, then, produces the following assertions:

I am free.
I am an apostle.

I have seen the risen Christ.
You are my workmanship in the Lord.

Russell Sisson's analysis of this sequence (1994) suggests that the second sentence provides the rationale for the first, and the last two sentences confirm the rationale:

Thesis: I am free,
Rationale: because I am an apostle,
Confirmation of the rationale: (I am an apostle),
because I have seen the risen Lord,
and you are my workmanship in the Lord.

If Sisson's analysis is correct, and I suggest that it is, 1 Corinthians 9 begins with a rhetorical syllogism. This is important for three reasons. First, Aristotle said that the most powerful way to begin a speech is with a syllogism; an alternative way is with an anecdote or story. Second, if a speech starts with a syllogism, it would be natural for it to continue with a series of argumentative devices that, in the end, present what rhetoricians in Late Antiquity called 'a complete argument'. Third, if 1 Corinthians 9 presents a complete argument, then it would be natural for Pauline discourse to contain complete arguments in other contexts that interpreters do not currently expect.

When people use syllogistic argumentation in public contexts, they do two things that are important for analysis of 1 Corinthians 9. First, customarily they present their conclusion first and their rationale for the conclusion second. This is important, for it helps us to see that the first question, and not the second or third, introduces the thesis for the chapter. Second, a person regularly states only one of two logical premises that support the conclusion (Mack and Robbins 1989: 69–84). This means that the statements in the discourse presuppose a second, unstated premise, and often it is very informative for an interpreter to reconstruct that premise. According to Sisson's analysis, the complete syllogism at the beginning is:

Unstated major premise: All apostles are free.
Minor premise: I am an apostle.
Conclusion: Therefore, I am free.

The argument at the beginning of 1 Corinthians 9 presupposes that all apostles have freedom. Immediately, as stated above, the question arises: What is the nature of this freedom? This is a question that receives answers as the text continues. The answer lies in the thick texture of 1 Corinthians, not only with historical phenomena but with social, cultural and ideological codes of understanding that were current in Mediterranean society during the first century. An exploration of the inner texture of the text reveals a presupposition that all apostles are free. As further analysis proceeds, the nature of this freedom will unfold.

After the first two questions present a syllogistic opening for the chapter, the next two questions confirm the rationale (minor premise). In other words, the statement about an apostle applies to Paul, because there is evidence that Paul has seen the risen Lord and performed the work of an apostle among the Corinthians. The *Rhetorica ad Herennium* 2.18.28–19.30 presents the confirmation of a rationale as a natural step at the beginning of an argument that begins with a thesis and a rationale. 1 Corinthians 9 opens, then, in a conventional manner with a thesis, a rationale and a confirmation of the rationale.

After the confirmation of Paul's apostleship (the rationale for the thesis about freedom), the discourse presents a summary statement that concludes the opening:

> If to others I am not an apostle, at least I am to you; for you are the seal of my apostleship in the Lord.

This summary repeats the rationale and the confirmation, emphasizing the role of the Corinthians as the 'seal' of Paul's apostleship and allowing the phrase 'in the Lord' to strengthen the assertion that Paul had seen the Lord. As a reiteration of the previous argument, it also is a rhetorical syllogism:

> Unstated major premise: The workmanship of an apostle in the Lord is the seal of his apostleship.
> Minor premise: You (my workmanship) are the seal of my apostleship in the Lord.
> Conclusion: Therefore, I am an apostle to you.

It is important to notice that this summary has advanced the argument in a particular way beyond its beginning point. While the initial argument was about the freedom of apostles and was grounded in the relationship of an apostle to the 'Lord Jesus', the evolving argument includes a community of people who are 'the work' of an apostle.

This opening for the chapter reveals a number of important things about the nature of the discourse in it. First, a section of argumentation in this discourse will regularly conclude with a summary statement. Second, a concluding statement will contain argumentative features that reformulate earlier syllogistic argumentation. Third, a summary will refocus the argument. Fourth, there will be movement back and forth between authority figures (e.g. the 'Lord Jesus') and 'Paul's work' among the people.

After the opening, the discourse contains an indicative statement, 'This is my defense to those who would examine me', followed by eight questions. The same observation applies to these questions that applied to the first four: their interrogative form is an emphatic way of making an assertion. Sisson's analysis indicates that the indicative statement and the first three questions restate the thesis about 'freedom' in terms of 'rights' (9.3–6). This unit, then, has the function of repositioning the thesis even further than the statement after the first three questions (9.2). The particular 'freedom' this discourse will address is 'the right to food and drink', the right to request and receive 'a living' from the people in the community where an apostle works. The strategy of the discourse at this point, then, is to 'delimit' freedom to a particular issue for which it is possible to formulate a strong argument.

After the repositioning of the thesis, the discourse presents an argument from analogy (9.7). The argument is amplified with three examples: soldier, vineyard planter, shepherd. Amplification is characteristic of this discourse; only one example would have been necessary but it provides three. The special function of an argument from analogy is to ground the reasoning in common social and cultural phenomena. The argument gains a 'public' appeal with its employment of 'everyday' commonplaces. The discourse claims not to be 'esoteric' or puzzling, but 'open' to all and persuasive to all who are 'reasonable'.

After the argument from analogy, the discourse presents an argument from written testimony (9.8–12). Wuellner's analysis (1986: 67–8) reveals the syllogistic nature of the argument. The unit opens with a self-deliberating question (9.8a) that polarizes 'human authority' with divine authority. Verse 8b appeals to Torah as 'written testimony' about social rights. Then verses 9–10, attributing the authority of the Torah first to Moses, then to God, presents a syllogistic argument:

Major premise: Moses wrote that you shall not muzzle an ox when it is treading out the grain. (9.9a)

Minor premise: In what Moses wrote, God was speaking not about oxen but about humans. (9.9b–10)

Conclusion: Therefore, if we have sown spiritual good among you, it is not too much for us to reap your material benefits. If others share this rightful claim upon you, we do still more. (9.11–12a)

Three unstated premises clearly underlie the argumentation in this syllogism:

(a) God spoke what Moses wrote.
(b) Spiritual good is equal to or greater than material good.
(c) We have sown more spiritual good among you than others.

The first premise accounts for the transition from Moses in the major premise to God in the minor premise. The second premise accounts for the juxtaposition of 'spiritual good' and 'material benefit' in the conclusion. The third premise accounts for the final statement about 'us' having more of a rightful claim than 'others'. A fourth unstated premise appears to be:

(d) Everything God spoke to Moses is for the sake of humans.

We will see in the section on oral–scribal intertexture below that this conclusion may have been influenced by the presence of statements about humans on both sides of the verse in the Torah (Deuteronomy 12.1–25.3; 25.5–19). There are other considerations also, which the analysis will explain below.

There are three major points for us to notice in this context. First, the argument from written testimony brings a new 'authoritative' set of presuppositions into the discourse. These presuppositions broaden the authoritative base beyond 'apostleship in the Lord Jesus' to 'God himself through Moses'. In other words, the preceding argument from analogy established a 'general' premise to support the claims in the discourse; now the argument from written testimony transforms the premise into a 'specifically authoritative' claim within Jewish culture. This will be important in the exploration of 'cultural' intertexture in the chapter. Second, this unit brings 'authoritative' presuppositions into the argument by 'rerunning' the mode of the very beginning of the argument, namely, by means of a syllogistic argument. The discourse, then, adopts a 'logical' mode when it introduces personages, both divine and human, to 'author-ize' its assertions. Third, the final statement in the unit reiterates the topic of 'rights' (9.12a), the delimited form of the topic of 'freedom' that the restatement reformulated (9.3–6). As the final statement reiterates the topic, it evokes a polarity between 'spiritual good' and 'material benefit', and between 'us' (Paul and Barnabas) and 'them' (others who worked among you). Again the argument moves from the authoritative sphere – in this instance God, Moses and the Torah – to Paul (and Barnabas), 'other' apostles and the Corinthian community.

After the argument from written testimony, the discourse formulates an argument from the contrary (9.12b–18). For a particular set of reasons, Paul does not use the 'rights' which the argument thus far has established for the apostles. In contrast to the kind of argument from the contrary that simply 'reaffirms' the opening argument, this argument from the contrary 'repositions' the argument in a manner similar to the preceding units. The reasoning to this point raises the possibility that an apostle who does not exercise the 'freedom' to use his 'rights' may disqualify himself from his identity as an apostle. This discourse risks a 'dangerous' argument from the contrary as a way of unambiguously establishing a contrary mode of reasoning. In other words, this is an argument from the contrary that 'turns' the argument rather than recycles the assertion at the beginning.

The first component in the argument defines the contrary mode of action as a means to advance 'the gospel of Christ' without putting any obstacle in its way (9.12b). Prior to this point in the chapter, the discourse does not refer either to the gospel or to 'Christ'. The opening statement of the contrary repositions the language of 'apostle', 'Jesus the Lord' and 'God' in terms of the gospel of Christ.

The second component in the unit (9.13–14) repositions the previous arguments from analogy and from written testimony in terms of 'spiritual work', which the preceding unit juxtaposed with 'material benefit'. In the context of 'the gospel of Christ', the work of an apostle is directly analogous to the work of 'those employed in the temple', and the authoritative testimony for this resides in a 'command of the Lord (Jesus)' that those who proclaim the gospel should get their living by the gospel. The discourse could have contained this repositioning at the end of previous units. Its embedment in the argument from the contrary functions in a 'digressive' manner (a well-established technique in Pauline discourse: Wuellner 1979) that integrates previous argumentation into the new terminology of the argument.

The next component (9.15–17) introduces a third syllogistic argument into the chapter. Verse 15a presents the conclusion to the syllogism, namely that Paul does not make use of these rights and verse 15b provides the minor premise, namely that use of the rights would deprive Paul of his boasting. Verses 16–17, then, present a complete syllogism that confirms the minor premise concerning Paul's boasting. Put in syllogistic order, the reasoning is:

> Major premise: Preaching the gospel of one's own free will brings a reward, but preaching the gospel not of one's own free will makes it (only) an entrustment with a commission.
> Minor premise: Preaching the gospel is laid upon Paul as a necessity, an entrustment of a commission.
> Conclusion: Therefore, preaching the gospel as an entrustment gives Paul no ground for boasting (but preaching it of his own free will brings a reward).

Preaching the gospel against one's own will makes it an entrustment of a commission, which in turn gives no ground for boasting. Preaching the gospel out of one's own free will, however, brings a reward. What might that reward be? In the initial syllogism, Paul has indicated that his reward is to be able to boast. It is clear, then, that the unstated presupposition in the initial syllogism (9.15) correlates Paul's ground for boasting with preaching the gospel out of his own free will:

> Unstated major premise: My ground for boasting is doing this of my own free will.
> Minor premise: I would rather die than have any one deprive me of my ground for boasting (i.e. doing this of my own free will).
> Conclusion: Therefore, I have made no use of these rights, nor am I writing to secure any such provision (a decision of my own will).

Paul does not make use of these rights both because it would put an obstacle in the way of the gospel and because it would deprive him of his ground for boasting. Paul preaches of his own free will, rather than simply because it is laid upon him as a necessity. Then the discourse presents a summary:

What then is my reward? Just this: that in my preaching I may
make the gospel free of charge, not making full use of my right
in the gospel.

(9.18)

This summary does three things. First, it gathers the concepts of
'reward', 'preaching the gospel' and 'not making use of one's right
in the gospel' together in a statement that concludes the argument
from the contrary. Second, it reformulates Paul's 'boast', which is a
benefit for Paul alone, into 'making the gospel free of charge', which
is a benefit for people in the community. Third, it has reformulated
the issue from 'we' (9.12b) to 'I' (9.18). The discussion started
with Paul and the Lord Jesus (9.1), brought in Barnabas as an ally
(9.4–12) and introduced Moses, God and the Lord (Jesus) as guaran-
tors (9.9, 9.14). Now the argument turns the discussion decisively
away from 'others' to a decision of 'my' own will (9.17) which
focuses on 'my' preaching in which 'I' make the gospel free of
charge (9.18). At this point, then, the authority of the discourse
moves into the body and voice of the narrator himself.

The next unit continues with an argument from example
(9.19–23), building on the conclusion which the discourse reached
in the argument from the contrary. The introduction to the unit
(9.19) repositions the argument yet once more by integrating the
concept of being 'free' (9.1) with 'making myself a slave to all, that I
might win the more'. In other words, a restatement now removes
the limitation of freedom to 'rights' (9.4–6) so that the issue of 'freedom' can be juxtaposed to 'slavery'. The next two verses establish
the integrity of the 'one who made himself a slave' by his work not
only with 'Jews under the law' (9.20) but also with 'those outside the
law' (9.21) and 'the weak' (9.22). The goal of the work is to win
people for God, to save them. The division of humanity into three
groups rather than two builds in a special way on the appeal to the
law earlier in the chapter (9.8–10). A polarity between those under
the law and those outside it could result simply in differentiation
and dissociation (Perelman and Olbrechts-Tyteca 1969: 190–1,
324–5, 411–59). The inclusion of a group of people with the attribute of weakness moves beyond a polarity into associative discourse
that integrates multiple attributes of humanity. The concluding
statements (9.22b–23) summarize the meaning effect well:

^{22b}I have become all things to all, that I might by all means save some. ²³I do it all for the sake of the gospel, that I may become a full participant in it.

Humanity includes not only those under the law and outside the law, but also the weak. The discourse presents Paul as a person who has forgotten no one. He has become all things to all people. The final verse reiterates the topic of the 'gospel' which first appeared at the opening of the argument from the contrary (9.12b) where the discourse moved beyond authorizing 'the rights' of the apostle to an explanation of Paul's not making use of these rights. The discourse suggests that Paul's thought and action embody the inner nature of the gospel. The final clause introduces a new term in the chapter, translated here 'a full participant'. The term appears to have a double nuance. On the one hand, Paul has become a full partner, an intimate associate, of the gospel of Christ. On the other hand, Paul participates of his own will in the gospel, freely deciding to become a fellow associate of all people – those under the law, those outside the law and those who are weak.

The final unit presents an amplified conclusion (9.24–7) to the argument in the chapter. The opening question introduces the analogy of running a race, where only one runner receives a prize, and the next statement issues an exhortation to run in a manner that one may win the prize (9.24). The next component broadens the analogy to every athlete and introduces a polarity between the perishable crown they receive and the imperishable one 'we' receive (9.25). The final two sentences bring the chapter to a close with a focus entirely on Paul's embodiment of the gospel in the manner of the most seriously self-disciplined runner and boxer:

²⁶Well, I do not run aimlessly, I do not box as one beating the air; ²⁷but I pommel my body and enslave it, lest after preaching to others I myself should be disqualified.

Having started with the freedom of an apostle, the argument ends with the self-discipline of an athlete. After establishing the rights of an apostle (9.3–6) and supporting those rights by analogy (9.7) and written testimony in the Torah (9.8–12a), the change began in the argument from the contrary (9.12b–18), where Paul, an apostle, does not exercise the rights of the apostle but participates of his own will in the gospel. The argument from example immediately after it (9.19–23) reveals that this 'decision to offer the gospel free of charge' willfully takes the form of slavery to all people to 'gain' or 'win' Jews, those outside the law and the weak. In a context that establishes a polarity between a perishable and imperishable crown, the conclusion (9.24–7) employs the analogy of the self-disciplined athlete to exhibit Paul's embodiment of this slavery to the gospel and to exhort all to run the race so they may obtain the prize.

Argumentative texture, then, exhibits the internal reasoning in the discourse as it moves from the beginning to the end of the chapter. Between the beginning 'I' and the ending 'I' lies a skillful sequence of three complex syllogistic arguments in contexts of analogy, written and oral testimony, contrary and example. In 9.3, the discourse evokes the dynamics of a judicial defense. If the discourse in this chapter truly is judicial, the event in the past which called forth an accusation is the failure of Paul and Barnabas to accept support for their work among the Corinthians. The charge would be that the failure to accept support disqualifies them from the status of 'apostles'. A deliberative moment emerges in the chapter when the discourse exhorts the implied hearers to 'run' in such a manner that they may win the prize (9.24). But this appears to have emerged more as a natural part of a concluding statement than as a symbol of the rhetorical nature of the discourse in the chapter. The deliberative moment, however, may reveal that the discourse is epideictic rather than judicial.

Epideictic discourse, especially if it incorporates a significant negative tone, has significant affinities with judicial rhetoric. Instead of making a specific charge that someone has done something wrong in the past, epideictic rhetoric evaluates actions and intentions as good or bad for the purpose of confirming values that people already hold. The section of the chapter that functions as a 'refutation' of 'those who would examine Paul' (9.12b–18) moves far beyond a goal of acquittal to a goal of displaying the nature of the most genuine kind of preaching of the gospel. The discourse retains dynamics of a judicial defense, because it exonerates the life and work of the speaker himself in a context where people may misunderstand them. Nevertheless, the phrase 'life and work' is a signal that the discourse moves beyond judicial rhetoric toward the kind of goal envisioned by epideictic rhetoric. Judicial rhetoric would focus on a specific action in the past for the purpose of 'acquitting' the one who performed that action from guilt. Epideictic rhetoric, in contrast, moves naturally to the evaluation of a person's 'entire life and work' as a testimony to the values everyone prizes most.

In 1 Corinthians 9, defense of past action is a means to differentiate between people who engage in the work of the gospel in a manner that keeps the most treasured prize at the end in view, and those who do not. The purpose for evoking a differentiation between doing what one has the right to do and doing what saves the most people is to confirm that a focus on the gospel itself is the only means by which any real 'prize' is awarded to the runner. Anyone who focuses on material benefit is completely misguided. Only a person who keeps an 'imperishable crown' in focus will be running in a manner that has any possibility of achieving something worthwhile. Thus, in the end the goal of the discourse is to censure anyone who would emphasize the importance of material benefits and to praise all who enslave themselves to Jews, to people outside the law and to the weak for the sake of the gospel.

Sensory–aesthetic texture

Before moving to the chapter on intertexture, this section will deepen the analysis of 1 Corinthians 9 through aspects of its sensory–aesthetic texture. While there are various ways to do this, the focus here will be on the range of senses the discourse evokes and the manner in which the discourse embodies these senses (cf. Malina 1993: 73–82). A key to the discourse is the manner in which it, in the end, embodies the full range of the senses it evokes in an image it creates of the 'Paul' who embodies the gospel of Christ.

The first verse of the discourse begins with appeals to the entire body of Paul: Am I not free? Am I not an apostle? (9.1a, b). Then the discourse moves to the eyes of Paul: Have I not seen Jesus our Lord? (9.1c). Then it moves to the relation of the working body (or hands) of Paul to the entire bodies of the people whom the discourse is addressing: Are not you my workmanship in the Lord? (9.1d). The discourse begins, then, with appeals to the status of Paul's entire body, and the special function of his eyes and hands. The work of his hands establishes an important point of view concerning the status of the bodies of the people the discourse addresses: from the perspective of this discourse, the 'religious' status of their bodies is a product of Paul's working body. This sequence ends by evoking an image for all to see: the Corinthians are 'the seal' of Paul's apostleship in the Lord. People do not need to depend on Paul's eyes to know that he is an apostle of Jesus the Lord. Anyone can use their own eyes to look at the Corinthians: they are the visible medallion of honor that anyone with eyes can see.

In 9.3 the discourse shifts to judgments of the mind that people make concerning Paul. Paul begins with aspects of his mouth. With this letter he is making a defense, evoking a setting of speech from his mouth. He stays with the mouth as he discusses food and drink (9.4). Then he moves to entire bodies of people as they travel and as they are related to one another as wives and fictive kin. Then he shifts to entire working bodies and how they get living support and food for their mouths (9.7).

In 9.8–10 the discourse refers directly to Paul's own speaking mouth and then to written law that he claims comes from God's heart ('concern') and mouth. Then the discourse uses the image of working bodies that sow grain to interpret the words Paul and his associates have spoken to the Corinthians and the harvest it would be appropriate for them to reap from the Corinthians. At this point, spoken words have attained the value both of agricultural work that produces food and of holy work that produces spiritual nurture.

In 9.13 the discourse shifts to people who work with their bodies in temples and get their food from this work – eating temple and altar food. In 9.14 the discourse claims that the mouth of the Lord commanded that those who use their mouths to proclaim the gospel should get their living from this work. An attendant result of this imagery can be the implication that the people who receive the gospel are like a holy temple and altar with which apostles and their associates work. In 9.15–16 Paul claims that he does not use these rights to receive food so he can use his mouth for boasting in addition to preaching the gospel.

In 9.17 the discourse evokes the function of the will. Is the will located in the mind? Or is it in the liver or intestines? Wherever it is located, suddenly the imagery has moved beyond body, eyes and hands to the will in the body. Using his own free will, when he preaches with his mouth without taking food for his mouth, a reward or wage emerges on its own. The reward is that Paul can make the gospel free of charge.

In 9.19 Paul moves to the social identity of his body. Though his body is free from all people, he makes it a slave. He makes his body Jewish to win Jews, outside the law to win those outside the law, and weak to win the weak. In other words, he makes his body socially different to win socially different people.

In 9.24 the imagery shifts to the feet as it refers to runners. In 9.25 it refers to athletes, another social identity for the body, and asserts that all of them exercise self-control in all things. In this concluding setting, the discourse again refers to a visible phenomenon signaling honor. In this instance it is the wreath regularly placed on the head. The wreath of athletes regularly withers up and is temporary. For exercising self-control as they preach the gospel, refusing support so they can offer the gospel free of charge, Paul asserts that they compete for an imperishable wreath. He ends by referring to his feet not running aimlessly and his hands pommeling his own body, rather than shadowboxing in the air, to subdue his entire body, lest after using his mouth to preach the gospel he be disqualified.

The focus on parts of the body throughout the chapter crescendos to running with the feet and pommeling the entire body with the hands as an image of exercising control over the body. Aesthetically this imagery calls for implanting the gospel in one's complete body. Simply having the gospel in one's mind, mouth, eyes, feet or hands alone will not suffice. The discourse makes two moves here. On the one hand, it insists that the gospel must be fully embodied, or perhaps the body must be fully gospelized. On the other hand, the discourse creates the image of Paul as one who fully embodies the gospel, or perhaps whose complete body has been gospelized.

As Paul uses words to explain what appear to be ordinary phenomena, the words begin to transcend their usual meanings to create aesthetic meaning effects that evoke an image of mind, heart, will, strength and hope all focused on 'bodily' living the gospel of Christ. This discourse, then, evokes a deeply embodied aesthetic. Mind over matter is not nuanced richly enough to describe the aesthetic. Rather, the image is fully embodied freedom–slavery. In the end, there is neither concern for body nor concern for freedom, even though both body and freedom are significant topics of reasoning and argumentation. Freedom is slavery, slavery is freedom, bodily concerns are spiritual concerns and spiritual concerns are bodily concerns. They do not cancel each other but fulfill one another.

CONCLUSION

Inner texture, then, covers a wide spectrum of phenomena, meanings and meaning effects in a text. Since repetition itself is a progression from one occurrence to another, repetition is an important phenomenon out of which flows progressive texture. The interplay of repetitive and progressive texture establishes beginning–middle–closing texture.

While repetitive, progressive and opening–middle–closing texture emerge first and foremost out of the signs on a page of text, narrational texture emerges when signs are given voice. Narrating voice creates the context for narrational repetition and progression. The interplay of narrational repetition and progression establishes narrational patterns. As we have seen, narrational patterns can vary from alternation between narration and speech attributed to characters to repetition of interrogative and declarative speech throughout a chapter of text.

Argumentative texture moves beyond sign and voice into the inner reasoning in the repetition and progression in the text. At this point, logical and qualitative progressions effect myriads of techniques with language that evokes images of authority, persuasion, emotion and myriads of other meanings and meaning effects that rhetoricians throughout the ages have investigated and discussed.

Sensory–aesthetic texture moves beyond inner reasoning into the evocative power of all the senses available to human life and imagination. The very images the discourse selects to communicate its meanings stimulate dimensions of the body that transcend explanation and understanding. In the realm of the aesthetic, communication occurs in ways that quite fully escape our ability to describe. We can point, and we can dance and sing with the text. All this is simply designed to release the text to do what it alone can do. The aesthetic of our language, of course, will intercept in one way or another the aesthetics of the text. Yet, attempts to enter the aesthetic texture of the text may open vistas of its aesthetic that may otherwise remain dormant as a result of our other strategies of analysis and interpretation.

At the end of this chapter on inner texture, it is important to realize that intertexture, social and cultural texture and ideological texture have stalked us all the way. They have been present all along, even though our focus has turned our attention away from them. This chapter employs an authoritative narrational voice that every reader should recognize now, if they have not already, as problematic. Analyses and displays of repetitive texture may choose to emphasize one aspect of repetition over another. Discussions of progressive texture may select phenomena in a highly different manner in the text. Analyses of opening–middle–closing texture may place a priority on one rather than another effect of the ordering. Analyses of narrational texture may observe one kind of phenomenon rather than another. Investigations of argumentative texture may draw one kind of conclusion rather than another. Moreover, interpretations of aesthetic texture may explore one range of nuances rather than another in a text.

Does this mean that inner textual analysis is fully arbitrary? The answer is no. It means that every construal of the inner texture of a text is located somehow in particular ways of hearing, seeing, understanding, envisioning and imagining. It may be of interest to the reader to know that when Joop F. M. Smit responded to the analysis above of 1 Corinthians 9 at a meeting of doctoral students funded by the Netherlands Research Foundation in March 1994, he challenged the analysis of the argumentative texture with an assertion that the discourse of the chapter begins with 1 Corinthians 8.13: 'Therefore, if food is a cause of my brother's falling, I will never eat meat, lest I cause my brother to fall'. Following the analysis of Margaret M. Mitchell (1992), he argued (as many interpreters do) that the overriding topic in the argumentation is the food practices of early Christian believers in Corinth in a social context where Jewish purity rituals and Greco-Roman religious practices are creating different perceptions of responsibility and opportunity (cf. Smit 1994). If an interpreter emphasizes the presence of 1 Corinthians 9 in the context of the discussion of food in 1 Corinthians 8.1–11.1, the argument about apostleship in the chapter is a subsidiary theme in an argument about freedom, responsibility and embodiment of the gospel in a context where people with a range of loyalties to Jewish and Greco-Roman views of the world have gathered together in local communities. This subordination creates a different function for the topic of food and drink throughout 9.3–13. This different function, in turn, creates alternative functions for the arguments from analogy, previous judgment, contrary and example.

A major alternative that surfaces in analysis and interpretation of 1 Corinthians 9, then, is whether the interpreter has a greater interest in the nature of Paul as a leader or in the nature of Pauline communities as syncretistic religious communities characteristic of Hellenistic-Roman society and culture. The variations in interests and concerns between these alternatives can create significantly different construals of the inner texture of 1 Corinthians 9.

During the last three years, students who have used the guidelines in this chapter to write inner textual studies have regularly manifested two alternative ways of reading the inner texture of a unit. For example, with Mark 10.17–22, the rich man and Jesus, a major alternative is whether the opening of the story is simply the narrational comment 'And as he was setting out on his journey, a man ran up and knelt before him', or whether the introduction also includes the additional comment 'and he asked him, "Good Teacher, what must I do to inherit eternal life?"'

If the opening is simply the introductory narrational comment, the story contains two major units in the middle characterized by an initial statement from the rich man followed by a response from Jesus. From this perspective, the story focuses on the rich man in every unit of the story: (a) opening (10.17a); (b) middle (10.17b–19, 20–1); (c) closing (10.22). The rich man approaches Jesus, asks Him about eternal life, speaks openly about his faithful observance of God's commandments, and decides not to risk a transfer of his loyalties and responsibilities to Jesus. In the context of the attributed speech, the three narrational comments emphasize the rich man's initial attraction to Jesus (10.17a) to which Jesus responds with attentiveness and love (10.21a) and to which the rich man responds with sorrow and departure (10.22). In the context of these actions and reactions, richly repetitive and progressive speech attributed to Jesus (9.18, 9.21) reaches its high point in Jesus' call to the rich man to follow him as a disciple.

If, however, the opening includes the speech attributed to the rich man in 10.17, the story contains three attributed sayings in the middle part: (a) 10.18–19: Jesus; (b) 10.20: rich man; (c) 10.21–2: Jesus. In the middle, then, Jesus has the first and last word. This analysis highlights the manner in which the rich man comes to Jesus filled both with action that has led him toward Jesus (10.17a) and with speech that has led him into conversation with Jesus (10.17b). In the end, however, Jesus' call for him to follow causes the man to lower his face, to lose all ability to speak, to move away from Jesus and in sorrow to maintain his possessions rather than to begin new social and economic relationships with Jesus and his followers. This interpretation emphasizes the chreia-like nature of each unit of the story, including the passive action-chreia in 10.22. In the mode of anecdotal narration in Mediterranean society, sequential attribution of action and speech to both the rich man and Jesus features movement from a confident rich man who confronts Jesus in a conventional narrational mode of challenge and response in Mediterranean society. When Jesus responds to the rich man in the form of an expanded sayings-chreia (10.18), the rich man responds with a brief response that provides the context for elaborating the topic of Jesus' initial response with language, themes and argumentative figures characteristic of early Christian discourse during the last three or four decades of the first century. In other words, the story is really not about the rich man. The purpose of the story is to evoke a context for creating a particular persona for Jesus by attributing speech and action to him in a mode characteristic of anecdotal biography in Mediterranean society during the first century. Particular analyses of inner texture of texts, then, are intimately related to an interpreter's overall interests, whether these remain implicit or are explicitly stated by the interpreter.

At the conclusion of this chapter, therefore, we must recognize that analysis and interpretation of the inner texture of a text, even in highly sophisticated and systematic ways, not enough in biblical interpretation. Historical, social, cultural and ideological issues have been not only on the doorstep but in the house of interpretation itself throughout this chapter, whether or not we have recognized it. To deal with the presence of issues that have accompanied inner textual analysis and interpretation of inner texture, sociorhetorical criticism explores three additional arenas of texture in addition to inner texture in texts. At the end of this chapter, then, we evoke the need for systematic investigation of arenas of practice and thought beyond the inner texture of texts. The discussion turns first to intertexture, then it will turn to social and cultural texture, and, last of all, it will return to ideology.

4

INTERTEXTURE
Every comparison has boundaries

INTERTEXTURE IN
SOCIO-RHETORICAL CRITICISM

A second arena is intertexture. In socio-rhetorical terminology, in this arena the interpreter still interprets the text as a 'work', the production of an author. This means the interpreter works in the area between the author and the text, not between the text and the reader. The appearance of the book entitled *Intertextuality in Biblical Writings* (Draisma 1989), produced by a team of international scholars, has brought a new focus to this arena of texture in New Testament texts. As words stand at all times in relation to other words both inside and outside any particular text, so texts stand at all times in relation to other texts. While analysis of the intertexture of a text requires an exploration of other texts, the object of the analysis is, nevertheless, to interpret aspects internal to the text under consideration.

Intertexture in a text covers a spectrum that includes: (1) oral–scribal intertexture; (2) historical intertexture; (3) social intertexture; and (4) cultural intertexture. Intertexture concerns the relation of data in the text to various kinds of phenomena outside the text. Each kind of intertexture has its own range of relationships. It is not possible to be exhaustive in one's intertextual analysis. Rather, a representative range of intertextual phenomena enables an interpreter to begin to address the myriads of ways a text participates in networks of communication that reverberate throughout the world. Whether every text has a theoretically infinite relation to

things in the world is debatable. It is clear, however, that every intertextual analysis and interpretation establishes boundaries. As we
will indicate below, these boundaries are the means by which interpreters establish or accept implicit and explicit canons of literature
within which they work.

ORAL–SCRIBAL INTERTEXTURE

Socio-rhetorical criticism includes analysis and interpretation of
oral–scribal intertexture. Analysis of oral–scribal intertexture
includes recitation, recontextualization and reconfiguration of other
texts, both oral and scribal, in the foregrounded text. I begin with
analysis of an essay by Gail O'Day that carries the subtitle 'A Study
in Intertextuality' (O'Day 1990). This essay vividly introduces both
the arrival of the concept of intertextuality on the scene of New
Testament studies and the limitations of intertextual studies that
locate themselves in traditional theological and canonical criticism.
O'Day's approach is inspired and informed by Michael Fishbane's
'inner biblical exegesis' (O'Day 1990; Fishbane 1980, 1985, 1986).
In the first paragraph of her essay, O'Day defines intertextuality as
'the ways a new text is created from the metaphors, images, and
symbolic world of an earlier text or tradition' (p. 259). She gets this
definition from T. S. Eliot's essay on 'Tradition and the Individual
Talent' (Eliot 1920), and the focus of the definition is on the 'metaphors, images, and symbolic world' an author has used from an
antecedent text to 'create' a new text. This is a definition that
focuses on the author's 'production of the text'. O'Day is interested
in Paul's creation of 1 Corinthians 1.26 out of words, structures
and aspects she calls 'substantive theological parallels' that exist in
Jeremiah 9.22–3.

In the second paragraph of her essay, O'Day establishes
firm poetic boundaries for her analysis. She does not investigate
Hellenistic-Roman literature where the Greek words in Pauline discourse for 'wise', 'powerful' and 'well-born' occur (Wuellner 1973:
671). Rather, she excludes resources characteristic of the *Religionsgeschichtliche Schule* by adopting canonical criticism as practiced by
Brevard Childs and James Sanders. The circular nature of her statements in this paragraph reveals how a disciplinary approach encodes
its own authority internally. She uses canonical criticism for her
intertextual analysis, because 'canonical criticism . . . presupposes
the conceptual framework of intertextuality'. Then she adds:

'Shared texts and traditions, used and reused throughout the history of a particular faith community, provide the interpretive pieces in this method' (O'Day 1990: 259). Her disciplinary boundaries, then, are secured by 'a particular faith community'. In other words, a theological code invests the disciplinary practice with religious authority, and this disciplinary practice establishes boundaries that exclude Greco-Roman literature from her investigation.

The final paragraph in her introduction announces the rigor of the approach. Her analysis will use the method of inner biblical exegesis developed by Michael Fishbane, and this method, she announces, is '[t]he single most important contribution to the study of intertextuality in scripture . . .' (p. 259). This method 'is not simply "literary or theological playfulness", but "arises out of a particular crisis of some sort"'. Moreover, it is grounded in 'the most characteristic feature of Jewish imagination', its 'textual-exegetical dimension' and 'Paul, the Jewish apostle to the Gentiles, shared in this textual-exegetical imagination'. This method is not interested, therefore in 'theoretical constructs', she informs us, but instead 'works with remarkable methodological clarity, precision, and thoroughness to uncover the richness of inner biblical exegesis . . .' (p. 260). This statement, one notices, pits 'theory' against 'clarity, precision, and thoroughness', and let us notice its implications. Its unstated premise is that theoretical constructs are unclear, imprecise and partial, in contrast to her approach, which is obvious, exact and complete. With O'Day's intertextual approach we see, then, an interpreter who evokes firm boundaries that canonical and theological criticism have established in biblical study. Her analysis and interpretation will remain strictly within Hebrew Bible and Jewish literature. O'Day expresses no desire to go around, over, under or through these boundaries. Boundaries, in other words, offer the possibility for this intertextual interpretation to attain assured, complete results (notice 'precision' and 'thoroughness' above).

As O'Day begins, analysis of 'inner texture' stands in the forefront. But the essay does not start with 1 Corinthians. It begins with analysis of the antecedent text, Jeremiah 9.22–3, then moves to 1 Corinthians 1.26–31. The antecedent text takes precedence over 1 Corinthians, because it provides the material that Paul remolded. In contrast with a socio-rhetorical approach, then, the priority does not lie with the inner nature of the argument in 1 Corinthians but in authoritative biblical tradition that Paul has refashioned in a setting of crisis.

As the inner exegesis of Jeremiah 9.22–3 and 1 Corinthians 1.26–31 proceeds, the essay is interested, as mentioned above, in 'substantive theological parallels' rather than 'verbal and structural parallels' (p. 267). Substantive theological parallels, the essay asserts, give us 'intertextuality at its fullest'. Paul makes 'explicit reference to the received text and interweaves it thoroughly into the fabric of his new text' (p. 267). We are to understand that the analysis and interpretation 'helps to correct a misreading of vv. 27–29' that was also 'theologically dubious' (p. 265). Further, we are to understand the approach as scientific, grounded thoroughly in itself and in strategies that derive from the data itself. The essay has not added or subtracted anything from the text. The conclusions are there in the data, and the essay has simply called them to our attention.

I start with analysis of this intertextual interpretation, because it illustrates more clearly than some studies how intertextual interpretations, including my own, function within definite boundaries. I disagree with limiting the boundaries for intertextual interpretation of New Testament literature to Hebrew Bible and Jewish literature, since the Hellenistic-Roman world was the context of its intertexture. Nevertheless, other interpreters challenge my limiting of intertexture to Mediterranean literature. Theoretically, the intertexture of any piece of literature may be with 'every culture in the human world'. It is impossible, however, to study everything at the same time. For this reason, we establish boundaries. The manner in which we establish the boundaries and refer to those boundaries after we establish them, however, is an important issue.

A major reason for the difference between the boundaries O'Day establishes and the boundaries I establish is ideological. Therefore, let us anticipate the discussion of ideology in chapter 5 by observing some basic aspects of the ideology that drives the interpretation in O'Day's essay. A major dimension in the ideology underlying her intertextual interpretation, from my perspective, is 'oppositional' rather than 'dialogical' reasoning. The interpretation focuses on positives and negatives rather than dialogical aspects of the discourse. A manifestation of this emerges in the pitting of theory against precision and clarity. Another emerges in the perception that Paul's discussion is a fight rather than a strategy of arbitration. Paul's statements, in her view, are oriented not toward negotiation but toward setting the Corinthians right. In addition, in my opinion, oppositional ideology has guided the establishment of the outer framework of the unit the essay analyzes, and it accompanies the analysis and interpretation throughout the article. Thus the essay emphasizes that Paul presents first a negative view of boasting then a positive view (p. 261). It asserts that the content of 1 Corinthians 1.26 – whether people are wise, mighty and rich – is not an issue of sociological content and import, but an issue of whether the social location of the Corinthians precludes a full hearing of the theology of the verse. Paul, it tells us, was disabusing the Corinthians of categories 'on which they had falsely based their individual and communal identities'. Thus, he is making a critique of 'false sources of security' and offering a 'christocentric presentation' based on 'the authoritative voice of Jeremiah'.

Despite my interests in the intertextual strategies O'Day uses in the essay, I respond negatively to the many places I perceive an oppositional ideology to be at work. For me, the discourse of 1 Corinthians aims at negotiation and reconciliation (cf. the title of Mitchell 1992). The informative thing, so far as socio-rhetorical criticism is concerned, is the manner in which this ideology accompanies every arena of texture either she or I addresses. Also it guides what we include or exclude in our analyses. First, I would like the essay to tell the reader that the wording Paul asserts to be 'as it is written' never occurs in this exact form in Jeremiah 9.22–3 or anywhere else in scripture. Paul has condensed and inverted language from scripture to create a succinct statement that sounds like an authoritative maxim. Second, I would like the essay to analyze both the Jeremiah and 1 Corinthians passages rhetorically. The essay refers to the last part of the Jeremiah passage as 'a secondary addition to the text', rather than describing its rhetorical function in the extant unit. This fracturing of the Jeremiah text influences the analysis of the text in 1 Corinthians, where the essay does not observe that Paul's reference to 'as it is written' is the well-known rhetorical figure of 'an authoritative judgment from ancient testimony' (see Mack and Robbins 1989: 28–9, 38, 41, 52, 54–7, 60–1, 100–1, etc.). From my perspective, the inner biblical exegesis in the essay fractures the rhetorical argumentation in both the antecedent unit and 1 Corinthians. Third, I would like to see a full exploration of the Greek Septuagint text in addition to the Hebrew MT. While the essay asserts that 'Paul's use of Jeremiah is mediated by the Septuagint translation of the Hebrew text' (p. 260), it uses the Hebrew MT throughout and mentions only in passing that the same wording in which the essay is interested stands in the Septuagint text of 1 Samuel 2.10 (the song of Hannah) as well as in Jeremiah 9.22–3 (p. 261). This causes the essay to miss nuances of agreement and difference between the Greek of 1 Corinthians and the Greek of Jeremiah 9, and in one instance this strategy creates a strange sentence as follows: 'The adversative *alla* [Greek] in 1 Corinthians 1.27 has a similar function to the -ki 'im [Hebrew] of Jeremiah 9.23 and receives comparable rhetorical stress'. The essay should have said that the adversative *alla* [Greek] has a similar function to the 'alla ē [Greek] of Jeremiah 9.23. Fourth, the lack of use of the Septuagint leads to a lack of use of the 1 Samuel 2 Septuagint passage. This is damaging to the argument on p. 267 that 'Paul introduces a term into the text, Christ Jesus, that is clearly foreign to the Jeremiah text'. The problem is that the Septuagint passage in 1 Samuel 2.10 ends with *kai keras christou autou*, 'and will exalt the horn of his christ, his anointed one'. Different ideologies, then, establish different boundaries for intertextual analysis and these different boundaries encourage significantly different strategies of interpretation.

Again, there are four reasons for starting this chapter with such a full critique of O'Day's essay. First, the goal is to show that O'Day and others have been bringing intertextual analysis and interpretation explicitly into the field of New Testament study. Second, the goal is to introduce the awareness that every intertextual analysis occurs within either implicit or explicit boundaries. Third, the goal is progressively to introduce ideologies, including my own, that attend interpretations throughout the chapters in this book. Fourth, the goal is to call attention to the symbiotic relation among all the arenas of the texture in a text and among all the arenas of an interpreter's analysis. Strategies an interpreter uses for analysis of intertexture regularly have a close relationship to the strategies an interpreter uses for analysis of inner, social, cultural, ideological and theological texture.

To take the discussion of intertextual analysis a step further, let us turn to Richard Hays' recent work. His intertextual analysis has a significantly different tone, but he also excludes the resources characteristic of the *Religionsgeschichtliche Schule* from his analysis. Like O'Day, he is interested in reading the letters of Paul 'as literary texts shaped by complex intertextual relations with Scripture' (Hays 1989: xi). For his particular approach, he uses John Hollander's investigations of 'echo' in literature as a major resource

(Hollander 1981). Hays considers the following criteria to underlie his judgments about the presence of echo in a text:

(1) *Availability.* Was the proposed source of the echo available to the author and/or original readers? ...

(2) *Volume.* The volume of an echo is determined primarily by the degree of explicit repetition of words or syntactical patterns ...

(3) *Recurrence.* How often does Paul elsewhere cite or allude to the same scriptural passage? ...

(4) *Thematic Coherence.* How well does the alleged echo fit into the line of argument that Paul is developing? ...

(5) *Historical Plausibility.* Could Paul have intended the alleged meaning effect? ...

(6) *History of Interpretation.* Have other readers, both critical and pre-critical, heard the same echoes? ...

(7) *Satisfaction.* With or without clear confirmation from the other criteria listed here, does the proposed reading make sense? ...

(Hays 1989: 29–31)

Functioning within these criteria, Hays in fact analyzes a whole range of uses of scripture in Pauline discourse almost without discrimination. Intertextual analysis needs a more systematic approach if interpreters are going to use it in place of conventional historical-critical practices. Socio-rhetorical criticism offers a refinement of analytical practices. First, it distinguishes between oral–scribal and cultural intertexture. Hays' work collapses the two into one. I will argue below that both reference and echo represent cultural rather than oral–scribal intertexture. Second, socio-rhetorical criticism expands intertextual analysis beyond oral–scribal and cultural intertexture to social and historical intertexture. For analysis of oral–scribal intertexture, which is the particular topic of this section, socio-rhetorical criticism explores the following spectrum in a text:

(a) recitation;
(b) recontextualization;
(c) reconfiguration.

This terminology refers to the rhetorical use of other texts in a text. Third, socio-rhetorical criticism expands echo beyond the confines of scripture to literature within the Hellenistic-Roman world. We will see this expansion in the work of other interpreters as we

102

explore intertextual analysis further in this chapter. At present, however, the task is to introduce rhetorical procedures for analyzing oral–scribal intertexture in a text.

The first manner in which a text uses another text is *recitation*. Recitation is the presentation of speech or narrative or both, either from oral or written tradition, in words identical to or different from those the person has received. Recitation was the first exercise the rhetoricians recommended that students be taught when they composed a chreia (Hock and O'Neil 1986: 94–5; Robbins 1993b: 120). A quotation of exact words occurs in Luke 4.4: 'Jesus answered him, "It is written, 'One does not live by bread alone'"'. Inside this chreia (a saying attributed to Jesus) is recitation of the same words that are present in Deuteronomy 8.3 in the Greek Septuagint. It is important to observe that one of the meaning effects of the recitation is that the words in their new context function like a maxim or proverb. Jesus appears to be presenting 'wisdom' that everyone should know.

Second, recitation may also occur with omission of some of the words. Luke 4.9–11 contains the following words:

> And he [the devil] took him [Jesus] to Jerusalem, and set him on the pinnacle of the temple and said to him, '. . . for it is written, "He will command his angels concerning you, to protect you," and "On their hands they will bear you up, so that you will not dash your foot against a stone."'

This chreia contains words from Psalm 91.11–12, but the wording in the first part of the recitation is slightly different from the Septuagint. The exact words in Psalm 91.11 are (with varying words italicized):

> *For* he will command his angels concerning you,
> to protect you *in all your ways*,
> On their hands they will bear you up,
> so that you will not dash your foot against a stone.

The chreia in Luke does not add words to the text of the Psalms, except for 'and' which it adds between the verses, making it appear that more than one context in Scripture supports the devil's argument. However, the chreia omits words: the conjunction 'for' and the phrase 'in all your ways'. The absence of these words helps the saying to function efficiently and directly in its new context, namely Jesus standing on the pinnacle of the Temple in Jerusalem. Thus, conjunctions (and, for, but, etc.) and qualifying phrases (like 'in all your ways') may be removed or added when a verse from scripture is put on the lips of a speaker in New Testament narrative.

Another example of omitting words in a saying occurs in 1 Corinthians. The scriptual verse underlying Paul's discourse is Jeremiah 9.24:

> 'But *in* this *let him who boasts boast*, understanding and knowing that I am *the Lord* who does mercy and justice and righteousness on the earth; for in these things are my will', says the Lord.

Paul's discourse skillfully abbreviates this verse to 'Let him who boasts, boast in the Lord' (1 Cor. 1.31). The rhetorical effect of its abbreviated form is, of course, remarkable. Again the recitation has not added new words to scripture; rather it has conveniently removed words. Now the verse can function as a short, crisp proverb to support Pauline argumentation in more than one context (cf. 2 Cor. 10.17). It is disappointing that even interpreters who have focused on the intertexture of 1 Corinthians 1.26–31 have given the impression that Pauline discourse repeats the scriptural text without significant modification (cf. O'Day 1990: 267). Wording in the verse is both abbreviated and rearranged for rhetorical purposes in Pauline discourse.

A third way is to recite with different words. Deuteronomy 6.13 reads:

> *Fear* the Lord your God and serve him
> *and cleave to him and swear by his name.*
> (Wevers 1977: 122–3)

The chreia in Luke 4.8 reads: 'Jesus answered him, "it is written, '*Worship* the Lord your God, and serve *only* him.'"' The recitation in the Gospel of Luke changes one of the key words, adds the word 'only' and omits the two final statements. The modification of 'fear' to 'worship' is a matter of adapting the wording of the verse to the new context, where the narrator uses 'worship' in relation to the devil (Luke 4.7; cf. Matt. 4.9–10). Omission of the last two statements again gives the recitation a crisp, proverbial function in the verbal contest between Jesus and the devil.

A fourth way is to recite an episode using some of the narrative words in biblical text plus a saying from the biblical text. Acts 7.30–2 reads as follows:

³⁰Now when forty years had passed, *an angel appeared to him* in the wilderness of Mount Sinai, *in* the *flame* of a *burning bush*. ³¹When *Moses* saw it, he was amazed at *the sight*; and as he approached to look, there came the voice of the *Lord*: ³²'*I am the God of Abraham, Isaac, and Jacob*'. *Moses* began to tremble and did not dare to look.

This recitation contains words (in italics) that appear in Exodus 3.2–6. This is an excellent example of recitation in an abbreviated form, which is the sixth exercise in compositional exercises with the chreia (Hock and O'Neil 1986: 100–1). The recitation not only abbreviates the narrative wording. In Exodus 3.6 the saying of the Lord reads: 'I *myself* am the God *of your father, the God* of Abraham, and *the God of* Jacob, and *the God of* Isaac'. Once again the New Testament recitation omits words from the biblical text. The abbreviation of both the narrative and the saying creates a dramatic chreia that features a short proverbial saying. Abbreviation of the saying is especially noticeable in this context, since the words in the Septuagint text are explicitly attributed to the Lord God. One might imagine that direct speech of God would be recited exactly the same.

A fifth way is to recite a narrative in substantially one's own words. Mark 2.25–6 reads:

And he said to them, 'Have you never read what *David* did when he and the ones *with* him were hungry and in need of food? He entered the house of God, when Abiathar was high priest, and ate *the bread of the Presence*, which it is not lawful for any but the *priests* to *eat*, and he gave some to his companions'.

Words that occur in 1 Samuel 21.1–6 are in italics. The remaining words are different from the biblical text. A remarkable feature of this recitation is that it does not get the story quite right. There were no companions with David on the occasion, and he did not give any of the bread to anyone else to eat. The priest in the story is Ahimelech, whom the recitation does not mention, and the wording concerning Abiathar in the Markan text makes it unclear whether the statement about him is correct. Abiathar was not high priest at the time of this event. In addition, the narrator might have used the saying of David, 'Give me five loaves of bread, *or whatever is here*' (1 Sam. 21.3), to support the action of plucking and eating grain on the Sabbath, but the saying does not appear in the recitation. The function of Jesus' recitation of the story in the context of the plucking of the grain on the Sabbath raises fascinating issues (Mack and Robbins 1989: 107–41; Robbins 1993a: 97–105).

Sixth, a recitation may summarize a span of text that includes various episodes. Luke 17.26–7 reads:

> [26]Just as it was in the days of *Noah*, so too it will be in the days of the Son of Man. [27] They were eating and drinking, and marrying and being given in marriage, until the day Noah entered the ark, and the flood came and destroyed them all.

This recitation presents a summary of the biblical text in Genesis 6.1–24. It is informative to see what the recitation adds and what it leaves out of the biblical account. There is no reference to 'eating and drinking' in the biblical account. This appears to be a result of the characterization of the Son of Man's 'eating and drinking' (Matt. 11.19/Luke 7.33). The reference to 'marrying and being given in marriage' summarizes the following statements in Genesis 6.2, 6.4:

> The sons of God saw that the daughters of men were fair; and they took to wife such of them as they chose. . . . The Nephilim were on the earth in those days, and also afterward, when the sons of God came in to the daughters of men, and they bore children to them.

The recitation in the New Testament does not mention that the marrying was between 'sons of God' and 'daughters of men'. It also does not mention that Noah and all of his household went into the ark (Gen. 7.1, 7.7). The recitation makes it sound as if Noah might have survived alone. The focus on Noah alone is surely the result of the comparison between 'his days' and 'the days of the Son of Man'.

Recitation, then, may replicate exact words that exist in another text, it may omit words, it may change a few words, or it may recount the content of the other text in different words. The kind of recitation that exists in a particular text reveals important socio-rhetorical information about its discourse. For instance, if a text recites one kind of text with nearly verbatim wording while it recites another in its own words, this variation in pattern may display the use of one arena of tradition authoritatively to reconfigure another tradition with which it is competing in its context.

Recontextualization, in contrast to recitation, presents wording from biblical texts without mentioning that the words 'stand written' anywhere else. This covers a spectrum from extended word-for-word replication of a biblical text to the poignant use of a word, phrase or clause from scripture in a new context. 1 Peter 2.3 is a good example of recontextualization of a line from scripture: 'Like newborn babes, long for the pure spiritual milk, that by it you may grow up to salvation; for you have *tasted the kindness of the Lord*'.

This verse of Petrine discourse puts words from Psalm 34.8 in a new context without telling the reader that the words stand in scripture. The words in the Psalm are: 'Taste and see that the Lord is kind'. 1 Peter omits the 'seeing' from the line, making it a statement about 'tasting' that focuses on basic attitudes and actions of kindness which the discourse considers to be the 'spiritual milk' that will nurture a person into salvation.

Reconfiguration refers to the restructuring of an antecedent tradition. Recitation and recontextualization may be part of the reconfiguration of a past tradition, but they may also simply present the past tradition, like Acts 7.30–2 above. An excellent example of reconfiguration occurs in Luke 4.1–2:

> And Jesus, full of Holy Spirit, returned from the Jordan and was led by the Spirit for forty days in the wilderness, tempted by the devil. And he ate nothing in those days; and when they were ended, he was hungry.

First, this wording reconfigures the context in which Moses received the ten commandments. Exodus 34.28 states that Moses spent 'forty days and forty nights' with the Lord, and during this time 'he neither ate bread nor drank water'. Second, the wording evokes Elijah's flight into the wilderness when Jezebel threatened to kill him. When he went a day's journey into the wilderness and was sleeping under a broom tree, an angel touched him and told him to arise and eat. The third time the angel made the command, 'he arose, ate and drank, and went in the strength of that food forty days and forty nights to Horeb the mount of God' (1 Kings 19.8). The story of Jesus' testing by the devil in Luke, then, begins with a situation that reconfigures the situation both of Moses and Elijah.

Another instance of reconfiguration occurs in 1 Peter 2.22–25a:

... Christ also suffered for you. ... He *committed no* sin; *no guile was found on his lips.* When he was reviled, he did not revile in return; when he suffered, he did not threaten; but he trusted to him who judges justly. He himself *bore our sins* in his body on the tree, that we might die to sin and live to righteousness. *By his wounds you have been healed.* For you were *straying like sheep* ...

In this passage, the tradition of the suffering servant of Israel is reconfigured in terms of the crucifixion of Jesus. The story of Jesus' death is told in words from Isaiah 53, without reference to these words standing written in another place. The extended use of the wording exhibits more than simply recontextualization. The tradition itself is reconfigured in terms of bearing our sins 'in his body on the tree'.

This, I suggest, represents the range of oral–scribal intertexture in texts. Through reference and echo in texts, which is the next subject of discussion, oral–scribal intertexture flows into cultural intertexture. A rhetorical approach makes this clear. The boundaries both O'Day and Hays establish for their analyses occur as a result of establishing 'poetic' (Hays 1989: 176) rather than rhetorical boundaries. It would be extremely difficult for Hays to justify a limitation of Paul's echoes to scriptural echoes if he were interpreting the rhetoric of Paul's text. As rich as Hays's analysis and interpretation are, they reveal a highly limited perspective on the intertexture of Pauline discourse. Let us move quickly on, then, to cultural intertexture.

CULTURAL INTERTEXTURE

The book referred to earlier which bears the title *Intertextuality in Biblical Writing* (Draisma 1989) presupposes the existence of cultural intertexture, but even this book manifests an inconsistent pursuit of intertextuality in New Testament texts. In an essay comparing intertextuality with redaction criticism, Willem Vorster discusses intertextuality as a decisive move beyond previous source and redaction methods of analysis in biblical studies. He asserts that the intertexts of real importance are those which have been used in comparable contexts. Thus, 'birth stories' or 'speeches about the future' are important intertexts for one another (pp. 21, 25–6).

In his actual analysis, Vorster refers to the Didache, 4 Ezra and extracanonical gospels (pp. 22–4) and on one occasion he refers to speeches in Thucydides in relation to Jesus' speech about the future in Mark 13 (p. 25). There is, however, no programmatic reference either to Hellenistic Jewish or Greco-Roman literature in his discussion or analysis. His perception is that the 'fragments of texts' in New Testament discourse are primarily from 'canonical texts' plus a few extracanonical Jewish and Christian texts.

James Voelz begins his essay on 'Multiple Signs and Double Texts' by quoting Roland Barthes: 'The text is a tissue of quotations drawn from innumerable centers of culture' (p. 27). In the remainder of his essay, however, there is not one reference to literature outside the biblical canon.

Jean Delorme makes a strong assertion about the manner in which intertextuality breaks canonical boundaries in biblical analysis:

> The limits of the scriptural canon do not apply to intertextuality of the biblical books. Intertextuality of a text cannot be confined to previous or subsequent texts presenting a similarity in expression or content. The Bible does not allow itself to be confined to the cultural heritage of the West whose art and literature have been inspired by it. It should be confronted for example with Buddhist writings. The cultural worlds are not impermeable and the writings of one world can be understood in another one. With intercultural and interreligious dialogue, the Bible cannot be a prisoner of an original context from which it escaped a long time ago.
>
> (p. 36)

Again, however, throughout the remainder of the essay, which discusses aspects of the Gospel of Mark, there is no reference to literature outside the biblical canon, except for an offhand remark about 'Snow White' (p. 38).

Throughout the remainder of the book, neither Ellen Van Wolde's essay on the nature of intertextuality nor the intertextual readings by eleven New Testament scholars refers to literature outside the biblical canon. This evidence suggests that Thaïs Morgan, a literary critic, is right when she says:

> despite its formal apparatus of linguistic models and terminology, intertextuality is finally a conservative theory and

practice. Like the methodology of source, influence, and biography which it replaces, the location of intertexts, intratexts, and autotexts takes place within a circumscribed field of literature that overlaps significantly with the canon or tradition proposed by early modern critics. . . . In effect, the 'best that is known and thought in the world' is redefined as that set of text(s) on which the greatest number of intertexts converge.

(Morgan 1989: 272)

While the spectrum of oral–scribal modes of production and composition is an important issue, then, an even more important issue is the limitation of intertextual analysis to biblical literature. To open intertextual analysis at least to Greco-Roman as well as Jewish cultural intertexture in New Testament texts, socio-rhetorical criticism features analysis of reference and echo in texts.

Reference is the occurrence of a word, phrase or clause that refers to a personage or tradition known to people in a culture. In Mark 6.15, 'But others said, "It is Elijah"', refers to a 'prophet' who is the center of attention from 1 Kings 17 to 2 Kings 2 in the Bible, in certain extra-biblical literature and in scattered references to him in other literature of the time. Socio-rhetorical criticism uses the term 'cultural' to refer to the status of a phenomenon that appears in a wide range of literature that spans many centuries. By the first century, Elijah was a cultural rather than simply a textual figure. People could refer to him without reference to any particular oral or scribal text. Likewise, Acts 14.12, 'Barnabas they called Zeus, and Paul they called Hermes, because he was the chief speaker', presupposes stories in Homer's *Iliad* and *Odyssey* and other literature in Mediterranean antiquity about the 'father' of gods and about the special 'messenger' of this and other gods. Simple reference to personages like this evokes a wide range of meaning effects that are more properly called cultural than oral–scribal.

Echo represents yet another aspect of cultural intertexture. Echo occurs when a word or phrase evokes, or potentially evokes, a cultural tradition. The nature of echo is such that scholars will regularly debate the presence or absence of an echo of a verse in the text under consideration. To explore this phenomenon in its broader context characteristic of socio-rhetorical criticism, let us turn to the work of Abraham Malherbe.

Abraham J. Malherbe's investigations of Cynic and Stoic discourse in Pauline letters have contributed decisively to analysis and interpretation of the broader world of cultural intertexture in New Testament literature. He has worked primarily off reference and echo in Pauline discourse to set the stage for analysis of the recontextualization and reconfiguration of Cynic and Stoic cultural discourse in Pauline discourse. For many, Malherbe introduced this kind of analysis of cultural intertexture in his article '"Gentle as a Nurse": The Cynic Background to I Thess ii' (1970). Malherbe set the context for his analysis of 1 Thessalonians 2 with statements in the text 'that could be understood as denials of accusations':

> our visit . . . was not in vain (*kenē*) . . . but in the face of great opposition (*agōni*) (vss. 1–2), not from error (*planēs*) or uncleanness (*akatharsias*), nor with guile (*dolō*); but . . . (vss. 3–4), not to please men, but to please God . . . (vs. 4), neither . . . with words of flattery (*kolakeias*) . . . nor a cloak for greed . . . nor seeking glory (*doxan*) from men, nor . . . making heavy demands . . . but we were gentle (*ēpioi*) among you (vss. 5–7).

The language Malherbe exhibits in this manner may appear to be strictly 'Pauline' discourse. Malherbe exhibits it entirely in Greek in his article, then he systematically shows how this language is either used by or associated with moral philosophers in Greco-Roman literature. In other words, Malherbe analyzes reference to, and echo and recontextualization of, moral philosophical discourse in 1 Thessalonians 2.

Malherbe proposes that the statements in the discourse of 1 Thessalonians 2 are related to different types of philosophers. First, there are resident philosophers who do not appear in public at all; they are useless (*anōpheleis*), refusing to enter the contest (*agōn*) of life (pp. 205–6). Here Malherbe is working with intertextual echo in 1 Thessalonians 2.2. Paul's statement which is usually translated 'in the face of great opposition (*agōn*)' is really a reference to 'the great contest (*agōn*)' which is the arena in which he preaches the gospel. This is simply the beginning point for Malherbe's exhibition of Mediterranean cultural discourse embedded in Pauline discourse. Second, there are Cynics who are hucksters; they deceive (*planan*, *apatan*) people with flattery (*kolakeuein*, *thōpeuein*) instead of 'speaking with the boldness and frankness of the true philosopher'. They go around for their own glory (*doxa*), personal pleasure (*hēdonē*) and money (*chrēmata*) (pp. 205–6). Here Malherbe is interpreting the cultural echoes in

1 Thessalonians 2.3, 2.5–6. Third, there is a type of Cynic who 'was difficult to distinguish from rhetoricians'. They make speeches that lack substance, and the people themselves are vain or empty (*kenos*). They are 'like a physician who, instead of curing his patients, entertains them' (p. 207). This analysis concerns especially the echoes in 1 Thessalonians 2.1, 2.7. Fourth, there are serious Cynics who speak with the boldness (*parrēsia*) of 'the philosopher who has found true personal freedom'. He speaks in this manner out of a desire to benefit people, his *philanthrōpia*. He adapts his speaking to the people's needs to lead them to virtue and sobriety, 'partly by persuading and exhorting (*peithōn kai parakalōn*), partly by abusing and reproaching (*loidoroumenos kai oneidizōn*) . . . also admonishing (*nouthetōn*) them in groups every time he finds opportunity, with gentle words at times, at others harsh' (pp. 208–9). Malherbe fills his own English discourse with Greek words that occur both in the discourse of Paul and the discourse by and about moral philosophers in Mediterranean culture. His analysis shows the close intertextual relation of Paul's discourse to the discourse in the Greco-Roman literature he is citing. He is analyzing 'cultural' intertexture, since Cynics represent a particular sector of Greek philosophy, which is particular to Greek culture. When he presents a typology of Cynics, his approach acquires the nature of a 'sociology of culture', an analysis of culture with a typology common to sociological analysis.

As Malherbe brings his discussion of the four types of Cynic to a conclusion, he includes statements by pseudo-Diogenes, Dio Chrysostom and Plutarch about the combination of gentleness with bold admonishment, rebuke or even a whipping by a father or a nurse (pp. 212–14). At this point, he is exhibiting cultural echo in 1 Thessalonians 2.7:

> But we were gentle (*ēpioi*) among you, like a nurse (*trophos*) taking care (*thalpē*) of her children (*tekna*).

Then he moves to a discussion of *katharōs*, which may mean either 'speaking plainly and clearly' or 'speaking with purity' rather than deceit or guile (pp. 214–16). This speaks to the issue of 'uncleanness' in 1 Thessalonians 2.3. The discussion then leads to the conclusion that Paul's description of his ministry to the Thessalonians 'is strikingly similar to the picture sketched by Dio, both in what is said and in the way in which it is formulated' (p. 216). There is, however, a further task:

the Cynics differed among themselves as to what they meant by the same language. The further step must be taken of coming to a clearer perception of the self-understanding(s) of the Cynics before investigating Paul's thinking on his ministry against the background.

(p. 217)

Malherbe's analysis, then, is 'cultural' – it concerns particular self-understandings within particular contexts. He is not investigating Cynic philosophy as a general social phenomenon – the kind of knowledge that most people in Mediterranean society would already have. Rather, he is investigating particular cultural understanding – the kind of knowledge that only people 'on the inside' of this particular sphere of culture will have. Malherbe's analysis is also 'intertextual'. His analysis stays close to the precise wording of texts at every point. He is interested in the culture of the Cynics as it is 'textualized'; and he is interested in the manner in which Pauline discourse has 'textualized' language attributed to or associated with Cynics. At the end of the article, he is raising the issue of the 'particular configuration' of 'self-understanding' in the discourse of different Cynics and in the discourse of Paul. From a socio-rhetorical perspective, this is analysis and interpretation of 'cultural intertexture', and it is analysis of an exemplary kind.

Burton Mack's analysis of the Gospel of Mark, which appeared at the end of the 1980s, carried this kind of analysis of cultural intertexture beyond Pauline discourse into the Gospels. His analysis of Mark 4 is an exemplary exhibition of his approach. Mark 4 contains images of 'the field, sowing, seeds, miscarriage, and harvest' that are characteristic of 'Jewish apocalyptic, wisdom, and prophetic literatures'. These images, however, occur in a literary context that uses a Greco-Roman mode of rhetorical elaboration to unfold the mysterious nature of the kingdom of God in Jesus' activity. As the discourse displays the meanings and meaning effects of the kingdom, it echoes topics that are commonplace in Greco-Roman discussions concerning *paideia* – instruction or education. Mack presents comparative texts that exhibit the presence of reference and echo to *paideia* in Greco-Roman discourse (Mack 1988: 155–60; Mack and Robbins 1989: 145–60):

The views of our teachers are as it were the seeds. Learning from childhood is analogous to the seeds falling betimes upon the prepared ground.

(Hippocrates, *Law* III)

113

As is the seed that is ploughed into the ground, so must one expect the harvest to be, and similarly when good education is ploughed into your persons, its effect lives and burgeons throughout their lives, and neither rain nor drought can destroy it.

(Antiphon, fr. 60 in Diels, *Vorsokratiker*)

Words should be scattered like seed; no matter how small the seed may be, if it once has found favorable ground, it unfolds its strength and from an insignificant thing spreads to its greatest growth.

(Seneca, *Epistles* 38.2)

If you wish to argue that the mind requires cultivation, you would use a comparison drawn from the soil, which if neglected produced thorns and thickets, but if cultivated will bear fruit.

(Quintilian, *Institutio Oratoria* 5.11.24)

The initial quotation from Hippocrates concerns cultural echo in Mark 4.1–9, 4.13–20. The first verse states that Jesus 'began to teach' the people, and the second verse says that 'he taught them many things' and that he said specific things 'in his teaching'. Thus, Mark 4 introduces Jesus as a teacher, which is the topic of the quotation from Hippocrates. The next assertion of the quotation is that the 'views of our teachers' are 'the seeds'. This is precisely the assertion in Mark 4.14: 'The sower sows the word'. Then throughout Mark 4.15–20, Jesus' interpretation of the parable of the sower explains 'the analogy' between 'the seeds' falling betimes on the prepared ground', to use the language of the Hippocrates quotation, and the learning of people about the kingdom of God.

The quotation from Antiphon, which is second above, discusses 'the harvest', which is the topic of Mark 4.8, 4.20. The yield, Antiphon says, relates directly to the ploughing of the seed into the ground. In other words, if the seed is not successfully ploughed into the soil, because it 'falls along the path' or 'falls on rocky ground' where the plough will not turn the soil over, this seed will not be productive (cf. Mark 4.4–6, 4.14–17). If it is successfully ploughed into the soil, however, it is like good education that causes lives to be fruitful, because neither rain nor drought can destroy it (cf. Mark 4.6, 4.8, 4.20).

The quotation from Seneca asserts that words should be scattered like seed (Mark 4.14) and discusses the smallness of the seed. No matter how small the seed may be, if it finds favorable soil, it will find strength and grow to its greatest growth. This is the topic of the parable of the mustard seed in Mark 4.30–2.

The quotation from Quintilian refers to 'cultivation of the mind', 'thorns and thickets' and 'bearing fruit'. The mind is a special matter of concern in Mark 4.18–20, where a problem is that cares of the world, delight in riches and desire for other things enter in and choke what has been heard so that a person is unfruitful. The problem, in Markan terms, is whether a person is able to 'hear the word and accept it' (4.20). It is a problem, then, of the cultivation of the mind. If the mind is not cultivated properly, thickets and thorns overtake it, precisely the topic of Mark 4.7, 4.18–19.

Reference and echo to topics in Greco-Roman discourse about teaching, learning and its effects, then, are deeply embedded in Markan discourse about Jesus' teaching of the kingdom of God in parables (analogies). The great strength of Mack's analysis is the analysis of the integration of both Jewish and Greco-Roman cultural discourse in Markan discourse in the chapter. Thus, in contrast to previous interpreters, he does not claim that the discourse is 'strictly Jewish' or 'strictly Greco-Roman'. Even in analysis of the letters of Paul, it has been most common for interpreters to analyze either Jewish cultural intertexture or Greco-Roman cultural intertexture, rather than merging the two in the same analysis. My analysis of the Gospel of Mark in 1984 activated a similar kind of 'bi-cultural' analysis and interpretation (Robbins 1992a), and one of the major goals of socio-rhetorical criticism is to move interpretation beyond an activity on one side or the other of a boundary between Jewish culture and Greco-Roman culture.

Cultural intertexture, then, concerns symbolic worlds that particular communities of discourse nurture with special nuances and emphases. The special challenge with analysis of the cultural intertexture of New Testament texts lies in the interaction among Jewish and Greco-Roman topics, codes and generic conceptions in New Testament discourse.

SOCIAL INTERTEXTURE

In the context of intertextual analysis, an interpreter may become interested in *social* intertexture. Gerd Theissen exhibited this interest especially in his study of 1 Corinthians 11, where he investigated concepts and wording in texts that described practices and conventions in settings of eating in Mediterranean society (Theissen 1982).

First, Theissen focuses on wording in 1 Corinthians 11.20–21a:

> When you meet together, it is not the Lord's supper (*kyriakon deipnon*) that you eat. For in eating, each one (*hekastos*) goes ahead with his own meal (*to idion deipnon*) . . .

Theissen finds two Greek inscriptions containing language especially pertinent to this verse. One uses the words *kyriakon*, 'lord's', and *idios*, 'one's own', to distinguish between the imperial and private treasuries and another uses the phrase *ek tōn idiōn*, 'from their own', to refer to an object that was paid for by a donor. The evidence, in Theissen's view, suggests that 'his own meal' would refer to food that individuals brought with them and that the words of institution, 'This is my body, etc.', would have the effect of 'converting a private contribution into community property' (pp. 148–9). In other words, the inscription referring to an object that was donated suggests to Theissen that the wealthier Christians were bringing 'their own food', and at the point where food was distributed for 'the Lord's supper' the food became a 'donation' to the community. The problem, in Theissen's view, was that no one shared food until the words of institution. Here Theissen has worked from reference and echoes in the text toward a particular social practice. The analysis does not remain at a cultural level, like the analysis of Malherbe and Mack. Rather, it moves into social meanings of terms that support conventional practices in certain kinds of social settings.

Second, Theissen focuses on wording in 1 Corinthians 11.21b–22:

> . . . and one is hungry and another is drunk. What! Do you not have houses to eat and drink in?

For this part of the passage, Theissen cites a fragment of Eratosthenes that criticizes a public feast where 'each one drinks from his own flask which he has brought along', and he examines a lengthy quotation from Plutarch which discusses how companionship (*to koinon*) fails where each guest has his own private portion (p. 149). Again, Theissen works on the basis of intertextual references and echoes to ascertain the meaning effects of certain social practices.

116

Then Theissen continues with a series of social issues related to the first two analyses. He thinks 1 Corinthians 11 suggests that the wealthy Christians began to eat before the congregational meal began, and the 'individual eating' may have extended into the Lord's supper itself (pp. 151–3). He cites evidence for an established practice in associations or clubs in Antiquity of having different portions of food and drink for people who donated different amounts to certain causes (p. 154). In addition, different qualities of foods were served to people of different social status at private meals. Thus, if wealthy patrons invited guests of their own social status, it would have been 'necessary' for them to give guests preferential treatment (pp. 155–9).

Theissen concludes that some wealthier Christians in the Corinthian community who donated bread and wine for all at the meals were treating the common meal as a 'private' meal. In turn, regular members of the community would be expecting to have some 'special' food at the gathering, which they would not get. These members of lower social status were experiencing disappointment as the wealthier members ate and drank with their associates during the common meal and did not share any of their food with members outside their group. Paul speaks strongly to the wealthier members of the community, exhorting them with both social and theological arguments to create images and motivations for community and sacramental activity together (pp. 160–8).

From a socio-rhetorical perspective, Theissen worked in an environment of intertextual reference and echo to investigate an aspect of the 'social intertexture' of Pauline discourse in 1 Corinthians. The analysis is intertextual, because it works so closely with the wording both of 1 Corinthians and of Greco-Roman inscriptions and literature. The analysis concerns 'social' phenomena, since it focuses on customs and practices that are widespread throughout Mediterranean society, potentially affecting almost every person at some time during their life. The phenomena are not simply 'cultural', for two reasons. First, it is not only people 'on the inside' who understand what is happening, but people throughout society. People of many ranks and stations would know about these customs, even if they were never allowed to participate in them. Second, Theissen has identified a social practice, not simply a cultural belief, conviction or concept. This phenomenon, in other words, has a social manifestation – the text points toward a particular social activity that occurred regularly among the Corinthian

Christians. From the perspective of socio-rhetorical criticism, this is not 'historical' intertexture, since this term is reserved for specific events during specific periods of time. Theissen did not attempt to pinpoint the year this practice began, the years during which it occurred and the year in which the Corinthians changed the practice, if indeed they did. If the text yields this kind of information, it contains historical intertexture. Theissen only pursues data concerning a social practice. Thus, Theissen analyzed social intertexture in 1 Corinthians 11.17–34, and this is an important mode of socio-rhetorical analysis.

HISTORICAL INTERTEXTURE

As mentioned above, another aspect of intertextuality is *historical* intertexture. This kind of intertexture 'textualizes' past experience into 'a particular event' or 'a particular period of time'. Historical intertexture differs from social intertexture by its focus on a particular event or period of time rather than social practices that occur regularly as events in one's life. J. Louis Martyn's study of the Gospel of John introduced analysis of historical intertexture to New Testament studies in a decisive manner toward the end of the 1960s (1968). Beginning with careful analysis of the drama that unfolds in seven scenes in John 9, Martyn gathered information in support of the view that the three statements about exclusion from the synagogue in John 9.22, 12.42, and 16.2a exhibit a historical event of recent occurrence in early Christianity. Martyn's procedure is implicitly socio-rhetorical, since it works carefully with the inner nature of the Johannine text itself in a manner that allows the rhetoric of the Johannine text to provide new information about the history of early Christianity. The first essential step was to break with the referential world of Jesus' lifetime itself and to enter the fictive drama of the text itself. Martyn paves the way for this with the observation that the statement 'You are a disciple of that one but we are disciples of Moses' (John 9.28) is 'scarcely conceivable in Jesus' lifetime, since it recognizes discipleship to Jesus not only as antithetical, but also as somehow comparable, to discipleship to Moses' (p. 19). This step breaks the interpreter's uncritical allegiance to a referential world of historical realism for Jesus' life and prepares the way for the interpreter to enter the narrative world of the text itself. The second essential step was to analyze the rhetoric of the narrative drama in such a manner that it evoked social, cultural and historical echoes about early Christianity. This was a matter of working with the process of the author's production of the text in an intertextual manner oriented toward social and cultural issues, rather than in a manner that focused on 'literary sources'.

The analysis begins with significant exploration of the inner texture of the healing of the blind man in John 9 (pp. 3–22). The careful attention to the stages of the drama and the nature of the discourse at each stage entailed the adoption of an approach such as a literary critic would take to a play or a novel. After analyzing the inner texture of the drama, Martyn investigated the inter-texture of the statements about exclusion from the synagogue. Working with oral–scribal intertexture on the basis of the term *aposynagogos*, 'excluded from the synagogue', Martyn moved into social intertexture, namely the social phenomenon of exclusion from synagogues in early Christianity. The rhetoric of the Johannine text itself, namely the statement that 'The Jews had already agreed that . . .', convinces Martyn to move beyond oral–scribal and social intertexture to historical intertexture. He posits that leaders of the Jewish community in which the Fourth Gospel was written had recently introduced guidelines for identifying Jews who wanted to hold a dual allegiance to Moses and to Jesus as Messiah. In Martyn's terms:

> Even against the will of some of the synagogue leaders, the Heretic Benediction is now employed in order formally and irretrievably to separate the church from the synagogue.
>
> (pp. 40–1)

At this point Martyn has circled back to the home base of a historical critic. But a new step in New Testament exegesis occurred when a fictive drama became the medium for a new datum in the history of early Christianity. Moreover, once Martyn had posited this new historical datum, he returned to the inner texture of the Fourth Gospel to show both the nature of Johannine discourse and the nature of the conversation in early Christianity. Only after careful analysis of John 5 and 7 in the context of the entire narrative (pp. 45–88) does he posit the theological terms that functioned in the conversation (pp. 91–142). Again, this is essentially an interdisciplinary mode of analysis, namely an exploration of fictive narrative to reconstruct a particular social and historical context.

Since Martyn's book does not use explicit rhetorical resources in its analysis, it is only embryonically socio-rhetorical. The approach, however, was a harbinger of the new paradigm in New Testament studies. The decisive move beyond a historical–critical paradigm occurred when Martyn used the discourse and drama of a narrative he considered to be fictive to inform the reader about the social, historical and theological terms of a situation in post-70 Christianity. In Martyn's analysis, the Johannine drama is a symbolic representation of the terms and dynamics of conflict in the Johannine community, much as a modern novel or short story may be a commentary on our own times. The manner in which Martyn correlates his insight into the narrative's dramatic fiction with the social and theological experience of exclusion from synagogues creates an essentially interdisciplinary mode of analysis. Written in 1968, the study is not formulated in interdisciplinary terms; rather, it operates in the domain of historical–critical interpretation and moves outside this domain only by the manner in which it enters seriously into the narrative drama and explores its meanings. The absence of explicitly literary or rhetorical resources also keeps the analysis of the argumentative texture of the pertinent Johannine passages closer to the mode of historical–critical exegesis. Nevertheless, the procedure itself and its conclusions point forward to an approach that works systematically out from the discourse in the text to wider and wider circles of meaning.

This is the place where socio-rhetorical criticism challenges traditional historical criticism on its own turf. Among the most highly debated issues in New Testament studies, as a result of the emergence of socio-rhetorical practices of interpretation, is the historical intertexture of portions of the Gospels with the historical Jesus, with Christianity throughout the Galilee during the first quarter of a century after Jesus' life, and with subsequent relationships among various groups and movements in early Christianity.

INTERTEXTURE IN 1 CORINTHIANS 9

At this point we return to analysis and interpretation of 1 Corinthians 9. Moving beyond inner textual analysis, which was the interest in the last chapter, we move to intertextual analysis. The analysis of 1 Corinthians 9 begins with oral–scribal intertexture.

Oral–scribal intertexture

One of the most recognizable forms of intertexture, we recall, occurs when wording from other written or oral texts appears in the text under investigation. In a rhetorical culture like early Christianity, people regularly recite written text orally and oral text scribally. One of the results of this dynamic is variation in wording that results from abbreviation, substitution of different wording, amplification or reordering of words, phrases or clauses.

1 Corinthians 9.9 contains a clear instance of scribal intertexture: 'For it is written in the law of Moses, "You shall not muzzle an ox when it is treading out grain"'. This is an instance of *recitation*, that process in which a person formally restates a tradition from the past in either verbatim wording, slightly modified wording or significantly newly formulated wording. In this instance, Pauline discourse transmits a line of scriptural text that contains four Greek words. This means that the Septuagint (Greek) version of scripture contains the intertext for this verse. In this instance, there is no inversion of the order of any of the four words in the recitation, as there often is, but there is variation in the first two letters of the verb 'you shall (not) muzzle'. In many New Testament manuscripts, and in the Septuagint text, the verb begins with the two letters *ph* and *i* (*phimoō*). Another common word in Greek for muzzling an animal was formed in exactly the same way except that the first two letters were *k* and *ē* (*kēmoō*). Some New Testament texts start the word with *phi-* and others start it with *kē-*. Since it is more likely that early scribes changed the spelling so that it agreed with the Septuagint (*phimoō*, since it purports to be a recitation of it) than that any scribe changed it so that it varied from the Septuagint text, it appears that Pauline discourse did not use the verb as it stands in the Septuagint but used the alternative verb in contemporary Greek meaning 'to muzzle'. Recitation in this instance, then, has four words, like the Septuagint text, but it spells one of the words differently.

After the Pauline discourse recites Deuteronomy 25.4, it engages in interpretation:

> [9]Is it for oxen that God is concerned? [10]Does he not speak entirely for our sake? It was written for our sake . . .
>
> (1 Cor. 9.9–10)

Pauline discourse applies the biblical verse to humans rather than oxen. A look at the verse in its context in Deuteronomy reveals that all the laws in fifteen chapters before and two chapters after the verse concern humans; only one verse in seventeen chapters speaks about animals without reference to humans. Thus, it would have been natural for interpreters to consider this verse also to be meant for humans rather than, or in addition to, oxen. The reason the discourse gives for thinking the verse applies to humans rather than oxen is not, however, the reason we have just presented. Rather, the stated reason is an argument from analogy based on traditional social logic: just as a plowman and a thresher both expect to get a share of the crop when it is harvested, so it is to be expected that God's statement about an ox being allowed to eat while it works actually refers to humans. This means that Pauline discourse allows traditional social logic to guide the interpretation of a verse from scripture. This will gain in importance as the analysis of the chapter proceeds.

Later in chapter 9, Pauline discourse presents a *recitation* of a saying of Jesus. At this point, the interactive relation between transmission of written and oral text in early Christianity becomes even more evident. 1 Corinthians 9.14 reads as follows:

> In the same way, the Lord commanded that those who proclaim the gospel should get their living by the gospel.

An expanded version that enumerates items an apostle should not take is present in Matthew 10.9–10:

> Take no gold, nor silver, nor copper in your belts, no bag for your journey, nor two tunics, nor sandals, nor a staff; for the laborer deserves his food.

The negative enumeration of items appears clearly to be an expansion of 'the laborer deserves his *food*'. An alternative form of expansion exists in Luke 10.7–8:

> And remain in the same house, eating and drinking what they provide, for the laborer deserves his wages. Whenever you enter a town and they receive you, eat what is set before you.

In this instance there is expansion both before and after 'the laborer deserves his *wages*'. The Matthean version refers to 'food' in a context that discusses items other than food that are not to be taken and the Lukan version refers to 'wages' in a context that discusses food.

Underlying these varying expansions lies the Q tradition of the saying 'For the laborer is worthy of his food/wages [reward]', (Matt. 10.10/Luke 10.7). There are important points here for our present discussion of oral–scribal intertexture. Pauline discourse recites 'in its own words' a saying it attributes to Jesus. In other words, even though Paul's recitation has a direct relation to the saying attributed to Jesus in Matthew and Luke (and thus is Q), not one word of the Pauline recitation is the same as the recitations in the gospel tradition. Pauline discourse recites this saying with two articular occurrences of the noun 'gospel' (*to euangelion*). Moreover, it uses a favorite verb in Pauline discourse, 'to proclaim' (*katangello*). Thus, instead of 'the laborer' as the one who receives, Pauline discourse refers to 'the one who proclaims the gospel' (*tois to euangelion katangelousin*). Neither the noun 'gospel' nor the verb 'proclaim' occurs in the Q material (Kloppenborg 1988: 220, 223). Rather, he who labors, labors for 'the kingdom' (Matt.10.7/Luke 10.9). In other words, Pauline discourse reconfigures the conceptualization of the 'worker' in terms of 'the one who proclaims the gospel'. As we saw in the inner textual analysis of 1 Corinthians 9, one of the effects of Pauline discourse is to evoke the image of 'one who proclaims the gospel' as one who uses all dimensions of the body 'to do the work' of the gospel. In the process of communicating this concept, which is embedded in the vocabulary of the saying attributed to Jesus, Pauline discourse takes 'the language of the saying' over into its own vocabulary field. In a very forceful way, therefore, the recitation of a saying of Jesus in 1 Corinthians 9.14 'Paulinizes' language that it attributes to Jesus.

The remaining words in 1 Corinthians 9.14 show how completely Pauline discourse has taken over the language of the saying attributed to Jesus. The Q tradition says that the worker 'is worthy of' or 'deserves' (*axios*) either his 'food' (Matthew: *hē trophē*) or his 'wages' or 'reward' (Luke: *ho misthos*). Pauline discourse recites this in terms of 'getting a living' (*zēn*). This is also very interesting, since other verses of 1 Corinthians 9 refer specifically both to eating (9.4, 9.7, 9.13) and to receiving a 'wage' or 'reward' (9.17, 9.18). Pauline discourse again reconfigures the conceptuality of 'reward' or 'wage', however, by embedding it in discussion of 'the gospel':

What then is my reward/wage? That in my preaching of good news (*euangelizomenos*) I may make the gospel (*to euangelion*) free of charge, not making full use of my right in the gospel (*en tō euangeliō*).

(1 Cor. 9.18)

Pauline discourse recites the language of Jesus tradition in 'the words of' Pauline discourse and by this recitation it reconfigures the saying so it supports Pauline conceptuality concerning proclaiming the gospel rather than the conceptuality of the Q tradition.

Oral–scribal intertexture clearly appears in 1 Corinthians 9, then, in a recitation of Deuteronomy 25.4 and a saying of Jesus. The recitation of Deuteronomy 25.4 supports the custom of workers receiving food for their labor. The recitation of the saying of Jesus supports the concept that proclaiming the gospel is a form of work that is 'freely' performed if it offers the gospel free of charge. Thus, Pauline discourse reconfigures the conceptuality from 'laboring for the kingdom' to 'laboring freely for the gospel'. In other words, Pauline discourse in this context recites scriptural testimony in nearly verbatim language, but it 'Paulinizes' the language of the saying it attributes to Jesus. Since we have commented earlier on the places in the argument where these recitations appear, we will not pursue those matters further here. In this context, however, we want to call attention to the fact that Pauline discourse in 1 Corinthians 9 reconfigures the language and conceptuality of speech it attributes to Jesus. Pauline discourse does not simply transmit the language of other Christians within its own circles. Rather, it rewords, reconfigures and reconceptualizes this language, creating a distinctive discursive culture in early Christianity.

Historical intertexture

Another easily recognizable form of intertexture in argumentative discourse is reference to prior events, namely *historical intertexture*. This kind of intertexture is present in nine verses that represent five contexts in 1 Corinthians 9. The first instance occurs in 9.1: 'Have I not seen Jesus our Lord?' This statement evokes the image of at least one event in the past when Paul saw the Lord Jesus. Whether the statement is true or not, or exactly what the nature of that event might have been, the discourse does not say. The reader must go to evidence available outside this chapter to explore that intertexture, just as the reader must go to a text like the Septuagint, Gospels or other discourse to explore the nature of oral–scribal intertexture.

The second instance of historical intertexture occurs in 9.11: 'If we have sown spiritual good among you, is it too much if we reap your material benefits?' This verse refers to one or more events in the past when Paul and Barnabas (9.6), and perhaps some other associates, worked among the Corinthians to initiate a particular kind of spirituality. The nature of that spirituality will emerge as the analysis continues. At present, the issue is the reference to past activity among the Corinthians which creates historical intertexture in the text.

The third instance occurs in 9.12: 'Nevertheless, we have not made use of this right, but we endure anything rather than put an obstacle in the way of the gospel of Christ'. This verse refers to something which has *not* happened in the context of the activity of Paul and his associates with the Corinthians. Historical intertexture occurs again as the discourse refers to past (and perhaps present) endurance of hardship which comes from the necessity to provide their own livelihood as they work among them. We will return to the last half of the verse, which provides a rationale for not making use of the right. Only the first part of the verse contains historical intertexture.

Historical intertexture appears for the fourth time in 9.15: 'But I have made no use of any of these rights, nor am I writing this to secure any such provision'. This is a reiteration of the reference in 9.12 with an addition that characterizes the discourse in the present letter as a historical event. The formulation, sending and arrival of this letter is an additional historical event; this event is not to be construed as a request for money or any other kind of provision, just as none of the other previous events were. Historical intertexture, then, may be oriented toward the future, the present or the past. This verse refers clearly to past and present, and perhaps implicitly to the future: (a) in the past Paul did not request or accept provisions for his livelihood from the Corinthians; (b) the present activity of the writing of the letter is not a request for provisions; (c) when the letter arrives and is read to the Corinthians, the letter will not at that time be a request for provisions.

The fifth occurrence of historical intertexture appears in 9.19–22 and contains a series of statements:

¹⁹For though I am free from all men, I made myself a slave to all, that I might win the more. ²⁰To the Jews I became as a Jew, in order to win Jews; to those under the law I became as one under the law – though not being myself under the law – that I might win those under the law. ²¹To those outside the law I became as one outside the law – not being without law toward God but under the law of Christ – that I might win those outside the law. ²²To the weak I became weak, that I might win the weak.

This is the final instance of historical intertexture in the chapter, and it occurs just before the conclusion (9.24–7). These verses function as a summary, stated in positive terms, of events that did *not* occur when Paul and his associates worked among them. In positive terms, what Paul did *not* do – namely, he did not accept food or drink – was a matter of 'becoming a slave to all people'. This means that every time Paul worked with the Corinthians in the past, he found other means to live – either he lived extremely frugally, depriving himself, or he labored at some task like tentmaking to support himself. The point of interest here is the assertion that these activities did and did not happen in the past. The language of the discourse, then, is evoking an image of the history that leads up to this moment of writing the letter. This, again, is the nature of historical intertexture in a text. The discourse defines the past activity by using the image of a slave. Also, it divides the activity in terms of having become 'a Jew to Jews', 'one outside the law to those outside the law' and 'weak to the weak'. We will return to this aspect of the discourse in the discussion of social and cultural intertexture in the chapter.

In the Pauline discourse of 1 Corinthians 9, then, historical intertexture occurs in the form of references to the past when Paul saw the risen Lord and when Paul and his associates worked among the Corinthians to nurture a particular kind of spiritual life among them. In addition, Paul refers to the present event of writing the letter and, at least implicitly, to the future event when this discourse will be read to the Corinthians. Historical intertexture in Pauline discourse does not concern the baptism of Jesus and the exorcisms, healings and controversies he performed (Jesus' enactment of his 'authority') but the calling and work of Paul (Paul's enactment of 'his' authority). Pauline discourse, then, fills Christian discourse with a significantly different historical intertexture. The historical activity of Jesus is much less important than the historical activity of Paul and his associates. On the night Jesus was betrayed he broke bread and drank wine (1 Cor. 11), he was crucified and buried and he was raised (1 Cor. 15). This is the full extent of historical intertexture concerning Jesus in Pauline discourse. The really important historical intertexture concerns the work of Paul and those around him. Thus, much as Pauline discourse reconfigures and reconceptualizes the speech of Jesus, so it reconfigures and reconceptualizes the important historical episodes in Christian discourse.

Social intertexture

Social intertexture occurs when the discourse refers to information that is generally available to people in the Mediterranean world. The presupposition is that the discourse evokes images of 'social reality' that every member of Mediterranean society could describe in a series of sentences.

There are nine instances of explicit social intertexture in 1 Corinthians 9:

(a) 9.7: 'Who serves as a soldier at his own expense?'
(b) 9.7: 'Who plants a vineyard without eating any of its fruit?'
(c) 9.7: 'Who tends a flock without getting some of the milk?'
(d) 9.10: 'the plowman should plow in hope and the thresher thresh in hope of a share in the crop'.
(e) 9.13: 'Do you not know that those who are employed in the temple service get their food from the temple, and those who serve at the altar share in the sacrificial offerings?'
(f) 9.17: reference to being a steward.
(g) 9.19: reference to being a slave.
(h) 9.20 reference to being a Jew.
(i) 9.24–7: reference to being an athlete.

The first five instances refer to six common social roles in the Mediterranean world: soldier, vineyard planter, shepherd, plowman, thresher and temple worker. Dale Martin's research has shown that 1 Corinthians 9.17 refers to the managerial position of a steward (*oikonomos*) in Mediterranean society (1990: 80–1). These positions were generated by wealthy people who needed their household watched over when they went away or needed to have someone who would hire people to work in their fields or vineyards. 'Stewards' regularly did not have to work with their 'bodies', so their work was more prestigious than the work of laborers. Also, these positions allowed people to do other people favors – stewards functioned as 'brokers' of the benefits of the patron over them – and they allowed stewards more freedom than laborers to establish their own times of working and to do things in ways they themselves preferred.

Dale Martin's investigation shows, in addition, that many stewards in Mediterranean society were 'slaves' – middle-level 'managerial' slaves. The existence of this level of slave calls into question many previous interpretations of 1 Corinthians 9. This evidence suggests that Paul is not completely demeaning himself, but is referring to a type of slavery that could, in fact, be a means to attain upward social mobility. '[N]aming oneself the slave of an important person was a way of claiming status for oneself' (p. 48). Thus, Martin suggests, being a 'slave of Christ' could offer people of lower status a way of attaining a higher status among their peers. In addition, being a slave entrusted with a stewardship gives a person a higher status than someone who receives a wage (pp. 80–1). This would mean that Pauline discourse uses the term 'wage' (*misthos*) in 9.18 ironically to refer to that which Paul receives for his preaching of the gospel: Paul does not actually receive a 'wage'; he receives 'a reward', the opportunity to 'boast' that he offers the gospel 'free of charge' to people 'of his own free will'.

In 1 Corinthians 9.20, Pauline discourse refers three times to 'Jew(s)' and juxtaposes four occurrences of the phrase 'under the law' with the term. This is another instance of social intertexture, since it was widespread knowledge that Jews submitted themselves in special ways to the laws of their founder Moses. It will be necessary to comment further about the categories of those 'without the law' and 'the weak' under Pauline culture below.

The last four verses of the chapter contain resonant social intertexture when they refer to various kinds of athletes. Martin does not explore this social aspect of Pauline discourse in the context of the slave imagery in the chapter. Russell Sisson has supplemented Martin's analysis with evidence that the movement from the image of the slave to the image of the athlete is natural as the result of the widespread use of the image of the athlete in the literature of the moral philosophers of the time (Sisson 1994). But this takes us into cultural reasoning, so let us turn from social intertexture to cultural intertexture.

Cultural intertexture

Cultural intertexture refers to the logic of a particular culture. This may be an extensive culture essentially co-extensive with the boundaries of an empire, or it may be what Clifford Geertz describes as a 'local' culture. The overall context of Pauline discourse is Mediterranean culture. Many cultural voices constitute Mediterranean culture, and many of these voices are in dialogue in Pauline discourse. To facilitate analysis of the cultural voices in dialogue within Pauline discourse, it is helpful to distinguish the following spheres of cultural discourse: (a) Jewish diaspora discourse; (b) Greco-Roman discourse; (c) Palestinian Jesus discourse; and (d) Pauline discourse. I have not included biblical discourse here, simply for reasons of space. Certain aspects of what Richard Hays discusses under 'echo' are properly called 'biblical cultural intertexture'. This refinement of his work will need to be left for other contexts. Here we move beyond biblical culture to other cultural discourse in dialogue in Pauline discourse.

Jewish diaspora discourse

One of the spheres of great importance for Pauline discourse is Jewish diaspora discourse. Paul was born outside Syria-Palestine in the context of diaspora Judaism, and the Epistles attributed to him in the New Testament were written in Greek, the major language of diaspora Judaism. The writings of Philo of Alexandria are a major corpus of literature representing Jewish diaspora culture. Philo, like Paul, wrote in Greek, and his discourse exhibits substantial dialogue among multiple cultural voices in Mediterranean society.

The first instance of intertexture with Jewish diaspora discourse in 1 Corinthians 9 is the interpretation of Deuteronomy 25.4 in 9.8–10: 'Do I say this on human authority? Does not the law say the same? . . . Is it for oxen that God is concerned? Does he not speak entirely for our sake?' The 'law' to which the discourse refers is not Roman law, Greek law, or Egyptian law – it is Jewish Torah. Torah is not a common social phenomenon; it is a cultural phenomenon created by a particular group of people in the environs of the Mediterranean world. Torah is part of a complex network of presuppositions, dispositions, attitudes, thoughts and actions embodied in people to whom literature during the first century refers as Jews.

In 1 Corinthians 9.8–10, the discourse establishes a polarity between 'human authority' and 'the law of Moses'. Then the discourse tells the reader that 'God' was referring 'not to oxen' but to 'humans'. In other words, the discourse purports to give an 'authoritative' interpretation of the passage in the Torah which 'God' spoke. While the context of the verse about oxen resides, as mentioned above, in a setting of seventeen chapters of sayings that concern humans, a special principle had been formulated in diaspora Jewish culture that 'the law does not prescribe for unreasoning creatures, but for those who have mind and reason' (Philo, *Special Laws* 1.260; Loeb vol. 7: 251). On the other hand, in another place Philo specifically refers to 'the kindly and beneficent regulation for the oxen when threshing' (Philo, *On the Virtues* 146; Loeb vol. 8). It appears, then, that both the context of the verse in the Torah and a general approach to Torah in diaspora Jewish culture support the approach in Pauline discourse, even though it would have been possible to focus on the oxen themselves.

Another instance of intertexture with diaspora Jewish discourse is the athletic imagery which appears at the end of 1 Corinthians 9. When Pauline discourse begins to use athletic imagery, it refers to running a race (9.24). Running a race was obviously a well-known social phenomenon among Mediterranean people, but it was a particularly Greco-Roman cultural phenomenon in its origin and perpetuation. Because of its widespread presence, this phenomenon was readily accessible to a person in Jewish diaspora culture. Philo used the imagery of running a race in his discussion of the pursuit of moral or religious virtue and its rewards (Philo, *Allegorical Interpretation* III.48; Sisson 1994: 101). According to Philo, a person must keep on the racetrack during the race, which lasts one's entire lifetime:

> If on his way [the one who aspires to be good] does not become exhausted or give up and collapse, or carelessly swerve aside from the straight course but . . . completes life's race without falling, when he comes to the finish, he will receive crowns and prizes worthy of his efforts.
> (Philo, *Migration of Abraham* 133; Sisson 1994: 101)

Philo uses the analogy of the footrace to describe the obstacles that can cause one to fail in the pursuit of goodness (Philo, *De Agricultura* 180; Sisson 1994: 101). Thus, for Philo, the pursuit of a virtuous life is like running a race, and the race is not completed until the end of one's life. The race itself occurs on a racetrack directed toward God, and running off the track is a matter of running away both from 'oneself' and from God. The race itself is an obstacle course that regularly causes a person to stumble and fall. If people keep on track, however, and do not give up, they will win the greatest of crowns and prizes.

When imagery of athletic activity is extended beyond running a race, the nearest additional images regularly are wrestling and boxing. Philo frequently uses analogies of wrestlers and boxers in competition or training to describe the moral and religious life (Philo, *On Dreams* I.129–30; cf. II.145–6). In 1 Corinthians 9.26, Paul refers to shadowboxers, people who 'beat the air' with their hands. Philo compares the pretensions of 'sophists' who do not have training in dialectic to the exhibitions of shadowboxers who have no experience in real competition (Philo, *Worse Attacks the Better* 41–2; Sisson 1994: 103). Then in 1 Corinthians 9.27, Paul refers to the possibility of being disqualified. Philo also discusses disqualification in the context of the pursuit of virtue (Philo, *On Joseph* 138; Sisson 1994: 106). The concluding verses of 1 Corinthians 9 (9.24–7) refer not to one particular test or another, but to the test of one's entire life. Philo also considers the testing to refer to one's entire life (Philo, *On Rewards and Punishments* 4–6; Sisson 1994: 102, n. 56). If the virtuous person is able to endure the test, the prize is no ordinary prize but a special encounter with the divine:

> The task of him who sees God is not to leave the sacred arena uncrowned, but to carry off the prizes (*brabeia*) of victory. And what crown (*stephanos*) more fitting for its purpose or of richer flowers could be woven for the victorious soul than the power which will enable him to behold The One Who Is with clear vision?
>
> (Philo, *Change of Names* 81–2)

The language of Philonic discourse uses the same words for 'prize' and 'crown' as the Pauline discourse. For Philo, the prize is 'beholding The One Who Is'. Paul refers, in contrast, to an 'imperishable crown' (9.25). While Philo directs the focus on seeing God, which Moses came close to experiencing on Mount Sinai, Paul directs the focus on the enclothing of the perishable person with 'the imperishable', something which he perceives to have occurred in the resurrection of Christ (1 Cor. 15.42, 15.53).

In the midst of all of these similarities between Philonic and Pauline discourse, there is a striking difference in their use of the image of the slave. For Philo, the slave is the opposite of the athlete:

> The athlete and the slave take a beating in different ways, the one submissively giving in and yielding to the stripes, while the athlete opposes and withstands and shakes off the blows that are falling upon him.
>
> (Philo, *Allegorical Interpretations* III.201)

Philo characterizes the slave as a passive, slovenly person in contrast to the athlete, who actively engages in, and endures, the beating of his body. For Philo, the difference between the two is the result of using or not using 'reasoning' (*logismos*):

> The man of knowledge (*ho epistēmōn*) . . . stepping out like an athlete to meet all grievous things with strength and robust vigor, blows a counter-blast to them, so that he is not wounded by them but regards each of them with absolute indifference.
>
> (Philo, *Allegorical Interpretations* III.202)

Finally, then, the free person – the one not enslaved – is indifferent to death itself as well as to the hardships and disgraces that exemplify people who have a lower status in life:

> [H]e who adjusts himself and his to fit the present occasion and willingly (*hekousios*) and also patiently endures the blows of fortune . . . who has by diligent thought convinced himself that, while what is God's has the honor of possessing eternal order and happiness, all mortal things are carried about in the tossing surge of circumstance and sway unevenly on the balance, who nobly endures whatever befalls him – he indeed needs no more to make him a philosopher and a free man.
>
> (Philo, *Every Good Man Is Free* 23–4)

For Philo, slavery is something to be avoided. The athlete, who is the model of the one who seeks God and God's virtue, avoids slavery by using right reason. God's athlete, then, is truly free.

There is, however, an interesting tension in Philo's writings. While he regularly differentiates slaves and athletes, describing slaves as 'passive' and depraved in contrast to the athlete who endures the test and wins the prize, he knows about the kind of slaves Martin has called middle-level 'managerial' slaves (D. Martin

1990: 80–1). Moreover, Philo discusses this kind of slave in the context of 'freedom':

> There are others born as slaves (*douloi*), who by a happy dispensation of fortune pursue the occupations of the free (*eleutheroi*). They receive the stewardship (*epitropoi*) of houses and landed estates and great properties; sometimes too they become the rulers of their fellow slaves. . . . Still all the same they are slaves though they lend, purchase, collect revenues and are much courted.
>
> . . . But you say, 'by obedience to another he loses his freedom'. . . . For no one wills (*hekōn*) to be a slave. . . . [N]o one would deny that the friends of God are free. Surely when we agree that the companions of kings enjoy not only freedom but authority, because they take part in their management and administration as leaders, we must not give the name of slaves to those who stand in the same relation to the Olympian gods, who are god-lovers and thereby necessarily god-beloved.
>
> (Philo, *Every Good Man Is Free* 35–42)

In the end, Philo is not willing to use the term 'slave' for the one who is a slave but not enslaved. Paul, it appears, moved beyond this to say, 'I have enslaved myself to all' (1 Cor. 9.19). In order to put Paul's use in its proper context, and to bring to light the nuances of its distinctiveness, we must look beyond the boundaries of diaspora Jewish culture.

In summary, the writings of Philo of Alexandria reveal that a Jew living in the context of Mediterranean society could easily incorporate athletic imagery about running a race, wrestling and boxing. Evidence from Philo suggests that one of the most natural contexts for this imagery would be the pursuit of virtue as God requires it. Philo, in contrast to Paul, establishes a polarity between the slave and the athlete as he discusses the person of virtue. Nevertheless, Philo knows about 'managerial' slaves who, though slaves, are so free in their activities that they are not properly called slaves.

Greco-Roman discourse

The imagery of athletic competition – running, wrestling and boxing – has its natural home in Greek culture, not Jewish culture. Thus, Philo's incorporation of it is a matter of synthesis of Jewish and Greek culture in a context of first-century Mediterranean

society. Greco-Roman moralists also incorporated this imagery.
Russell Sisson has gathered intertexts together, using the research
of Malherbe, Horsley (1978) and Martin (Sisson 1994: 97–9).
The discourse of Epictetus describes the Cynic as one who is 'sent
(*apestaltai*) by Zeus to men' (Epictetus, *Discourses* 3.22.23–5).
Further on, the discourse adds that the Cynic also is 'a herald
(*kēruka*) of the gods' (3.22.69).

This Cynic must be 'free to go about among men, not tied down
by the private duties of men' if he is to be true to his calling
(3.22.69). Moreover, he thinks of his service (*diakonos*) to God as
something he willingly does, even though he was called by Zeus to
do it:

> I am free (*eleutheros*) and a friend of God that I might of my
> own free will (*hekōn*) obey him.
>
> (Epictetus, *Discourses* 4.3.9)

For the Cynic, the goal is to attain freedom from all things
(Epictetus, *Discourses* 3.13.11). The Cynic has been sent by God to
teach people this freedom:

> And how is it possible for a man who has nothing, who is
> naked, without home or hearth, in squalor, without a slave,
> without a city, to live serenely? Behold, God has sent to you
> the man who will show in practice that it is possible. 'Look at
> me,' he says. 'Am I not free from pain and fear, am I not free?'
>
> (3.22.46–8)

The Cynic does not show concern for just a few people, but cares
for all humans:

> The Cynic has made all humans his children; the men among
> them he has as sons, the women as daughters; in that spirit he
> approaches them all and cares for them all. . . . It is as a father
> he does it, as a brother, and as a servant (*hypēretēs*) of Zeus,
> who is father of us all.
>
> (3.22.81)

Epictetus describes the task of the Cynic sage called by God in
terms of athletic competition that produces hardship and requires
discipline (Epictetus, *Discourses* 1.24.1–2). For Epictetus, the
struggle is a discipline that trains the Cynic (Epictetus, *Discourses*
3.20.9). Epictetus speaks directly about the end result of athletic
training as self-control.

Instead of shameless, you will be self-respecting; instead of faithless, faithful; instead of dissolute, *self-controlled*.

(Epictetus, *Discourses* 4.9.17)

In the end, Epictetus says, the Cynic receives the crown as his reward (Epictetus, *Discourses* 3.24.51–2; cf. 2.18.28). The discourse emphasizes that this is not just any contest, but the greatest – Olympia itself (Epictetus, *Discourses* 3.22.51–3). Usually the discourse speaks of this activity as service (*diakonos*) and refers to the one who has been called as a servant (*hypēretēs*):

[Diogenes] became a servant (*diakonōn*) of Zeus, caring for men indeed, but at the same time subject (*hypotetagmenos*) to God.

(3.24.65)

But there is an extended discussion, as well, of the freedom of the Cynic in relation to slavery:

Is the paltry body which you have, then, free or is it a slave? . . . [T]here *is* something within you which is naturally free.

(3.22.40–2)

The goal of the Cynic is to become free in all things, because this is the truly natural state of humans (3.24.71). The point is that a person should allow no humans and no internal human desires to make them their slave. But then the discourse turns to God, using some of the same imagery of the Pauline discourse:

A good soldier does not lack someone to give him pay (*ho mistodotōn*), or a workman, or a cobbler; and shall a good man? Does God so neglect His own creatures, his servants (*diakonōn*), his witnesses, whom alone he sees as examples to the uninstructed . . . ? . . . I obey, I follow . . . For I came into the world when it so pleased Him, and I leave it again at His pleasure, and while I live this was my function – to sing hymns of praise unto God, to myself and to others, be it to one or to many. God does not give me much, no abundance, he does not want me to live luxuriously . . .

(3.26.27–31)

The issue, finally, is fear of death (3.26.38–9). Then the discourse turns directly to slavery:

And what, says someone, has this to do with being a slave? – Doesn't it strike you as 'having to do with being a slave' for a man to do something against his will (*akonta*), under compulsion (*anagkazomenon*)?

(4.1.11)

One of the ways, and one of the reasons, people enslave themselves is for food:

If [the freed slave] gets a manger at which to eat he has fallen into a slavery much more severe than the first.

(4.1.35–6)

Finally, the discourse distinguishes between 'microslavery' and 'megaslavery':

Call... those who do these things for certain small ends *microslaves*, and the others, as they deserve, *megaslaves*.

(4.1.55)

For the Cynic, it is the knowledge about freedom and slavery which allows him to live a free life:

What, then, is it which makes a man free from hindrance and his own master? ... In living, it is the knowledge (*epistēmē*) of how to live.

(4.1.63)

But there is another issue, namely, God. How can the Cynic, called by Zeus, be entirely free? The answer lies in making his own free will the same as the will of God:

But I have never been hindered in the exercise of my will, nor have I ever been subjected to compulsion against my will. And how is this possible? I have submitted my freedom of choice unto God. He wills that I shall have fever; it is my will too. He wills that I should choose something; it is my will too. He wills that I should desire something; it is my will too. He wills that I should get something; it is my wish too. He does not will it; I do not wish it. Therefore, it is my will to die; therefore, it is my will to be tortured on the rack. Who can hinder me any longer against my own views, or put compulsion upon me? It is no more possible to do this with me than it is possible for anyone to do this with Zeus.

(4.1.89)

In the end, then, the true philosopher submits his own will to the will of God so that he wills what God wills for him. This is an amazing similarity with Paul, compelled to preach the gospel but free, because he freely chooses to endure hardship to offer it free of charge.

What, then, is distinctive about Pauline discourse in the setting of Greco-Roman discourse? First, Pauline discourse orients itself toward the God of Israel, not Zeus. The God of Israel has made promises to special people whom he has selected to receive his benefits, if they live according to his will. Second, Pauline discourse concerns itself directly with the law the God of Israel gave to his people. The discourse of the moral philosophers grounds its discussion more in the 'moral laws of the universe' than in laws given by Zeus. Third, Pauline discourse focuses on a recent act of God in the death and resurrection of a crucified Messiah, who is a stumbling block to Jews and a folly to the nations (1 Cor. 1.23). Fourth, Pauline discourse robustly embraces the term 'slavery' to describe the commitment to all people for the sake of the gospel; the discourse of Epictetus maintains a restraint with slave language by emphasizing that the Cynic's work is 'service' (*diakonos*) and the Cynic himself is messenger, scout, servant (*hypēretēs*) and friend of God who cares for all people.

Palestinian Jesus discourse

To ascertain the manner in which Pauline discourse transforms the constellation of concepts and sentences in early Christian discourse, it is necessary to explore, for a moment, those aspects of 1 Corinthians 9 that are dialoguing with the discourse of Palestinian Jesus culture. We saw above how 1 Corinthians 9.14 reconfigured the language of a saying attributed to Jesus with vocabulary that conceptualized working for the kingdom in terms of 'proclaiming the gospel to get a living from the gospel'. Pauline discourse 'Paulinizes' other discourse characteristic of Q tradition as well. The Epistle of James is another interesting source for seeing the influence of Pauline discourse on Palestinian Jesus discourse (Wachob 1993). Other pre-gospel traditions also are sources for this discourse, but we will not attempt to employ them here.

There is no evidence that 'Jesus followers' in Palestine linked 'freedom' with apostleship. Those who talked about freedom would have been talking about the Torah as a 'law of liberty' (James 1.25; 2.12). Among these followers, the emphasis would have been on 'perfect' or 'mature' law (James 1.4; Matt. 5.48; 19.21). Freedom would be the result of being a 'doer' who is 'blessed in his doing' (James 1.25; Matt. 7.17–27), and a major focus of this doing would have been on 'loving one's neighbor' (James 1.8; Matt. 5.43–5; Luke 6.27–8). This would have been a Jewish discussion about fulfilling the *Shema* of Israel in the fullest, most perfect way: 'Love the Lord your God with all your soul, mind, and strength, and your neighbor as yourself' (Deut. 6.4; Lev. 19.18; Matt. 22.37–9). Paul knows this tradition (Rom. 13.9; Gal. 5.14), and in Galatians 5.13–14 he discusses it in the context of 'you' who were 'called to freedom'. Freedom, then, would have been linked with fulfilling the Torah, not with being an apostle. The linking of 'freedom' with 'apostleship' appears to have occurred within Pauline discourse. Thus, we will discuss it below under Pauline culture.

When Pauline discourse refers to being an apostle, this is an intertextual phenomenon that dialogues with Palestinian Jesus culture. Characteristic discourse among representatives of Jesus culture in Palestine was related to the following teaching attributed to Jesus:

> [2]The harvest is indeed great,
> but the laborers few.
> Pray, therefore, the lord of the harvest
> that he *send out* laborers into his harvest.
> [3]Go! Behold, *I send you* as lambs in the midst of wolves.
> . . . [7]Remain in the same house,
> eating and drinking what is provided by them;
> for the laborer is worthy of his reward.
> [8]And when you enter a city, and they receive you,
> eat what is set before you,
> [9]and heal those sick within it,
> and say to them,
> 'The kingdom of God has come near to you.
> . . . [16]Whoever hears you, hears me,
> and he who rejects you, rejects me;
> and whoever rejects me,
> rejects *the one who sent me*'.
> (Q 10.2–3, 10.7–9, 10.16; Jacobson 1992: 139–40; Sisson 1994: 84)

The emphasis was on a chain of 'sending': God sent Jesus and Jesus sends the apostle. The message being sent is that the kingdom of

God has come near. The roots of the 'sending' tradition lie within Jewish culture, where the *shaliach*, the sent one, is authorized fully to represent the one who sent him. The roots of the message of the kingdom of God lie in the proclamation of John the Baptist and its transformation in the teaching of Jesus.

Palestinian sending tradition featured a saying attributed to Jesus that 'the laborer is worthy of his reward/wage', which we have discussed in the section on oral–scribal intertexture. This 'reward/wage' referred to food and drink, but it seems also to have presupposed housing while the apostle was working in the area. But it is doubtful that people in Palestinian Jesus culture talked about this as a 'right' or 'authoritative privilege', using the term *exousia* as Pauline discourse does (1 Cor. 9.4–6). Rather, the term *exousia* was linked with 'healing the sick': apostles asserted *exousia* – rights or authoritative privilege – over demons on the basis of the nearness of the kingdom of God. It is clear, then, that Pauline discourse in 1 Corinthians 9 was significantly reconfiguring constellations of words and sentences about apostles and their rewards.

One of the most important issues is the use in Palestinian Jesus culture of the phrase 'to proclaim the gospel' (1 Cor. 9.14: *katangellein to euangelion*), which we also discussed in the section on oral–scribal intertexture. In Palestinian Jesus culture, 'proclaiming' was conceptually connected with the kingdom of God. The earliest verb appears to have been to 'herald' or 'announce' (*kērussein*) the kingdom. In this context, there was no reference to 'gospel' or 'preaching the gospel'. The concept of 'gospel' appears to have come into Jesus culture when Septuagint (Greek) passages were applied to Jesus' activity. Q tradition in Matthew 11.4/Luke 7.22 attributes to Jesus:

> Go and tell John what you have seen and heard: the blind receive their sight, the lame walk, lepers are cleansed, and the deaf hear, the dead are raised up, the poor have good news preached (*euangelizontai*) to them. And blessed is whoever is not scandalized by me.
>
> (Matt. 11.4/Luke 7.22)

This saying, which is an early summary of Jesus' activity by followers of Jesus, incorporates language from Isaiah 29.18–19; 35.5–6; 42.18; 61.1. The concept of 'preaching the good news' comes from Isaiah 61.1: 'He has sent me to preach good news (*euangelisasthai*) to the poor'. There are no sentences containing the noun 'the gospel' (*to euangelion*) at this stage of Jesus culture in Palestine; rather the activity of 'preaching good news' focuses on the kingdom and the recipients of the message are 'the poor'. The reader will notice the closeness of this usage to the beatitude 'Blessed are the poor for theirs is the kingdom of heaven'. The reader also will notice the new beatitude generated by Palestinian Jesus culture – 'Blessed is whoever is not scandalized by me' (Matt. 11.4/Luke 7.22) – in a context of 'preaching good news to the poor'. It is instructive that the Epistle of James presents argumentative discourse about responsibilities to the 'poor' because the 'kingdom' has been promised to them (James 2.5; cf. Wachob 1993) and throughout the Epistle there is no reference to 'gospel' or 'preaching the gospel'. In other words, the discourse of the Epistle of James, in this regard, reflects Palestinian Jesus discourse prior to its incorporation of Septuagint language from Isaiah that presents a summary of Jesus' activity which includes 'preaching good news to the poor'.

Pauline discourse in 1 Corinthians 9 continues the use of the verb 'to preach good news':

> For if I preach good news (*euangelizōmai*), that gives me no ground for boasting. For necessity is laid upon me. Woe to me if I do not preach good news (*euangelisōmai*).
>
> (9.16)

But Pauline discourse creates clauses with the noun 'the gospel' (*to euangelion*) as an object, and these clauses stand alongside clauses containing the verb 'to preach good news' (*euangelizōmai*). We saw in the section on oral–scribal intertexture how fully this Pauline discourse takes over and reformulates a saying attributed to Jesus. Pauline discourse, then, reconfigures the discourse of Palestinian Jesus culture by transforming speech attributed to Jesus into speech that uses the noun 'the gospel' and by creating new sentences using the noun 'the gospel'. Pauline discourse maintains continuity with Palestinian Jesus discourse by perpetuating the use of the verb 'to preach good news'. Pauline discourse also maintains continuity by referring to 'inheriting the kingdom of God' (e.g. 1 Cor. 6.9–10; 15.50), but it breaks decisively with discourse in Palestinian Jesus culture by never referring to 'proclaiming the kingdom of God'. In its place, Pauline discourse generates a significant list of phenomena which a person 'proclaims', including the gospel (Gal. 2.2), Christ crucified (1 Cor. 1.23) and the word of faith (Rom. 10.8). The next section will investigate the significance of this further.

There is little, if any, evidence that Palestinian Jesus culture used the metaphor of the athlete in relation to apostles. This imagery appears not to have been used in their discourse.

Pauline discourse in intertextual perspective

When a cultural phenomenon appears as intertexture in the discourse of an alternative culture, the discourse reconfigures it in the terms of that alternative culture. The presence of multiple cultural intertextures customarily signifies that the discourse is defining a distinctive culture in the context of other cultures. The task in this section is to describe the particular reconfiguration of cultural discourses in Pauline discourse.

First, in 1 Corinthians 9.12 Pauline discourse links 'freedom' with being an apostle. This connection, as mentioned above, appears to be new in Jesus culture. Discussion of freedom was present in diaspora Jewish culture, as we saw above, and the discussion included 'managerial' slaves and people who were 'friends of God'. In Greco-Roman culture, discourse about Cynics called by God included discussions of freedom in the context of being compelled to serve the needs of all people. Pauline discourse brings language about freedom and slavery into a discussion of the responsibilities of an apostle.

Second, Pauline discourse about receiving food and drink for one's work as an apostle reconfigures Palestinian Jesus discourse by calling this a 'right' or 'authority' (*exousia*), and by referring to this as getting a living 'by the gospel' as one 'proclaims the gospel'. Palestinian Jesus discourse, it appears, referred to 'proclaiming good news' (*euangelizōmai*). The kingdom of God and the day of the Son of Man were the special topics of the proclamation, the healing of a range of bodily disorders were accompanying benefits of the proclamation, and 'the poor' were the special recipients of the proclamation. In this context, the apostle received food, drink and housing wherever he went. Pauline discourse reconfigures this conceptual network with new sentences containing new words and new concepts.

Third, Pauline discourse links preaching the gospel as a 'stewardship' with making oneself a 'slave to all'. The concept of slaves who receive a stewardship over property and possessions is part of diaspora Jewish discourse. Enslaving oneself to God or to a king as a 'friend' is one thing; enslaving oneself 'to all' would appear to be problematic in diaspora Jewish discourse. Freely caring for all humans, however, is an integral part of a conceptual network of sentences among moral philosophers who talk about the Cynic as one sent by Zeus as a messenger, scout and servant to teach all people to be free from other humans, outside circumstances and internal desires that would enslave them. The Cynic distinguishes, in this context, between 'microslavery', which is a degrading enslavement to petty things like food, desire, other people, etc., and 'megaslavery', which is an enhancing form of slavery like slavery to Caesar. In the end, the Cynic decides to submit himself completely only to the will of God, so that he himself freely wills whatever God wills for him. Paul decides, in the context of his compulsion to preach the gospel, to offer the gospel free of charge, and offering it in this form is its own reward, indeed a ground for boasting.

Fourth, Pauline discourse creates a new discourse within Jesus culture by employing imagery of the athlete to describe the challenges and rewards of the apostle. This imagery was fully at home in diaspora Jewish discourse about the virtuous person and in Greco-Roman moral-philosophical discourse about the person sent by Zeus to all people.

Attention thus far has been on the inner texture and intertexture of 1 Corinthians 9. In the process, oral–scribal, historical, social and cultural intertexture of the text have emerged for interpretation. The reader will notice that the domains of inner texture and intertexture are the major domains of historical criticism and its subdisciplines. The new phenomenon that guides socio-rhetorical criticism is rhetorical criticism, which nurtures analysis of multiple argumentative dimensions of the text that historical criticism and its disciplines have regularly explored only in modes properly described as 'restrained' analysis (Wuellner 1987: 451–3). The next two domains of texture – social and cultural texture, and ideological texture – take the interpreter decisively beyond the domains of historical criticism and its subdisciplines.

CONCLUSION

There is a deep irony at present in the use of the term intertextuality in New Testament interpretation. When Julia Kristeva introduced the term, she emphasized that texts were a 'mosaic of quotations', and this insight presupposed Mikhail Bakhtin's claim that the 'literary word' is 'an intersection of textual surfaces rather than a point (a fixed meaning), as a dialogue among several writings: that of the writer, the addressee (or the character) and the contemporary or earlier cultural context' (Kristeva 1986: 36). The issue, it turns out, is 'the cultural context'. Some interpreters in the field of literary study stay within a 'canonic culture' as they perform intertextual analysis. Others reach more broadly beyond canonical boundaries into the surrounding culture of the time. A similar situation exists in the fields of both secular literary criticism and New Testament studies. From a socio-rhetorical perspective this is especially a great irony in the field of New Testament study, since the New Testament represents Jewish tradition in a Mediterranean mode that was objectionable to leaders of Pharisaic Judaism who carried Jewish tradition into the Mishnah and the Talmuds rather than into Gospels, Acts, Epistles and apocalypses. The challenge must be to investigate the full range of differences, including the use of Greek language as the primary form of discourse, between the New Testament and the other forms of Jewish discourses during the first century. Some scholars refuse to engage seriously in the investigation of the relation of New Testament literature to literature outside Jewish tradition. The reasons are many, and the discussion of the ideological texture of texts in chapter 5 provides an arena for exploring this issue in detail. At present, however, the issue is the social and cultural texture of texts, and the reader must learn to distinguish between analysis and interpretation of social and cultural *inter*texture, which maintains a close relation to words in texts both inside and outside the New Testament, and the social and cultural *texture* of texts, which uses sociological and anthropological theory to ascertain the social and cultural nature of New Testament discourse in the context of the full range of discourses in the Mediterranean world.

5

SOCIAL AND CULTURAL TEXTURE
Every meaning has a context

A third arena is social and cultural texture. This arena differs from the arena of intertexture by its use of anthropological and sociological theory to explore the social and cultural nature of the voices in the text under investigation. Study of a particular sector of early Christianity with sociological theory appeared in Wayne A. Meeks's study of 'The Man from Heaven in Johannine Sectarianism' (1972). Meeks analyzed both 'the special patterns of language' in the Gospel of John and the special logic of the myth of the descending and ascending redeemer (p. 44), integrating a close, rhetorical reading of the text with anthropological and sociological insights into the formation and maintenance of sectarian communities. His interpretation demonstrates the profound relationship in Johannine discourse between the redeemer who belongs to the 'world of the Father' yet comes into the 'world which does not know or comprehend' him, and those who are 'in the world' yet are drawn to the redeemer by 'believing' in him. In the end, the reader sees that the redeemer's foreignness to the world is directly related to the sect's perception of itself as foreign to the world – 'in it but not of it'. In Meeks's words:

> The Fourth Gospel not only describes, in etiological fashion, the birth of that community; it also provides reinforcement of the community's isolation. The language patterns we have been describing have the effect, for the insider who accepts them, of demolishing the logic of the world, particularly the

144

world of Judaism, and progressively emphasizing the sectarian consciousness. If one 'believes' what is said in this book, he is quite literally taken out of the ordinary world of social reality.

(1972: 71)

This article was a superb initial step toward analysis of the social and cultural texture of a text in a mode that is attentive to the inner texture of the text. It contains a limitation that certainly cannot be criticized for 1972, but which needs to be transcended today, namely the place where it stops its analysis and interpretation. The article does not use sociological theory that would give further insight into the nature of the counterculture under discussion. Meeks discusses the historical existence of a community of Johannine believers without expanding the reader's sociological understanding of the discourse. These people, in his view, set themselves apart from the Jewish people in their setting and the world in which they lived. There are different ways in which people set themselves apart from others, and sociologists and anthropologists have given us language to describe different ways in which people do this. Meeks did not take the next step of using these resources. Though Meeks has, in a number of articles, pursued the social and cultural dimensions of various kinds of discourse in a mode similar to the initial article on the Johannine Man from heaven (1977, 1983, 1985, 1991), a historical rather than sociological orientation has remained prominent in Meeks's books. As Meeks has moved to an interest in the moral world of early Christianity (1986b, 1986c, 1987, 1988, 1990a, 1990b, 1993), he has maintained a historical focus rather than carrying out a socio-rhetorical project that programmatically explores the social and cultural nature of various kinds of early Christian discourse (but see Meeks 1985).

The year after the appearance of Meeks's article on Johannine sectarianism, Jonathan Z. Smith presented a paper on 'The Social Description of Early Christianity' that called for the incorporation of highly developed anthropological theory in analysis and interpretation of early Christian data (1975; cf. Meeks 1975). In his article, Smith referred to an 'almost total lack of persuasive models' (p. 19), a seduction 'into a description of a *Sitz im Leben* that lacks a concrete (i.e., non-theological) seat' and offers only the most abstract understanding of 'life' (p. 19), the writing of social histories of early Christianity 'in a theoretical vacuum in which outdated "laws" are appealed to and applied . . . which no longer represent a consensus

145

outside the New Testament or church history fields' (p. 19), and 'unquestioned apologetic presuppositions and naive theories' (p. 20). He suggested, however, that there were many resources available to move ahead, including a few 'major syntheses, lacking only the infusion of new theoretical perspectives' (p. 20). Calling for 'careful attention to the inner history of the various religious traditions and cults' (p. 20) and analysis and interpretation that are 'both richly comparative and quite consciously situated within contemporary anthropological and sociological theory' (p. 21), he pointed to Meeks's article on the Johannine Man from heaven as a 'happy combination of exegetical and sociological sophistication' (p. 21). Smith's critical agenda introduces theoretical practices that move interpretation beyond the boundaries of a poetics that limits textual discourse to its 'inner' world toward a comprehensive, critical method for constructing a new picture of the social and religious nature of early Christianity. New Testament interpreters have been gradually adopting the critical insights of cultural anthropology in his four books since that time (J. Z. Smith 1978, 1982, 1987, 1990), but much needs yet to be learned from these profound analyses of early Christianity.

The same year as the appearance of Smith's initial paper (1975), John G. Gager's *Kingdom and Community: The Social World of Early Christianity* introduced models from twentieth-century sociology and anthropology for the study of early Christianity (1975). Gager's analysis was part of the same intellectual world as Smith's; but this was a distant world from the work of many other interpreters at the time. Many interpreters knew that these intellectual worlds should come together, but they also knew that the road would be steep and rocky. Gager broached the issue with a well-placed quotation from Peter Brown:

> The need to link disciplines is frequently expressed among us. Discussion of this need takes place in an atmosphere, however, that suggests the observation of an African chieftain on a neighboring tribe: 'They are our enemies. We marry them'.
> (P. Brown 1970: 17; quoted in Gager 1975: xii; cf. Gager 1982)

Gager himself used social anthropological studies of millennialist cargo cults in Melanesia, social-psychological studies of cognitive dissonance and a merger of cultural-anthropological and history-of-religions interpretations of myth to approach 'The End of Time and the Rise of Community' in first-century Christianity (Gager

1975: 19–65). Then he discussed the transition from charisma to canon and orthodoxy (pp. 66–92), the social class or status of early Christians (pp. 93–113) and a perspective on the success of Christianity (pp. 114–58) as major challenges for interpreters of early Christianity. Rich with sociological and anthropological insight as well as information about the first four centuries of early Christianity, this book established an agenda for a new paradigm of investigation and interpretation. While a number of its agendas have been pursued in one way or another, the task of incorporating its insights programmatically into exegesis of New Testament texts still lies in the future. Socio-rhetorical criticism sets forth a programmatic set of strategies to pursue, test, enrich and revise the provisional conclusions Gager advances in his book.

SPECIFIC SOCIAL TOPICS IN RELIGIOUS LITERATURE

While Meeks used the term 'counterculture' to describe Johannine sectarianism and Gager used studies of millennialist cargo cults to inform his analysis, neither used a comprehensive sociological theory about religious communities in their analysis and interpretation. James A. Wilde, in contrast, investigated the social response to the world in the discourse of the Gospel of Mark with the aid of Bryan Wilson's seven types of religious sects (Wilde 1974, 1978). An adaptation of Wilson's sociological definitions to socio-rhetorical descriptions of different types of religious discourse produces the following seven major responses to the world.

Conversionist argumentation considers the outside world to be corrupted because humans are corrupted. If people can be changed then the world will be changed. It takes no interest in programs of social reform or in the political solution of social problems and may even be actively hostile to them. The judgment on humans and events tends to be moralizing, because it is grounded in a belief that humans are entirely responsible for their actions. This argumentation encourages revivalism and public preaching at mass meetings rather than door-to-door activity. It encourages emotional, but not ecstatic, experiences.

Revolutionist argumentation maintains an eschatological position that nurtures a desire to be rid of the present social order when the time is ripe – if necessary, by force and violence. It awaits a new

147

order under God's direction when the people who use this argumentation will become the holders of power as the friends and representatives of God. This argumentation is hostile at one and the same time to social reform and to instantaneous conversion. It tends to explain the world in determinist terms, just as it tends to consider the fate of individuals to be pre-determined. The argumentation occupies itself in prophetic exegesis, in comparisons of inspired texts and in the relation between predictions and contemporary events. Since conversionist argumentation considers change to be an occasional and gradual occurrence, it nurtures discourse that familiarizes newcomers with a complex spectrum of beliefs and moves them toward an acceptance of their truth. Revolutionist argumentation, in contrast, speaks in a matter-of-fact, unemotional manner, simply asking a newcomer to believe that this is the way things are. God is viewed as a divine autocrat. There is little feeling of direct relationship with the divinity. The members are considered to be God's instruments, waiting for the decreed moment, agents of God's work and will.

Introversionist argumentation encourages people neither to convert the population nor to expect the world's overturn, but simply to retire from the world to enjoy the security granted by personal holiness. The argumentation is indifferent to social reform, to individual conversion and to social revolution. It may consider some particular inspirational experiences to be significant for the entire group, or it may consider them to be purely individual revelations that might help the growth of personal piety. This argumentation is concerned more with deepening than with widening spiritual experience. It holds a certain disdain for those 'without holiness' and does not encourage the believers to introduce others to their holiness. It nurtures meetings that are 'assemblies of the saved' (gathered remnant). It views the community as supporting the individual and does not encourage people to act in mission in the outside world. The argumentation exhorts the faithful to be a law unto themselves and to live apart from the world.

Gnostic manipulationist argumentation insists especially on particular and distinctive knowledge. By and large, it accepts the outside world and its goals. It proclaims a more spiritualized and ethereal version of the cultural ends of global society, but it does not reject them. Gnostic manipulationist argumentation tries instead to change the methods appropriate for attaining these ends. It sometimes claims that the only way of achieving its spiritualized goals is to use the special knowledge taught by the movement. This is the only true and worthwhile way of acquiring health, wealth, happiness and social prestige. Although reinterpreting 'worldly' activities, it offers special techniques and verbal modes of assurance that justify the pursuit and attainment of cultural goals. This argumentation offers means for learning the systems but does not provoke conversions since the important thing is for people to acquire spiritual attitudes rather than to offer specific activities or relationships. Anyone may accept the gnosis and use it for his or her own personal ends since its efficacy is not dependent on any relationship or on any mystical process.

Thaumaturgic argumentation insists that it is possible for people to experience the extraordinary effect of the supernatural on their lives. It encourages the seeking of personal messages from spirits, obtaining cures, effecting transformations and performing miracles. It defines believers in relation to the wider society by affirming that normal reality and causation can be suspended for the benefit of special and personal dispensations. This argumentation resists acceptance of the physical process of aging and death and encourages people to come together to affirm a special exception from everyday realities which assures individuals and their loved ones of perpetual wellbeing in the next world. For the present, the believers procure immediate advantages by accomplishing miracles. This argumentation does not claim a special knowledge, but calls upon spirits and other powers to perform oracles and miracles. The ends it seeks can be defined in terms of compensation for personal losses rather than the specific quest for cultural goals.

Reformist argumentation insists that social, political and economic institutions can serve good, rather than oppressive, ends. By encouraging a very strong sense of identity and study of the world, it attempts to encourage people to involve themselves in the world with good deeds. This argumentation nurtures a role of social conscience and acceptance of a place in the world without becoming part of the world or being made impure by it. In other words, it encourages active association with the world without becoming part of it.

Utopian argumentation asserts that people should inaugurate a new social system free from evil and corruption to run the world. This system will change the relation of everything and everyone in the world. This argumentation encourages partly withdrawing from the world and partly wishing to remake it into a better place. It is more radical than reformist argumentation, because it argues that the whole system should be changed. It is potentially less violent than revolutionary argumentation, because it argues that authoritarianism is one of the major evils in the world. It is more constructive on a social level than conversionist argumentation, because it argues that the system is the source of evil, rather than people, whose nature is more naturally good than evil. Utopian argumentation encourages the construction of the world on a communitarian basis. While it regularly encourages the establishment of colonies, it does so as part of a program for the reorganization of the world along community lines.

It would be rare for discourse in a text as long as a Gospel or an Epistle to contain only one kind of social response to the world. Rather, two or three modes of response interact, creating a particular social texture for the discourse. For Wilde, revolutionist discourse dominates the text of Mark, and the social texture of this argumentation is 'objectivist'. This means that the discourse focuses primarily on the world as an object to be dealt with. Among the seven types of discourse, four are objectivist:

(a) revolutionist, which says God will overturn the world;
(b) introversionist, which says God calls us to abandon the world;
(c) reformist, which says God calls us to change present social institutions so they function toward good ends;
(d) utopian, which says God calls us to replace the present social system with a new social organization from which evil is absent (Wilde 1978: 50; Robbins 1994b, 1994d).

Wilde concludes that the objectivist aspect of Markan discourse is revolutionist. People themselves will never be able to change the world sufficiently enough to bring salvation. Therefore, the discourse does not use either reformist or utopian argumentation. The discourse also does not encourage people simply to abandon the world. Rather, people are to engage in various kinds of activity until God intervenes and overturns the world.

What does this mean that people should be doing until God intervenes? For Markan discourse, according to Wilde, two other kinds of social response are embedded in revolutionist discourse: conversionism and thaumaturgic response. Conversionism is a subjectivist aspect of discourse (1978: 50–1), and Wilde concludes that '[d]eath makes sense in Mark only as a result of conversionism and only for the sake of revolutionism' (p. 64). Markan discourse challenges people to modify their predispositions, attitudes and beliefs toward a willingness to engage in 'a ministry of preaching, being delivered up, and death' (p. 64). A thaumaturgic response is a 'relationist' aspect of discourse (p. 50), according to Wilde, and it supports both the conversionism and the revolutionism by 'reflect[ing] or elicit[ing] a mountain-moving faith in God which has its reward both in a present and future age' (p. 66).

First of all, I want to emphasize the usefulness of this kind of approach for analyzing and interpreting the social and cultural texture of the discourse of a text. In rhetorical terms, this kind of analysis focuses on the 'special' or 'material' topics in the discourse (Aristotle, *Rhet.* 1.2.21–2; Kennedy 1991: 45–7 (esp. n. 71), 50–2). This means that the analysis works directly with the content of statements in the text. When the voice of Jesus in Mark 13.24–5 says, 'But in those days, after that tribulation, the sun will be darkened, and the moon will not give its light, and the stars will be falling from heaven, and the powers in the heavens will be shaken', this is a 'revolutionist' premise. Jesus, the major actor in the narrative discourse, asserts in these verses that there will be a future time when God will intervene in the present order of the world and completely change things. Likewise, Wilde's discussion of 'conversionist' discourse is based on verses like Jesus' assertion that one must 'repent and believe in the gospel' (Mark 1.15). In turn, Markan discourse voices a 'thaumaturgic' response to the world in such verses as Jesus' statement in Mark 11.23: 'Truly, I say to you, whoever says to this mountain, "Be taken up and cast into the sea", and does not doubt in his heart, but believes that what is said will come to pass, it will be done for that person'. The specific content of the discourse, then, asserts a social response to the world that is an underlying premise or 'first principle' of this kind of discourse (Kennedy 1991: 46).

Second, I want to challenge Wilde's analysis of Markan discourse at one point. My analyses suggest that Markan discourse is more 'gnostic manipulationist' in its orientation than conversionist (Robbins 1994d: 74–81). According to Wilde, conversionists are subjectivists who say, 'God will change us', while gnostic manipulationists are relationists who say, 'God calls us to change perception' (Wilde 1978: 50). I understand 'repent and believe in the gospel' (Mark 1.15) to be a call from divine authority to change perception.

Moreover, I consider the emphasis on listening, seeing, taking heed, accepting and understanding what is hidden, secret and mysterious to be more gnostic manipulationist in orientation than conversionist (Robbins 1994d: 75). Burton Mack's discovery that the language in the parables in Mark 4 has a close cultural relation to the system of *paideia* in Hellenistic-Roman culture is an important contribution to this insight (Mack and Robbins 1989: 143–60; Robbins 1994d: 76–9). A primary orientation of Markan discourse is to call people to change their perception of themselves and the world rather than to presuppose that God changes people so they see and think differently. Both conversionist and gnostic manipulationist dimensions are present in the discourse, but my conclusion is that gnostic manipulationist presuppositions dominate over conversionist presuppositions in Markan discourse.

In as much as I have engaged in dialogue with Wilde's analysis at this point, it may also be good to return to Meeks's analysis for a moment. If revolutionism, thaumaturgy and gnostic manipulationism are prominent in Mark, what types of social response are prominent in Johannine discourse? First, it would appear that there are strong thaumaturgic presuppositions underlying Johannine discourse. There is a 'relationist' dimension (Wilde 1978: 50) in common, then, with Markan discourse. Both accounts of the life of Jesus emphasize the extraordinary effect of the supernatural on individual people. The healing of the blind man in John 9 and the raising of Lazarus in John 11 point dramatically to the presence of thaumaturgic social response to the world in Johannine discourse.

Second, Johannine discourse does not move into strong revolutionist assertions like Markan discourse. Johannine discourse moves, instead, into assertions of separation from the world. This points to strong introversionist impulses in Johannine discourse. The emphasis is more upon God's call to abandon the world than it is upon an assertion that God will overturn the world (revolutionist), that God calls us to change present social institutions (reformist) or that God calls us to replace the entire social system in the world (utopian), though there may be a strain of this last one. Johannine believers are to gather in a community of those 'born of heaven' and deepen their spiritual experience in this context.

Third, it will come as no surprise to most interpreters that Johannine discourse contains gnostic manipulationist premises. Throughout the Fourth Gospel there is an emphasis on knowledge sent from heaven that comes into the world as light that shines in darkness. 'All who received him, who believed in his name, he gave power to become children of God' (John 1.12). The only way to receive this knowledge is through the Messiah Jesus, since 'No one has ever seen God; the only Son, who is in the bosom of the Father, he has made him known (John 1.18).

The remarkable thing about Johannine discourse is the manner in which it embeds conversionist premises in its gnostic manipulationist orientation. Throughout the narrative, there is a strong emphasis on God's changing of people. On the one hand, this occurs through the work of the Spirit Paraclete: 'The wind blows where it wills, and you hear the sound of it, but you do not know whence it comes or whither it goes; so it is with everyone who is born of Spirit' (John 3.8). On the other hand, it occurs through the work of Jesus on earth: 'Whoever drinks of the water that I shall give him will never thirst; the water that I will give him will become in him a spring of water welling up to eternal life' (John 4.14). In the Fourth Gospel a number of people are changed by Jesus to people who live with God's powers of life and truth in them: the Samaritan woman (4.7–30); many Samaritans (4.39–42); Nicodemus (7.50–2); a blind man (9.1–41); Thomas (20.24–9). The emphasis on change, then, is prominent. In fact, God's powers appear to effect much more profound and widespread change in people in the Fourth Gospel than in the Gospel of Mark. In Mark, the only people who experience profound change experience it through direct physical healing: the leper (1.45); the Gerasene demoniac (5.20); and blind Bartimaeus (10.52). This means that change is limited to thaumaturgic contexts. In Mark, people who do not experience physical healing do not undergo change that transforms them into believers who begin to receive the full benefits of God's powers in their lives. In the Fourth Gospel, in contrast, profound change occurs in people not only through the thaumaturgic powers of God but also through persuasive word of God. God changes people through powerful word as well as powerful thaumaturgic deed. This means that Johannine discourse is more prominently conversionist than Markan discourse. In Mark, people are either on the inside or the outside, and even those on the inside may discover in the end that they are without understanding and thus without the working powers of God in their lives.

Using a sociologically grounded typology of religious responses to the world, then, can exhibit the inner workings of the multiple discourses in the New Testament with more clarity and detail than interpreters have seen thus far. Fortunately, others have also been engaged in this kind of work, but often these analyses still need to be taken into a programmatic socio-rhetorical form of analysis and intepretation.

John H. Elliott used Wilson's typology in the context of 'sociological exegesis' of 1 Peter at the beginning of the 1980s (1981). For Elliott, the discourse of 1 Peter evokes a dominantly 'conversionist' response to the world (pp. 75–8, 102–6). Elliott embeds his insights in a comprehensive approach to exegesis he called 'sociological exegesis' in 1981 and now calls 'social-scientific criticism' (1990a). His approach has an important relation to the four-texture approach of socio-rhetorical criticism. Elliott began with analysis of a repetitive pattern in the inner texture of 1 Peter. The term *oikos* [*tou theou*] (household [of God]) occurs throughout 1 Peter in correlation with *paroikos* (resident alien), *paroikia* (alien residence or residence as aliens) and *parepidēmos* (visiting stranger). It is 'their recurrence at key points in the structure of the document', the pattern of repetition, that attracted Elliott's attention (p. 23). Elliott did not use rhetorical resources to analyze the discourse in the letter, however. He presented a 'periphrastic outline' toward the end of the book that 'attempts to reflect the literary structure and composition of the text as closely as possible while also explicating its integrating theme and emphases' (pp. 234–6). Thus, he gave significant attention to the inner texture of 1 Peter on which interpreters can now build with the aid of rhetorical resources.

Next, Elliott turned to oral–scribal intertexture on the basis of the Septuagint, apocrypha, pseudepigrapha, Philo, Josephus, New Testament, rabbinic literature and Greco-Roman literature (pp. 24–37). Again, Elliott did not seek rhetorical patterns that accompany the language. Therefore, he did not engage in a fully socio-rhetorical analysis of social and cultural intertexture. Nevertheless, his quoting of Ecclesiastes and Psalms of Solomon, and his gleaning of linguistic evidence in the *Encyclopedic Dictionary of Roman Law* (Berger 1953) gave considerable attention to the intertexture of the language in the repetitive pattern he identified in the discourse (Elliott 1981: 24–37).

Elliott contributed dimensions to interpretation that were decisively new when he turned to his analysis of the social and cultural texture of 1 Peter. In the process of developing a social profile of the addressees, he employed the sectarian typology of Bryan Wilson and proposed that the discourse reveals a 'conversionist response to the world' (pp. 75–8). To fill in the picture, Elliott explored the discourse for reference to geographical location; ethnic composition; legal, economic and social status; religious allegiance and the social form such religious affiliation assumes; and the nature and historical circumstances of the conflict in which they are involved. This analysis, guided by sociological theory, focused on specific social topics in the discourse and exhibited a new way for interpreters to proceed. In essence, Elliott approximated the activity of a sociologist taking a survey throughout the discourse of 1 Peter, and with this approach Elliott was showing interpreters a new mode of analysis and interpretation. With the next step, Elliott moved beyond specific social topics and focused on a widespread social institution in the Mediterranean world, namely the 'household' (pp. 165–266). From a rhetorical perspective, this is a move beyond specific social topics to a common social and cultural phenomenon in the discourse. This kind of exploration has become the trademark of social-scientific criticism and makes an excellent contribution to one's understanding of the manner in which early Christian discourse often employs and reconfigures common social and cultural perceptions in the political, economic and social arenas of the Mediterranean world.

In the final chapter, Elliott turned to the ideological texture of 1 Peter. He discusses 'group interests' in the discourse and explains how analysis of ideology moves beyond theological analysis and interpretation. Then he turns to 'self-interests' that appear to point specifically to a social location in Rome. Last, he analyses cultural conflict in the form of Christian and non-Christian ideologies (pp. 267–88). With this move, Elliott took his analysis through the four textures that provide the comprehensive framework for socio-rhetorical criticism. Also, Elliott's interest in the ideology of the text reveals that his investigation is at least implicitly rhetorical from beginning to end. Elliott's concern lies with the specific nature of the discourse in 1 Peter, thus it returns regularly to the text as it proceeds. Since Elliott did not use rhetorical resources, the investigation is not a full-fledged socio-rhetorical analysis. Nevertheless, the abiding interest in exegesis throughout the book pointed the way toward a truly interdisciplinary paradigm of interpretation. The special contribution of the book to socio-rhetorical criticism is threefold. First, it introduced social theory into a context of detailed exegesis. Second, it explicitly discussed ideology within New Testament texts, something that historical–critical interpreters have been, and in many instances still are, unwilling to do. Third, it moved programmatically through the four arenas of texture that are the most prominent in the new, interdisciplinary paradigm that has been emerging in biblical studies during the last two decades.

For this section of this chapter, the special interest is Elliott's use of Wilson's typology to analyze 1 Peter. Locating 1 Peter in Asia Minor, Elliott perceives the problems facing the Christians there to be a double one: 'Not only were they suffering at the hands of outsiders; this suffering posed a threat to their internal cohesion as well' (1981: 83). The conversionist nature of the discourse in 1 Peter sets negative and positive aspects of Christian life in tension with one another:

> On the one hand, 1 Peter presents the relation between the believers and nonbelievers as one of alienation and hostility. The former are being demeaned and abused by the latter as inferior 'strangers' and 'aliens' (1.1, 17; 2.11), fanatical zealots (3.13), and ridiculous 'Christ-lackeys' (4.14, 16). . . .
>
> On the other hand, this same document speaks in positive, optimistic terms concerning the eventual conversion of these outsiders (2.12; 3.1–2), supports a neutral, if not favorable, view of civil government (2.13–17), and utilizes the secularly popular model of the household to discuss the roles and relationships of distinctive Christian behavior (2.18–3.7; 5.1–5a).
>
> (Elliott 1981: 108)

Elliott's analysis and interpretation function in the context of a comprehensive sociological theory about the development of religious sects and the strategies of different kinds of sects. This kind of analysis also looks carefully at the specific, material topics of the discourse and uncovers the particular social response which the discourse evokes. The reader is left to wonder, however, if the discourse of 1 Peter limits itself to conversionist premises. Does it put a few revolutionist premises at the service of its conversionist discourse (2.12; 4.5, 4.7, 4.17)? Does it use conversionist premises toward utopian goals articulated in terms of blessed people living generously with one another and with leaders of human institutions (2.4–25; 3.1–12; 5.1–5)? By pressing questions like this, the interpreter can begin a program of analysis and interpretation throughout New Testament discourse that can display the configurations of social responses to the world that exist in New Testament discourse and those that do not. If we begin to see configurations that are conventional outside New Testament discourse but not inside it, we may begin to get a clearer view of the distinctive nature of Christian discourse in Mediterranean culture and society.

Robert Jewett's rhetorical and social analysis of 1 Thessalonians made an additional contribution to a socio-rhetorical mode of analysis and interpretation (1986). From the perspective of Wilson's terminology, Jewett analyzed the happenstances in relation to revolutionist discourse during a period of time that spans the writing of 1 and 2 Thessalonians. For Jewett, some of the people in Thessalonica misunderstood the revolutionist discourse in 1 Thessalonians in such a manner that they became convinced that the Day of the Lord had already come. Jewett's analysis, however, does not use Wilson's typology, and it does not move fully into a socio-rhetorical mode as it moves toward its goals. Rather, Jewett uses rhetorical criticism in the context of socio-historical criticism. His goal is to exhibit the historical and social intertexture of the discourse. In other words, his social analysis finally devotes most of its attention to the social actions of a group of people in Thessalonica during a particular span of historical time. For this reason, Jewett does not analyze the relation of revolutionist discourse in the letters to conversionist, reformist, gnostic manipulationist, introversionist, utopian and thaumaturgic discourse in the letters. As a result, rhetorical analysis becomes a subdiscipline of historical criticism rather than an interdiscipline with a goal of exploring the ongoing social and cultural aspects of religious discourse during the first century.

Philip Esler's study of the social and political motivations of Lukan theology also used Wilson's typology, and Esler concluded that the thaumaturgic and conversionist types of response are especially relevant for Luke-Acts (1987: 59). He characterizes the thaumaturgic response in Lukan discourse, however, as 'anti-thaumaturgic', pointing to the superiority of the gospel over the thaumaturgic activities of Simon Magus (Acts 8.9–13, 8.18–24); Elymas, the Jewish sorcerer in Paphos (Acts 13.6–12), and the books of magic at Ephesus (19.19) (1987: 59; cf. Garrett 1989). The conversionist response, in turn, is evident in

> its author's preoccupation with individual penance and acceptance of the Gospel in baptism, which enable the believer to enter a zone of Spirit-filled experience during the period

before the final consummation to be inaugurated by the returning Son of Man.

(Esler 1987: 59)

After showing that Lukan discourse does not engage in a revolutionist response (1987: 59–65), Esler does not continue to use Wilson's insights into religious sects. I have included a socio-rhetorical response to Esler's work in a recent study of Mary, Elizabeth and the Magnificat in Luke 1.26–56 (1994b). My conclusion is that Lukan discourse features an inner relation between thaumaturgy and conversionism that emphasizes reformist activity: for example, a significant change in the systems of distribution throughout the Roman empire. More recently, Esler has applied this kind of analysis to 4 Ezra and other texts (1994a, 1994b). We can look forward to refinements in this kind of social analysis in future studies.

Although John Kloppenborg has not, in the studies available to me, applied Wilson's typology to any text, his work has moved steadily toward socio-rhetorical analysis and interpretation of the social and cultural texture of texts. His article on Q and the Q people (1991) best exhibits the manner in which the overall movement of his work has been toward programmatic socio-rhetorical exegesis. First, he performs extensive analysis of the inner texture of texts and maintains a textual location as he explores other arenas and draws conclusions. The section on 'Form, Content and Rhetoric' in his study of the social history of the Q people vividly illustrates the careful attention he gives to repetitive–progressive, opening–middle–closing, narrational and argumentative texture in texts (1991: 81–5; cf. 1990c). He observes not only instructional rhetoric (1991: 81–5); but he analyzes abbreviated and elaborated chreiai that characterize Jesus as a founder of a movement (1991: 91–4). He enriches insight into the sayings through comprehensive analysis of oral–scribal intertexture, which he exhibits prominently in his book on Q (1987a). From the analysis of inner texture and oral–scribal intertexture, he moves to historical and social intertexture by investigating material and literary evidence concerning Galilee and the Decapolis (1991: 96–9). Within this context, he moves to social and cultural texture, exploring the countercultural nature of the sayings in the framework of hierarchies and interactions among people in the city and the rural areas of Roman Palestine. He has not attempted to move into programmatic analysis of ideology and theology in material available to me, but other articles signal the presence of this arena in his work (1986, 1987b, 1989, 1990a, 1990b, 1990c, 1990d). John Kloppenborg's work, therefore, has been contributing insights for socio-rhetorical criticism for a number of years.

Analysis of the special or material topics of early Christian discourse using Wilson's typology of religious sects, then, is well underway. Using the resources of rhetorical criticism, we can begin to display and analyze the configuration of premises both explicitly asserted and implicitly presupposed in the multiple kinds of discourse that exist in the New Testament as a result of the process of selection that occurred throughout the first centuries of early Christianity.

COMMON SOCIAL AND CULTURAL TOPICS

Another dimension of the social and cultural texture of a text concerns the social and cultural systems and institutions that it both presupposes and evokes. In rhetorical terms, this is a matter of analyzing 'common topics' in a text (Aristotle, *Rhet.* 1.3.7–9; 2.19–24; Kennedy 1991: 45–7, 50–1, 174–213). As the 1980s began, Bruce J. Malina introduced the concept of common social and cultural systems and institutions to New Testament interpretation, using cultural anthropology as his major resource (1981a; 1986a). A *Semeia* volume edited by John H. Elliott gathered together a group of studies inspired by this new work under the rubric of 'social scientific criticism' (1986a). Then a series of studies by Jerome H. Neyrey (see bibliography), a volume on the social world of Luke and Acts (Neyrey 1991), and a volume on social-scientific criticism and the New Testament (Elliott 1993) have appeared, which display the results of a decade and a half of work by Malina, Elliott, Neyrey, Paul W. Hollenbach, Richard L. Rohrbaugh, Carolyn Osiek, Douglas E. Oakman, John J. Pilch, Halvor Moxnes, Philip Esler, Dennis Duling, Mark McVann (see bibliography for works of each author) and others (cf. Barclay 1992, 1995) on common social and cultural systems and institutions in the Mediterranean world like honor and shame, limited good, kinship, hospitality, patron/client/broker, sickness and healing, purity, dyadic personality, conflict, city and countryside, temple and household, and meals and table-fellowship. This work has added a new dimension through its concentrated focus on those social and cultural phenomena that anthropological and sociological theory perceive to be common to all people in Mediterranean society. By now the work of these interpreters offers rich resources comparable to the overall historical phenomena that had become available to interpreters by the middle of the twentieth century. Most of the people engaged in this analysis consider themselves to be 'adding additional data' to the enterprise of historical criticism. Some in the group are trying to bring this data into contexts of interpretation informed by careful attention to the nature of texts as written discourse (cf. Robbins 1995).

Using the results of social-scientific criticism, Bernard Brandon Scott wrote a book on the parables that embeds analysis of social and cultural systems and institutions in close exegetical work on the texts themselves (1989). The book moves systematically through literary-structural analysis of each parable, explicit and comprehensive intertextual comparison and analysis, social and cultural analysis and at least implicit ideological and theological analysis. The manner in which Scott enacted this interdisciplinary analysis and interpretation virtually fulfills the goals of a socio-rhetorical study without claiming the designation. Scott's interest focuses on 'voice' in the parables, and his goal is to reconstruct 'the implied speaker/author of the corpus of the parables' (p. 65). His analysis features detailed exhibition of both repetitive–progressive and opening–middle–closing texture in the parables. After detailed analysis of inner textual features, he presents a line-by-line reading that identifies, among other things, the manifestation of social and cultural systems and institutions in the discourse of the parables. His analysis reveals three major systems and institutions of Mediterranean social life and culture in their discourse: (a) the institution of the family; (b) the social and cultural system of patron–client relations; and (c) the cultural symbol system of the artifacts of daily life of home and farm.

Scott's analysis of family life in the discourse of the parables suggests that the family is the major institution for organizing social exchange throughout the village, city and beyond (pp. 79–202). The center of the social map in the parables is the family, with the father as the prominent figure. This social map provides basic identity for people, defining their relation to one another in such a manner that it pervades their understanding of social activities in the village, the city and beyond to the ends of the world. In addition, '[t]his social map furnishes a metaphorical system for the kingdom of God' (p. 79). The kingdom is like a family where one son says he will go out to work and does not and another says he will not work but does (pp. 80–5). Also it is like a man who gives three loaves at midnight to a friend in his village who must offer hospitality to unexpected guests who have just arrived (pp. 86–92). Moreover, it is like two men in the city who went up to the Temple, and the one with social status prayed confidently while the one who was a social outcast asked for mercy (pp. 93–7). Within these parables and others, the social map of family relations that reach out to village, city and beyond functions as a metaphorical system for the kingdom of God. A major feature of their discourse is to reconfigure traditional expectations concerning who is securely an insider and who is certainly an outsider. Each parable in its own way uses the social map to show the unusual, unpredictable and regularly disturbing nature of the kingdom of God.

In another group of parables, the social and cultural system of patron–client relations functions on a vertical axis to organize power exchange in society. The obligations are based on long-term relations, and actions are legitimated by custom more than law. For most matters, in fact, there is no appeal within the legal system. This system for 'allocating resources, exchanging power and wealth, and legitimating the social structure' (p. 205) provides a metaphorical framework for parables that feature master and servants, traveling householders and stewards, creditors and debtors, farmowners and farmworkers (pp. 205–98). Again, these parables subvert the assumptions of the world. In this world of dependency and inequality, certain masters are generous to the complaint of some, others are hardhearted to the dismay of some, and some respond positively to crafty but illegal action to the surprise of many. Again this is a world where regular values and expectations are in upheaval. Working metaphorically for the kingdom of God, these parables exhibit a range of actions and responses embedded in patron–client relations. The parables intermingle the need to reassess how God works with judgment and mercy with a reassessment of people on earth who have power to judge and to have mercy and people who anticipate judgment or mercy.

In the third group of parables, the artifacts of daily life of home and farm function as the symbols of transcendent cultural values. Seed, an empty jar, leaven, a small coin, a net, a treasure, fig trees and sheep become symbols of the kingdom in ordinary, surprising and sometimes offensive ways. As these artifacts function as symbols for values associated with the kingdom of God, the hearer of the parable has to decide which risk to take, which value to choose or which failure to accept (pp. 301–417). The basic ingredients of daily life function metaphorically for the basic dynamics of the kingdom. Big celebrations for little things, good results from unclean things or failure, or ordinary results from everyday things, are all present in this metaphorical world of the kingdom.

Exploring the parables in the context of the social and cultural institutions and systems of the first-century Mediterranean world, Scott concludes that their discourse coordinates the everyday, the unclean and miracle. One of the most surprising results is that parables do not invoke the fantasy world of the peasant (p. 421). They feature everyday activities of cheating, anger, loss, envy, disappointment and surprise without assuring the hearer that everything will be all right in the end. Rather, in the end there may be failure, mercy, judgment, praise, dismissal, joy or simply dismay. This study, appearing in 1989, exhibits the promise of embedding close analysis of the inner texture of New Testament texts in investigation of the dynamics of social and cultural institutions and systems that function in them. Scott does not call this a socio-rhetorical study, but the close reading of the parables is rhetorical in nature and the exploration of the social and cultural nature of the discourse is comprehensive. From my perspective, this book exhibits a form of socio-rhetorical analysis.

In 1991, David B. Gowler systematically investigated the function of the social and cultural systems of honor and shame, patron/broker/client, limited good, kinship, hospitality, reciprocity, purity and challenge-riposte in the context of a highly developed approach to the narratorial texture of Luke and Acts. As Gowler applied his socio-narratological approach to the characterization of Pharisees in Luke and Acts, he interpreted extensive portions of Luke 5–7, 11–19 and Acts 5, 15, 23 and 26 (1991: 177–296). His investigation of common Mediterranean social and cultural systems in the context of detailed analysis of the narratorial texture of Luke and Acts contributes to analysis of social and cultural texture in the framework of socio-rhetorical analysis. His analysis of Luke 7.36–50 serves well to illustrate the manner in which it makes this contribution.

First Gowler analyzes the inner texture of the narrative in a narratorial mode. The narrator (7.37) and the Pharisee (7.39) directly define the woman as a sinner, and Jesus implicitly defines her in this way (7.47). The Pharisee Simon directly defines Jesus as a teacher (7.40), but his inner thoughts deny that he is a prophet (7.39). The narrator directly defines the Pharisee as the host (7.39), but Jesus names the host as Simon (7.40). Direct definition occurs, then, from points of view that alternate among the narrator, the Pharisee and Jesus (p. 219).

In this context, the woman defines herself indirectly through her action: she 'wet Jesus' feet with her tears, wiped them with her hair, kissed his feet, and proceeded to anoint them' (p. 220). Then the focus turns from the woman to the Pharisee, bypassing Jesus. But the Pharisee does not speak at this point; the narrator reveals his 'inner thoughts', which raise doubts that Jesus is a prophet or he would know the woman is sinful and would not allow her to touch him (7.39). The dialogue that follows introduces comparison and contrast. As Jesus speaks, the two debtors in the parable function by analogy with the Pharisee and the woman, and this analogy, plus Jesus' additional statements, set the woman and the Pharisee in contrast to one another. The woman, Jesus says, provided a greeting kiss and water and ointment for his feet, and the Pharisee provided none of these. Jesus' favorable response to the woman and the Pharisees' unfavorable response result in status reversal: norms are defamiliarized, Jesus affirms the unfamiliar and:

> the triangle of relationships between Jesus, Simon the Pharisee, and the woman forces readers to take sides and to identify with the woman's attitude toward Jesus. . . . Simon – as well as the reader – is forced to consider the fact that there is no qualitative difference between himself and the sinful woman, only a quantitative difference.
>
> (pp. 220–1)

After this exhibition of narratorial texture in the story, Gowler turns to the function of cultural scripts in it. The dialogue between Jesus and Simon is an honor and shame contest. When Jesus responds publicly to Simon's silent challenge, Simon is put on the defensive. Simon's honor decreases as he joins all the other Pharisees who have been bested by Jesus, and Jesus' honor increases. Social meanings associated with different parts of the body highlight implications of honor and shame. The head is a primary symbol of honor; washing someone's feet is a shameful task. Simon did not anoint Jesus' head nor supply water for his feet; the woman did not dare to anoint Jesus' head, but wiped his feet with the hair of her head, and kissed and anointed his feet. 'The stress upon her humiliation is shown by the seven-fold repetition of the word *feet* in these few verses' (p. 223).

At this point Gowler turns to Mediterranean hospitality and to patron–client relationships to interpret the honor and shame in the story. When a person outside a community is invited to dine or lodge in someone's house, that person changes from a stranger to a guest. Ambivalence is pervasive as the host gives precedence to the stranger over familiar guests. The host gains honor by the quality of his guests; guests in turn are expected to honor the host. Any implication that the host has slighted the guest brings dishonor to the host; any sign of ingratitude on the part of the guest brings dishonor to the guest. In this story, hospitality interacts with patron–client relations. Jesus' acceptance of the role of guest is also an acceptance of the role of a client to a patron. When the woman challenges Jesus' honor in this public setting, however, Jesus accepts her actions as a greater form of hospitality than Simon has offered and adopts the role of broker of God's blessings to her as a client. Jesus' roles as both client–guest and broker of God's blessings create a social fracas that the story does not resolve. The implication is that the Pharisee needs Jesus to function as broker of God's blessings to him also, which, of course, is an insult to the Pharisee's status as a religious leader in the community (pp. 222–6).

Gowler's interpretation investigates the function of common social and cultural systems in the discourse of the story. Thus, it takes a significant step toward socio-rhetorical analysis. The absence of rhetorical theory to analyze the argumentative texture of the story (cf. Mack and Robbins 1989: 85–106), of detailed comparative analysis to interpret the intertexture of the story, and of ideological investigation to analyze the stereotypes and ethnic strategies of the discourse prevent it from delivering a full-fledged socio-rhetorical analysis and interpretation (Robbins 1992a). Nevertheless, Gowler's analysis has contributed to the formulation of programmatic socio-rhetorical exegesis which integrates detailed social and cultural analysis with careful analysis of the inner texture of New Testament texts.

Building on the work of Malherbe and others, Stanley K. Stowers has taken analysis of cultural intertexture into a mode of rhetorical-critical interpretation that provides a 'thick description' of cultural codes and generic conceptions. His essay on 'Friends and Enemies in the Politics of Heaven' exhibits the procedure well (1991). Stowers, observing extensive language concerning friends and enemies in Paul's letter to the Philippians, explores discussions of the ancient institution of friendship in texts from Aristotle, Plato, early Stoics, Epicureans, Cicero, Plutarch, Dio Chrysostom and Diogenes Laertius. Informed by this data, Stowers analyzes the architecture and strategies of the discourse from the perspective of a letter of friendship. Within the contrastive models of friends versus enemies, the discourse presents Paul as the author of a hortatory or psychagogic letter to a community of friends (p. 108), God as the creator and completer of the Philippian community (p. 117) and Christ as both Lord and friend of Paul and the community (p. 119). Since the cultural codes of friendship concern not only individual personal relations but politics and business (p. 107), the discourse establishes a politics of heaven that informs roles, economics and personal relationships in God's community on earth. The symmetry among 'the relationship of Paul to the Philippians, the relationship the Philippians are to have with one another, and the relationship both have with Christ' (p. 119) creates a culturally encoded symbolic world which nurtures theological convictions that inform wide-ranging sectors of Christian life. Distinctive features emerge with the pervasive use of language from the lower end of the status spectrum of Greco-Roman friendship and patronage, namely servants or slaves (p. 120), and the particular drama of Christ's decision to live as a servant (p. 117). Paul's own imprisonment and adoption of hardship in the tradition of the Cynics contributes the additional *ethos* to make the text an authoritative treatise for Christian life.

Willi Braun brought analysis of social and cultural systems into a full rhetorical mode in his recent study of Luke (1995). The two major systems are honor and shame and the distribution of food and wealth in the context of the city. These social and cultural systems provide the dynamics for the exchange between Jesus and the Pharisees at the great banquet scene in Luke 14.1–24. First, Braun shows that Lukan discourse introduces the topic of greed, love of money and excessive banqueting with the presence at table, across from Jesus, of a man sick with dropsy. The disease of dropsy, being 'watery', which causes people to have unquenchable thirst and insatiable hunger, is a standard Cynic topic for describing wealthy people who waste their life and health with eating and drinking and who, though loaded with money, continually crave more of it. Here Braun has uncovered a primary feature of cultural intertexture in

Lukan discourse that traditional interpretation has missed. Second, with the insight into the meaning effect of a man with dropsy at the banquet table among Pharisees, Braun is able to identify the opening scene in the chapter as a 'mixed chreia', a brief episode that attributes both dramatic action and decisive speech to Jesus in a well-known social situation. Jesus' action and speech make up a sharp social comment in the context of a banquet hosted by a Pharisee, a representative of a group Lukan discourse stereotypes as 'lovers of money' (Luke 16.14), people 'filled with extortion' (Luke 11.39). Third, recognizing the extended discourse attributed to Jesus from 14.8–24 as rhetorical elaboration, the 'working out' (*ergasia*) of a set of topics in a special social situation, Braun presents an intricate analysis of the function of the internal 'units' in the discourse and the social and cultural values and topics in the analogies, examples, judgments and exhortations. Fourth, in the context of this analysis, Braun explores in detail the implications of honor and shame, distribution of wealth (and honor), living by the 'roads and hedges' outside the city-gates and wealthy people conspiring against 'peers' who violate the practices of the 'elite' by failing to honor the rich and put the poor in their place. In particular, Braun benefits from Rohrbaugh's recent study of the Lukan perspective on the ancient city in Luke 14 (1991b), the studies by Moxnes and Gowler on the Pharisees (Moxnes 1988a; Gowler 1989, 1991, 1993) and Scott's extensive study of parables of Jesus (1989). Braun's insights into rhetorical elaboration are deeply informed by the work of Mack and Robbins (1989) on patterns of argumentation in the Gospels. The study features throughout a rich use of traditional resources, both ancient and modern; the work of social-scientific critics associated with the Context Group (Elliott 1993; Malina 1993; Neyrey 1991); and the work of rhetorical critics who have explored the function of the rhetorical chreia and its elaboration in the Gospels (Mack 1990; Robbins 1993a). Braun's investigation contains some of the most mature socio-rhetorical analysis currently available in New Testament studies.

Analysis of common social and cultural topics in New Testament texts, then, is well underway. Beginning in seminal works in 1981 by Elliott and Malina, this kind of analysis and interpretation has reached an advanced stage characterized by rich collaboration with literary and rhetorical interpretations.

FINAL CULTURAL CATEGORIES

Analysis of cultural alliances and conflicts in New Testament discourse is in its infancy (Robbins 1993c). In contrast to analysis and interpretation of special and common topics, this calls for rhetorical analysis of 'final categories' in texts (*Rhet. ad Alex.* I.1421b, 21–1422b, 12; Lausberg 1990: par. 375; Mack and Robbins 1989: 38, 58). Mack's study of the Gospel of Mark in the late 1980s brought this kind of analysis and interpretation decisively into view (Mack 1988; Robbins 1991b), and his recent study of the earliest sayings material has advanced the project further (Mack 1993). In his studies, Mack investigates discourse in the Gospels as an archeologist investigates different kinds of data in a site. Mack's goal is to uncover 'local' voices embedded in the discourse of the Gospels. The task Mack faces at this point is one of 'cultural intertexture' – namely identifying early cultural voices among the followers of Jesus that attained a significant enough 'identity' that they can still be heard in the new discursive context.

Rather than explain Mack's work on its own terms, I will bring his insights into the context of the socio-theoretical project of analysis and interpretation explained in this volume. Mack builds on the work of earlier scholars who have detected early 'collections' of sayings, miracles, parables and pronouncement stories in Mark, Matthew and Luke. Putting this work alongside the discourse in the letters of Paul, he identifies five kinds of 'local' discourses among followers of Jesus during the first four decades after Jesus' life. Let us analyze them briefly in the context of the practices of socio-rhetorical criticism.

Paul Achtemeier identified earlier collections of miracle stories in Mark 4–8, which he called 'chains' or *catenae* of stories (1970, 1972). Mack observes that the discourse in these stories contains no antagonism or polemic toward other Jews. Rather, these stories perpetuate the discourse of the great traditions of Moses and Elijah in the Bible. God's mighty powers affect the sea, the wilderness and individual people in direct ways to protect, feed and heal them. The new mediator of these marvelous powers is Jesus, rather than Moses and Elijah, so this discourse has been recontextualized in new stories. Also, these powers occur through new stories in new locations, so the discourse is reconfigured. Echoes of God's feeding of the people in the wilderness occur in the miraculous feedings of 5,000 and 4,000 people in Markan discourse, as the people sit down in groups with numbers related to the division of people into groups during the wilderness wanderings. Also, echoes of Elijah and Elisha's miracles appear as Jesus raises a young girl from death to life (Mack 1988: 215–19, 230–8). In socio-rhetorical terms, this discourse is thaumaturgic. The special concern is individual people's lives, and Jesus is the person through whom the powers of God work to answer their needs and fears.

We can take this analysis a step further in terms of final social and cultural categories if we introduce a typology of cultures I have recently developed (1993c; 1994b: 189–194; 1994d). If we take a brief digression to look at different kinds of basic culture, then we can return to this Markan discourse with yet additional insight.

Dominant culture is a system of attitudes, values, dispositions and norms supported by social structures vested with power to impose its goals on people in a significantly broad territorial region. Dominant cultures are either indigenous or conquering cultures.

Subcultures imitate the attitudes, values, dispositions and norms of a dominant culture and claim to enact them better than members of dominant status. Subcultures are wholistic entities that affect all of life over a long span of time.

> [The term subculture] stand[s] for the cultural patterns of a subsociety which contains both sexes, all ages, and family groups, and which parallels the larger society in that it provides for a network of groups and institutions extending throughout the individual's entire life cycle.
>
> (Roberts 1978: 112, quoting Gordon 1970: 155)

Subcultures differ from one another according to the prominence of one of three characteristics: (a) a network of communication and loyalty; (b) a conceptual system; and (c) ethnic heritage and identity. In a *network subculture*, a chain of communication and loyalty among certain individuals, families and institutions is the most prominent feature. In certain circumstances, it is difficult to decide if a network is simply part of the dominant culture or is a subculture within the dominant structure. In a *conceptual subculture*, a system of basic presuppositions about life, the world and nature is the most prominent feature. An *ethnic subculture* has origins in a language different from the languages in the dominant culture, and it attempts to preserve and perpetuate an 'old system' in a dominant cultural system in which it now exists, either because a significant number of people from this ethnic culture have moved into a new cultural environment or because a new cultural system is now imposing itself on it.

A *counterculture* arises from a dominant culture and/or sub-culture and rejects one or more *explicit* and *central* values of the culture from which it arises (Roberts 1978: 114; Yinger 1960, 1982). The term is best reserved for intra-cultural phenomena; 'counter-culturalists are cultural *heretics* trying to forge a new future, not *aliens* trying to preserve their old culture (real or imagined)' (Roberts 1978: 121). Countercultures are 'alternative minicultures which make provisions for both sexes and a wide range of age groups, which are capable of influencing people over their entire life span, and which develop appropriate institutions to sustain the group in relative self-sufficiency' (at least twenty-five years) (Roberts 1978: 113). A counterculture is 'interested in creating a better society, but not by legislative reform or by violent opposition to the dominant culture', which are common characteristics of sub-cultures. The theory of reform is to provide an alternative, and to 'hope that the dominant society will "see the light" and adopt a more "humanistic" way of life'. In other words, 'social reform is not a preoccupation' of a counterculture (Roberts 1978: 121). Its constituents

> are quite content to live their lives and let the dominant society go on with their 'madness'. Yet, an underlying theme is the *hope* of voluntary reform by the dominant society in accord with this new model of 'the good life'. Hence, one would expect a fully developed counterculture to have a *constructive* image of a better way of life. In short, the term counterculture might best be reserved for groups which are not just a reaction formation to the dominant society, but which have a supporting ideology that allows them to have a relatively self-sufficient system of action.
>
> (Roberts 1978: 121)

The value conflict of a counterculture with the dominant society 'must be one which is central, uncompromising, and wrenching to the fabric of the culture. The concept of counterculture also implies a differentiation *between* the two cultures which is more distinct than the areas of *overlap*' (Roberts 1978: 121). There is, then, a 'fundamental difference between a counterculture and a subculture'. A subculture 'finds ways of affirming the national culture and the fundamental value orientation of the dominant society'; 'a counterculture rejects the norms and values which unite the dominant culture' (Roberts 1978: 112–13).

A *contraculture* is a 'short-lived, counter-dependent cultural deviance' (Roberts 1978: 124). It is 'a groupculture rather than a subculture'. Contracultures are deeply embedded in a dominant culture, subculture or counterculture. Contracultures are 'groups that do not involve more than one generation, which do not elaborate a set of institutions that allow the group to be relatively autonomous and self-sufficient, and which do not sustain an individual over an entire life span' (Roberts 1978: 113). A contraculture is primarily a reaction-formation response to a dominant culture, subculture or counterculture. One can predict the behavior and values in it if one knows the values of the society, subsociety or countersociety to which it is reacting, since the values are simply inverted (Roberts 1978: 123–4; Yinger 1960: 629; Stark 1967: 141, 153; Ellens 1971). In a contraculture, then, the members have 'more negative than positive ideas in common' (Roberts 1978: 124, citing Bouvard 1975: 119).

Liminal culture is at the outer edge of identity (Bhabha 1992: 444). It exists only in the language it has for the moment. In some instances, liminal culture will appear as people or groups experience transition from one cultural identity to another. In other instances, liminal culture exists among individuals and groups that have never been able to establish a clear social and cultural identity in their setting. The language of a liminal culture is characterized by a 'dialectic of culture and identification' that has neither binary nor hierarchical clarity (Bhabha 1992: 445). Speech is disjunctive and multiaccentual (Bhabha 1992: 445). It starts and stops without obvious consistency or coherence. It features 'minimal rationality' as a dialogic process that 'attempts to track displacements and realignments that are the effects of cultural antagonisms and articulations – subverting the rationale of the hegemonic moment and relocating alternative, hybrid sites of cultural negotiation' (Bhabha 1992: 443).

From the perspective of these different kinds of culture, the miracle discourse Achtemeier and Mack identified is 'subcultural' discourse that is conceptually related both to Jewish and Greco-Roman culture. Some of the final categories in this discourse are 'care', 'mercy', 'life and death', 'fear and cowardice', 'faith or trust' and 'the possible' (Robbins 1994d: 66–7). This discourse shows few 'countercultural' features like the discourse in the Gospel of John that Meeks analyzed. In other words, the discourse perpetuates strong thaumaturgic emphases present both in Jewish and Greco-Roman tradition. There is an ethnic subcultural base for this discourse in Mark. But there is no decisively 'alternative' or 'oppositional' cultural system at work in the discourse. Rather, people who tell these stories and live in their meaning effects locate themselves in a subcultural thaumaturgic world. Their world is subcultural, because it is a local variation of dominant Jewish and Greco-Roman traditions that feature the great healers of the past like Moses, Elijah and Asclepius (Robbins 1993c: 448–9). Markan discourse, then, embeds this subcultural, thaumaturgic discourse in its own discourse. Analysis of the fully-developed rhetorical nature of this discourse has been started recently (Robbins 1994d: 65–74); a full socio-rhetorical exploration of this discourse in its contexts in the Gospels awaits interpreters who are equipped to analyze and interpret it.

A second form of local discourse in the Gospels is the kind of parable discourse that appears in Mark 4. The preceding chapter in this book contains a brief discussion of Mack's analysis of the 'cultural intertexture' of *paideia* in the topic of seeds as words that fall on different kinds of soil and produce different amounts of 'fruitfulness' under different circumstances. In this chapter, we can take this analysis a bit further. On the basis of its specific social topics, the discourse in the parables in Mark 4 is gnostic manipulationist. Not everyone is able to understand this discourse. Some are on the 'inside' and some are on the 'outside'. Those who hear it and understand it will be able to endure and be fruitful (Mark 4.20). On the basis of its final social and cultural categories, this discourse evokes a conceptual subculture in Mediterranean society. People are invited to think their way into the kingdom of God. The realms of agricultural life (Mark 4.1–20, 26–32), light in a house (Mark 4.21–2) and the marketplace (Mark 4.24–5) provide the categories of 'mystery', 'worth', 'the visible' and 'the just'. This discourse shows few signs of a 'countercultural' stance. The discourse does not suggest that the world is decisively 'against' people who understand these things. Those who use this discourse do have both 'tribulation' and 'persecution' in view (Mark 4.17), but the discourse does not seem to envision a 'programmed' attack on those who understand. Rather, this is simply the lot of a 'subculture' that aspires to participate in the wealth of the dominant class but is regularly disenfranchised from it. The discourse envisions that certain members of the group 'give in' to 'the cares of the world, delight in riches, and the desire for other things' (Mark 4.19). Life is good enough that some slip into the 'ways of the world'. It is necessary, from the perspective of this discourse, to maintain a commitment to a special, subcultural view of the way salvation occurs. This, then, is an alternative subcultural discourse among some early followers of Jesus. This discourse does not give prominence to a 'thaumaturgic' response to the world but to a 'gnostic manipulationist' response where one seeks a full life by pondering and celebrating the mysterious ways God works in the world (Robbins 1994d: 74–81).

A third form of discourse appears in the large collection of sayings common to Matthew and Luke regularly referred to as 'Q'. Instead of being thaumaturgic or gnostic manipulationist, the discourse in these sayings was strongly conversionist in its earliest stages. The emphasis was on changing people's view of life in the world as a way of changing the world itself, and some of the final categories are 'being blessed', 'loving' and 'not judging' (Mack 1993: 73–80). This is a noticeably countercultural view of the world with decisive affinities with the alternative lifestyle Cynics in Antiquity commonly recommended to people. The view is not to follow the values and perspectives of either dominant cultures or their subcultures. Here is a wisdom that turns usual values upside down, like when Diogenes the Cynic said, 'Why should my body be buried so the birds can't eat it when I have eaten so many of them?' While this movement probably began as a contraculture in Galilee, within two decades it emerged as a counterculture with substantive rationales to support its ideology. One of the ways it began to support its ideology was with a revolutionist view of an abrupt change that would occur in the world. In the earlier stages of this discourse, wisdom traditions both from Jewish and Greco-Roman tradition nurtured its vision of the world. Within two decades, revolutionist presuppositions began to serve as rationales for the conversionist discourse. God will burn the chaff with a fire no one can put out; Sodom will have a lighter punishment than you; every one who admits in public that they know me, the Son of Man will acknowledge before the angels of God; whoever disowns me in public, the Son of Man will disown before the angels of God; I came to strike fire on the earth, and how I wish that it were already aflame; there will be wailing and clenching of teeth when you see Abraham, Isaac, Jacob, and all the prophets in the kingdom of God and you yourselves excluded (Mack 1993: 81–102). This revolutionist discourse fits naturally with the rising revolutionary discourse in Galilee during the 50s. The Q discourse is deeply grounded in conversionist presuppositions: God's powers can change the ways of people according to the discourse that lies at the base of the collection. But now the discourse exhibits an angry response to the world. It is so difficult to change the world that God, and his representative the Son of Man, will have to change it. Now what can mostly be done is to tell other people what the dire consequences will be if they do not respond. This discourse remains strongly countercultural. Representatives of this discourse have no choice but to be against the world, since the world does not share its point of view or heed its warnings. In the Q material, then, we see a countercultural movement in early Christianity that began with strong conversionist presuppositions and topics and gradually added revolutionist presuppositions to undergird its countercultural view of the world.

A fourth form of discourse appears in the pronouncement stories in Mark. This discourse is pitted not against 'the world' but against a particular group of people: leaders in charge of synagogues in Galilee. This discourse is not so countercultural as it is *contra*-cultural. This discourse selects a few matters of behavior and, by inverting them, argues that it stands for something entirely 'new' and 'different' from other people. Major final categories in the discourse are 'the lawful', 'forgiveness', 'the new' and 'the pure'. The discourse contains 'ethnic' strategies as described by Fredrik Barth (Barth 1969; Goudriaan 1992; Østergård 1992). It actually shares many values with the discourse it attacks. Rather than emphasizing any common ground, however, it concentrates on certain points of behavior that it 'turns on its head'. While this discourse is decisively contracultural in relation to the Jewish culture it holds before the hearer and reader, it is either subcultural or countercultural in relation to Greco-Roman culture (Mack 1988: 179–204).

A fifth form of discourse appears in the letters of Paul and in the passion predictions and passion narrative in the Gospel of Mark (Mack 1988: 249–312). This discourse focuses on the death and resurrection of Jesus as a means by which people have received salvation. The data in this discourse suggest that in its earliest stages it was significantly introversionist (cf. Esler 1994b), focusing on a particular thing that had been achieved for certain people. People gathered in small assemblies both to deepen their own experience of being in a secure position in relation to promises concerning death and to deepen their relationship with others who participated in the same 'victory' over the forces of death and suffering in the world. Some of the final categories in this discourse are 'the memorable', 'the worthy' and 'the perishable'. Paul reconfigured this introversionist response into a significantly utopian response with reformist tendencies. We will expand on this in our discussion of 1 Corinthians 9, to which we will turn after a brief summary.

SUMMARY

Analysis and interpretation of the social and cultural texture of New Testament discourse begin to give us a significantly new look at first-century Christianity. The discourse embedded in the earliest texts furnishes the resources to deconstruct and reconfigure the story of the 'victors' as they told it in the Acts of the Apostles. Many scholars have known that the standard story of the beginnings of Christianity in Acts is highly schematized and embedded in a distinctive ideology of its own. Its social response to the world is both conversionist and reformist. The goal is to change people and institutions significantly in ways that will change principles of distribution of food and honor among people. It presents a picture of Christianity as the extension of the history of Israel in a context where 'leaders of the Jews' continually attempt to subvert their activity and get them imprisoned, killed or at least run out of town. This 'contracultural' discourse in relation to leaders of Jewish synagogues is embedded in 'subcultural' discourse that presents Christians as people who espouse the highest values of the emperor, namely peace (*pax*) and salvation. In other words, Jewish contraculture discourse interweaves with Mediterranean subculture discourse in Acts to present a favorable view of Christians in the Mediterranean world.

Traditional historians of New Testament literature presuppose that the account of early Christianity promulgated by the Acts of the Apostles is accurate in its essential outline. The view is that even if the account smoothes over disagreements that existed among various factions, schematizes Paul's activity in terms of two or three missionary journeys, and shows no knowledge of things as substantial as Paul's letters to various communities with which he worked, any significant 'reworking' of the history of Christianity as Acts presents it exhibits a scepticism that is disrespectful of 'scripture'. The problem with this view is that Acts presents a particular configuration of 'voices' within early Christian literature in a very particular way. What about the 'voices' in the Gospels of Mark, Matthew and John? They are 'scripture' also. It is obvious that Acts presents a picture of early Christianity in terms of the 'great traditions' of Israel. Both Stephen and Peter rehearse the 'history of Israel' in terms of its 'great leaders' and only certain early Christians – namely Peter, Stephen and Paul – are the major 'leaders' and 'movers' of Christianity in the context of these 'great traditions'.

The New Testament literature itself asserts that there were at least twelve men who were close associates of Jesus during his lifetime, plus a group of women who followed Jesus during his time in Galilee and through the travel that led to Jerusalem and his death. What about the voices of these early followers of Jesus? Where are these voices in the New Testament? Where is the voice of James the son of Zebedee and John his brother, whom the accounts call the sons of thunder (Mark 3.17)? Where are the voices of Andrew, Philip and Bartholomew? Where are the voices of James the son of Alphaeus, Thaddaeus and Simon the Cananaean? We now have a Gospel of sayings attributed to Thomas, which Greek fragments and careful analysis of the text show was written as early as the other Gospels that currently exist in the New Testament. Should we give any attention to voices attributed to Thomas? Or should we just ignore this voice? Also, there is a Gospel that attributes the voices in it to Matthew. Should we pay careful attention to those voices, or should we ignore them also? And there is a Gospel that attributes voices to John. Should we ignore them? And what about the voices Paul refers to but overspeaks? Should we pay any attention to them? Many voices speak out in New Testament literature, but it is common practice in interpretation to drown most of them out in favour of a 'story' that recounts the 'significant' events in terms of the 'great traditions' of Israel. Few have attempted to write a story of Christianity that begins with a group of early followers whose belief system focused on parables of Jesus that contained the 'mysteries' of God's ways of working in the world. Few have taken seriously the large collection of sayings of Jesus that a group took seriously for its lifestyle in Galilee during the early decades of the movement. Few look seriously at those groups who emphasized the special powers of God to heal their diseases, remove the evil spirits that afflicted them, provide food for them in miraculous ways and indeed be able to calm the raging waters of the sea. Few include in this story a group of early followers who fought about issues of leadership in synagogues throughout Galilee. The implication seems to be that taking all these movements seriously would be disrespectful of scripture, since the Acts of the Apostles is the authorized 'scriptural' account of the history of early Christianity. But perhaps the time has come to undertake a complete rewriting of the history of first-century Christianity on the basis of the multiple kinds of discourse that exist in New Testament texts. A major question in the coming years, then, is not the relation of the Acts of the Apostles to the letters of Paul, but the relation of Acts to discourse throughout the New Testament.

SOCIAL AND CULTURAL TEXTURE IN 1 CORINTHIANS 9

Specific social topics in 1 Corinthians 9

Analysis of the social and cultural texture of 1 Corinthians 9 begins with Bryan Wilson's typology of sects. This Pauline discourse shows no signs of being *introversionist*. This discourse does not focus on retiring from the world to enjoy security granted by personal holiness. Nor is it indifferent to social change or individual conversion. As Meeks observed some time ago, Pauline discourse does not encourage people to 'go out of the world' (1979). The discourse in 1 Corinthians 9.19–22 evokes an image of moving out to Jews (those under the law), to those outside the law and to the weak. This chapter, then, does not show significant dimensions of introversionist discourse.

This discourse is also not significantly *thaumaturgic*. It does not encourage a focus on obtaining cures, receiving special, personal dispensations and performing miracles. In certain contexts Pauline discourse evokes the presence of thaumaturgic interests in early Christianity (e.g. 1 Cor. 12.9–10), but it does not feature healing and miracles as a major response to the world. To be specific concerning 1 Corinthians 9, the discourse does not say, 'To the weak I became a healer, that I might through God's power make them strong' (cf. 9.22). Responses other than thaumaturgic are central to Pauline discourse.

Nor is this discourse *reformist*. It does not encourage investigation of the world to encourage and inform people as they involve themselves in it by good deeds. 1 Corinthians 9.3–14 does not evoke an image of changing the way in which the institutions of apostle-ship, military life, vineyard keeping, shepherding sheep and goats, agricultural work or temple service operate. The discourse pre-supposes that these social structures are basic systems of life and does not imply that they could be changed.

There are four more kinds of social response – conversionist, revolutionist, utopian and gnostic manipulationist – and strains of all of these four kinds of response are present in this Pauline discourse. First, in the mode of *conversionist* response, Pauline dis-course considers the outside world to be corrupted. Jews consider Christ to be a 'stumbling block' and the nations consider him to be 'folly' (1 Cor. 1.23). This discourse seems to imply that if these views of people changed, the world would be changed. 1 Corinthians 9 evokes the image of proclaiming the gospel 'to win' people (9.14, 9.19). The goal is for people to change. The discourse in 1 Corinthians 9, then, does appear to contribute to a vision that the speaking and doing of the gospel create a context in which God's spirit changes people and this change is an important aspect of deal-ing with what is wrong with the world (cf. 1 Cor. 3.5–9).

This discourse is also significantly *revolutionist*. Pauline discourse maintains that God will change the present social order when the time is right (1 Cor. 7.31). In fact, 1 Corinthians 15.51–8 merges conversionist and revolutionist discourse: at a particular time in the future God will act decisively (revolutionism) and the result will be that all people will be changed (1 Cor. 15.51–2). There are definite limits concerning what can be achieved on earth. No matter how many people respond positively to this discourse, it will not be possible for people to change everything or for God's spirit to change everyone in it. This can only occur with a decisive moment in the future when God will change all things.

Pauline discourse also has *utopian* strains. It encourages the creation of a perfect society (1 Cor. 13), but this utopianism is modulated by conversionist and revolutionist presuppositions. Utopian discourse is more radical than reformist argumentation – more change is necessary than the world could ever tolerate – and Pauline discourse has a strain of this radicality. Pauline discourse is also less violent than single-minded revolutionary discourse: more can be done in the world than facilitating God's overturn of this world, even though God soon will overturn it. This *more* that can be done has utopian dimensions. Community is a very special thing, and if the world could become a community like the communities

Pauline discourse envisions, the world would be changed. This discourse is more constructive on a social level than conversionist argumentation often is. There are aspects of world construction that envision communitarian living. The dimensions of conversionism and revolutionism in the discourse mute the utopian impulses, yet utopian impulses hover in the background.

Pauline discourse in 1 Corinthians 9 also has *gnostic manipulationist* dimensions. Underlying the claims by Paul that he is able to be a slave to all – a Jew to Jews, like one under the law to those under the law; as one outside the law to those outside the law; weak to those who are weak – lie presuppositions concerning the possession of a divine gift that gives him strong cognitive abilities which include the ability to live according to the demands of virtuous life (cf. Malherbe 1995: 234). In other words, in the context of an emphasis in Pauline discourse on changing others (conversionism) so that all live in harmonious community with one another (utopianism) until God acts decisively to change all (revolutionism), Pauline discourse evokes a self-image of the narrator that is decisively gnostic manipulationist in social and cultural terms. The character of Paul is grounded in a deliberate 'adoption of Stoic categories' (Malherbe 1995: 232) that emphasize divinely given cognitive powers that hold the potential for winning the imperishable crown rather than being disqualified (1 Cor. 9.25–7). For the personage of Paul himself, the discourse does not so much evoke an image of change (conversionism) as it evokes the image of a person whom God has endowed with cognitive strengths (gnostic manipulationism). No 'external things' like living under the law, living outside the law or living in a mode of weakness distract him from living according to the self-controlled virtuous life. In other words, no aspects of social identity and no mental, sexual or physical 'needs' or temptations are able to make him veer off the track of the divine race he is running. In accord with the nature of gnostic manipulationist discourse, Pauline discourse articulates a significant number of the values and goals of moral philosophers in the world outside the Christian community (Malherbe 1995). The distinctiveness of Pauline discourse in this context is its particular configuration of conversionist, revolutionist, utopian and gnostic manipulationist discourse. The moral philosophers appear to be much less optimistic about the possibilities for people to change, primarily because they do not share the view of Pauline discourse about the workings of God's power and spirit in people's lives. Also, the moral philosophers do not share the view of God's imminent changing of all things into a new form, which includes the changing of people into an imperishable nature. This means that the major overlaps appear to lie in the arenas of utopianism and gnostic manipulationism. Pauline discourse evokes an image of harmonious relationships inside Christian communities that is similar to emphases among some philosophical groups. In addition, Pauline discourse emphasizes the virtue-oriented cognitive powers that reside as a divine gift in those whom God has called for a special task among humans.

Pauline discourse in 1 Corinthians, then, configures conversionist, revolutionist, utopian and gnostic manipulationist responses to the world into a distinctive pattern in the Hellenistic-Roman world of the first century. None of the four types of response appears to constitute the total focus of the discourse. Rather, a vision of being 'all things to all people' for the purpose of 'winning them' so they live together 'with one mind' until 'God changes all' weaves a particular tapestry of social responses together in a particular manner.

Common social and cultural topics in 1 Corinthians 9

A way to 'thicken' the analysis and interpretation of social and cultural texture in 1 Corinthians 9 is to explore the manner in which the discourse dialogues with common social and cultural systems and institutions in Mediterranean antiquity. From a social and cultural perspective, the emphasis on slavery is particularly interesting. This was a well-established institution during the first century which Pauline discourse addresses in 1 Corinthians 7.20–4 (Bartchy 1973) as well as in the letter to Philemon (Petersen 1985). Paul's assertion that he has made himself a slave to all people appears to be grounded in his preaching of Christ crucified (1 Cor. 1.21–5). He describes his work among the Corinthians as a manifestation of 'knowing nothing' among them but 'Christ crucified', which led him to be with them 'in weakness' (1 Cor. 2.2–3). It is noticeable that this is not the message that members of the Palestinian Jesus movement proclaimed. Their message concerned the kingdom of God or perhaps the day of the Son of Man without emphasis on the crucifixion of Jesus. Perhaps a key verse in Pauline discourse, finally, is Romans 1.16 where Paul asserts that he is not 'ashamed' of the gospel, by which he means the gospel of Jesus' death and resurrection (1 Cor. 15.3–5). As Jesus took the form of a slave (Phil. 2.7), so Paul takes the form of a slave. Evoking the well-known institution of slavery, the discourse locates the work of Paul in the domain of the steward (*oikonomos*). As a steward of God's mysteries (1 Cor. 4.1), Paul freely enslaves his life to the gospel of Christ. Pauline discourse, then, does not overturn the institution of slavery in the Hellenistic-Roman world. Rather, it locates itself in discourse about slavery in a manner that correlates Hellenistic-Jewish discourse (e.g. Philo) with Hellenistic-Roman discourse (e.g. Epictetus).

Pauline discourse 'thickens' the discourse about proclaiming Christ crucified by embedding language about athletes and athletic competition in the language about slavery. In 1 Corinthians 9, discourse about slavery emerges in the argument from example that stands at the end of the elaborate rhetorical argument that spans 1 Corinthians 9.5–23. Then the athletic imagery emerges in the conclusion, 9.24–7, at the very end of the chapter. Of special importance for socio-rhetorical analysis and interpretation is the observation that discourse about athletes and athletic competition (*athlētēs, agōn, agonizomai*) does not occur in Palestinian-based Q material that transmits discourse attributed to Jesus (Kloppenborg 1988: 213) – even though the potential would have been natural, as Luke 13.24 shows: 'strive (*agōnizesthe*) to enter the narrow door'. This discourse did, in contrast, employ discourse about slaves (Kloppenborg 1988: 217–18). Lukan discourse introduces language of stewardship in Luke 12.42: 'Who then is the faithful and wise steward, whom his master will put in charge of his household staff?' Q material, then, uses the image of the one who does the work of the kingdom as a slave (cf. Matt. 8.9/Luke 7.8; Matt. 24.46–51/Luke 12.43–6; Matt. 22.3–4, 10/Luke 14.17, 21–4; Matt. 25.14–29/Luke 19.12–23), but it does not use the imagery of the athlete and athletic competition. Also, the Q material does not associate the work of the kingdom with a slavery that is like Christ's becoming like a slave through his crucifixion and death. Pauline discourse, then, effects a substantive shift in the social and cultural image of one sent by God in relation to the speech and work of Christ. Discourse about 'the gospel of Christ crucified' is absent from Palestinian Q material. Paul's public emphasis on the crucifixion of Christ brought a new dimension to conversionist Christian discourse. 1 Corinthians 9 brings discourse about both slaves and athletes – representatives of two major social and cultural institutions in the Mediterranean world – into the service of Christian discourse. This discourse, which adds significant gnostic manipulationist dimensions to the image of the 'one sent by God', acquires 'persuasive power' through its skillful use of these two well-known institutions that other moral and religious philosophers use. As we have seen in the last chapter, the use of these 'common social topics' is part of the reconfiguration of the concept of the work of the gospel that exhibits itself in the attribution of new language to Jesus in 1 Corinthians 9.14: 'The Lord commanded that those who proclaim the gospel should get their living by the gospel'. This 'command of the Lord' creates a context in which Paul freely enslaves himself to the gospel, exercising self-control as the noblest of athletes to win the imperishable crown. Common social and cultural topics contribute to thickly configured discourse in first-century Christianity.

Analysis of the common social and cultural topics in 1 Corinthians 9 can be taken still further by following the lead of E. A. Judge, who called attention to three cultural systems that Pauline discourse was engaging: (a) the social patronage system; (b) the system of self-esteem or boasting; and (c) the culture of higher education (1983: 11–13).

Judge's conclusion is that Pauline discourse broke with the social patronage system when Paul refused to accept gifts and benefactions. Sisson entertains the possibility that Paul challenges the system from the premise of his function as a 'steward' of God's blessings, which in patronage terms is to function as a 'broker' between the members of the communities who are clients of the patrons God and Christ (1994: 119). Sisson uses Moxnes's analysis of apostle/brokers in Luke-Acts (Moxnes 1991a: 261–3) and suggests that Pauline discourse in 1 Corinthians 9 functions in a similar manner.

Judge's language is stronger concerning the system of self-esteem or boasting. Here he claims that Pauline discourse 'deliberately' tears down 'the structure of privilege with which his followers wished to surround him'. The reason, according to Judge, is that 'it [the structure of privilege] enshrined the beautiful and the strong in a position of social power' (Judge 1984: chap. 3).

When Judge discusses the relation of Pauline discourse to the culture of higher education, he uses the language of 'replacement' rather than 'breaking with' or 'tearing down'. Pauline discourse, he asserts, occupies 'the territory that belonged to higher education' by 'asserting a new source and method of knowing about the ultimate realities of the world, and about how one should live in it'

(1983: 12). This was a matter of promoting a new kind of community education for adults. Epictetus emphasizes that the major function of the Cynic is fulfilled among the people to whom he goes by his teaching about freedom from those things that enslave people to fears, desires and comforts. The openly argumentative nature of Pauline discourse in 1 Corinthians 9 gives it a strong didactic quality. The presupposition in the discourse that people in the community will communicate the content and urgency of its message can well be seen as a new kind of community education for adults in the context of Mediterranean society.

When Wuellner incorporates insights from Judge's analyses into his analysis of 1 Corinthians, he says that Paul 'broke with the social patronage system', 'broke with the system of self-esteem or "boasting"' and broke with 'the educational system' (Wuellner 1986: 76–7). In other words, Wuellner pits Paul decisively against major social systems in Hellenistic-Roman society. The counterpart of this is that Wuellner asserts that the new social order Paul works for is 'compatible with "the hope of Israel", the kingdom of God' (Wuellner 1986: 73). Judge's presentation of the relation of Pauline discourse has identified major 'common social and cultural topics' in Pauline discourse. To negotiate the issues raised by Judge, Wuellner and Sisson, it is necessary to move to the realm of 'final categories'. How does Paul relate himself to the social and cultural institutions of Judaism and Hellenistic-Roman society and culture? The answer lies in moving beyond the identification of the common social and cultural topics in the discourse to the final categories of Pauline argumentation. Let us move on to ask about the inner cultural nature of Pauline discourse in relation to both Jewish and Hellenistic-Roman culture.

Final cultural categories in 1 Corinthians 9

Analysis of final cultural categories in 1 Corinthians 9 takes us to the list of final categories in the *Rhetoric of Alexander*: right, lawful, expedient, honorable, pleasant, easy, feasible, necessary (Mack and Robbins 1989: 38). The issue is the relation of Paul's final categories to the final categories of discourse from other sectors of Mediterranean culture.

Pauline discourse in 1 Corinthians 9 suggests a fairly clear role for one sent by God within the Mediterranean patronage system. Dale Martin's analysis (1990) shows that Paul's use of language of stewardship and slavery in 1 Corinthians 9.17–23 evokes the image of middle-level 'managerial' slaves, and we have presented a passage from Philo that shows his understanding of the freedom such a person enjoys. The final category here would appear to be the 'necessary'. Epictetus presupposes something like the following: megaslavery is 'necessary' for one called by God; microslavery is 'shameful'. Paul appears to share the same final category in 1 Corinthians 9 as Epictetus concerning slavery. In addition, wandering Cynics in particular prided themselves on offering their teaching 'free of charge'. The final category here appears to be 'purity', the 'true' or the 'genuine'. A well-known charge against sophists was that their acceptance of money prevented their ability to teach virtue. In other words, accepting pay corrupted, made false or made inauthentic their teaching of virtue. A person would teach what was pleasant, expedient or feasible rather than what was genuine, true or uncorrupted. Paul's break with patronage, then, challenges 'other Christian apostles' on the basis of teaching the 'genuine gospel', rather than challenging the system of patronage itself. The relation of Pauline discourse to the conventional patronage system was 'subcultural'. Pauline discourse evokes an image compatible with wandering moral philosophers who accept severe hardships to bring the 'true' message to all people. Their break with conventional brokerage is a result of being sent by Zeus. Rather than live in abundance they live in 'freedom' from those things that enslave other people. The benefits are intrinsic to the mode of life itself. In other words, this mode spiritualizes the patronage system in Mediterranean society: the Cynic submits to the ultimate patron Zeus, and Zeus, in turn, provides the Cynic with all he needs. Pauline discourse is subcultural to this conceptual subculture in Mediterranean society, recontextualizing a final category in moral philosophers' discourse (cf. Malherbe 1995). To the extent that Pauline discourse is countercultural in Mediterranean society, then, it has allies within the realm of contemporary Greco-Roman moral philosophy. One must be very cautious about suggesting a 'break with' the patronage system in Pauline discourse. Rather, Pauline discourse appears to have a strong subcultural relation to Greco-Roman discourse in Mediterranean society that spiritualizes the patronage system in terms of Zeus as the father of all human beings. Paul's 'break', it would appear, is with 'final categories' in other spheres of early Christian culture.

Second, the relation of Pauline discourse to the system of self-esteem or 'boasting' in Greco-Roman culture must also be nuanced. Here the final category appears to be the 'honorable'. It is honorable to boast about oneself only in particular ways and circumstances (Betz 1978). Pauline discourse emphasizes that people who boast should put their boast in the Lord (1 Cor. 1.31). It also invests Paul with a boast that 'of his own free will' he offers the gospel free of charge. Paul emphasizes that he has enslaved himself to all people, and he indicates that, if he is able to hold fast, there may be an 'imperishable crown' at the end for him. This discourse does not immediately qualify as breaking with the system of self-esteem or boasting (Wuellner 1986: 77). Again, Judge's comments are much more nuanced than Wuellner's. Judge refers specifically to 'the coupling of physical bearing with quality of speech' (1983: 13), to a system that 'enshrined the beautiful and the strong in a position of social power', and to 'the structure of privilege with which his followers wished to surround him' (1984: chap. 3). With the first two, Judge is talking about something very specific in dominant Greco-Roman culture; and with the last one, Judge is talking about something specifically within the early Christian movement. Taking the last first, rejecting a system of privilege that is being pressed upon Paul by fellow Christian apostles is one thing; rejecting a system of self-esteem is another. We must not identify other Christian apostles with a Greco-Roman social and cultural system for the purpose of arguing that Paul rejected Greco-Roman society. Paul's rejection of other Christian apostles is a matter of rejecting another cultural sphere within the Christian movement. The means by which he rejects them is very important. If, in fact, a person reads carefully through Plutarch's discourse on self-praise, it appears that Paul follows most of the guidelines quite carefully. One of the strategies of persons of privilege should be to deflect praise from oneself. What Judge is pointing to is Paul's inversion of the system that puts those who are 'beautiful, strong, and eloquent' in privileged positions of social power. When we encounter an inversion of a system, we may be seeing a *contra*cultural phenomenon. A contracultural phenomenon is so deeply embedded in the alternative culture that the majority of its dimensions remain in place. Yet the contraculture will invert particular aspects of that cultural system, and it will not provide well-developed rationales for that inversion. The relation of Pauline discourse to the Greco-Roman system of self-esteem appears to be contracultural. It inverts the emphasis on the beautiful, strong and eloquent, but it does so in a cultural framework that does not disregard the honorable, beneficial and genuine. Paul has his boasts, as other people do, but he does not boast about the same things they do. Paul claims his position of privilege with the Corinthians: he is their father, the builder of the foundation and the planter of the field. But all of these claims are a matter of being 'a slave to all people for the sake of the gospel'. It is not clear that Pauline discourse tears down the cultural system itself; rather it inverts certain social behaviors within that system.

Third, Judge's assertion that Pauline discourse replaces the cultural system of adult education evokes an image of a 'counterculture'. He uses language of 'replacement' and refers to 'a new source and method of knowing about the ultimate realities of the world, and about how one should live in it'. A major issue is whether this 'counterculture' promotes or rejects explicit and central values of dominant Mediterranean culture. If there is a value conflict that is 'central, uncompromising, and wrenching to the fabric of the culture', then the alternative education system is countercultural. If, in contrast, the alternative system fulfills central values of the dominant culture better than the dominant system, then the alternative system is subcultural. Yet we also remember the contracultural option where an alternative culture is so deeply embedded in the dominant culture that a majority of its values are compatible with it, yet it inverts some of the behaviors or practices in the dominant culture without providing a well-developed system of theses and rationales in support of the alternative behavior.

Judge's choice of language would suggest that Pauline discourse is countercultural in the domain of adult education. If an alternative system has a 'new source and method of knowing' that 'replaces' the dominant system, that system would appear to have well-developed alternative theses and rationales. In this domain, then, Pauline discourse has a very different relation to Hellenistic-Roman culture from that which it has with patronage or the system of self-esteem. With patronage, it appears that Pauline discourse simply found a particular subcultural location in the system; with self-esteem it appears that Pauline discourse, like Cynic discourse, simply inverted some of the conventional behaviors in a contracultural mode; with education, it appears that Pauline discourse may have presented a significantly countercultural source and method of knowing the ultimate realities of the world and how to live in it. Still, we must be extremely careful here. The close relationship between some aspects of Pauline discourse and discourse attributed to Epictetus calls attention to another aspect of counterculture, namely that the term refers to 'intracultural phenomena': 'counter-culturalists are cultural *heretics* trying to forge a new future, not *aliens* trying to preserve their old culture (real or imagined)' (Roberts 1978: 121). On the other hand, Pauline discourse has an ethnic subcultural relation to the discourse of a moral philosopher like Epictetus. When Pauline discourse talks about Moses and the Lord Jesus, it is alien to Greco-Roman moral philosophy. When Pauline discourse talks about freedom, slavery, athletes and crowns, however, it is more of a 'cultural heresy trying to forge a new future' in Mediterranean society. Thus, Pauline discourse appears to be embedded in a countercultural relation to dominant Hellenistic-Roman culture. This countercultural discourse, how-ever, has some strong subcultural and contracultural features supporting it.

Another angle that can help to clarify the social and cultural nature of Pauline discourse is to describe its relation to Jewish culture. In the midst of describing Pauline discourse as compatible with 'the hope of Israel, the kingdom of God', Wuellner qualifies the assertion with a statement that Pauline discourse is not com-patible with 'zealotic Jewish nationalism' (Wuellner 1986: 73). This qualification sends a signal that we also must seek precision in our description of the relation between Pauline culture and Jewish culture, just as much as we must seek precision with its relation to Hellenistic-Roman culture. Pauline discourse is, without any ques-tion, deeply embedded in Jewish culture. Nevertheless, Pauline discourse takes issue with Jewish culture at very important points. One of these points is the Torah. Why is it that Paul thinks that Torah enslaves rather than frees? Does he articulate truly good reasons? I think the answer to this may be 'No'. Paul simply 'knows' that the Torah enslaves believers in Christ. The final category here may be that which is 'beneficial'. He can tell us that God gave it to Israel as a temporary benefit, and many other things about it. But he provides only a few rationales for how and why it enslaves rather than frees. For the most part, Pauline discourse simply inverts Jewish discourse when it speaks about believers in Christ: Jews see the Torah as beneficial; Paul asserts that the Torah is not beneficial to believers in Christ. Likewise with circumcision. Paul can explain that Abraham was saved by faith before being circumcised, but he presents few rationales for believing that circumcision is not a benefit for a male who was not circumcised as a child. Jews circumcise, arguing that it is 'necessary'. Pauline discourse 'inverts' the argument, saying it is not necessary because it is not a benefit to uncircumcised people. In relation to Jewish culture, then, Pauline culture is significantly *contra*cultural.

The result of our analysis of social and cultural texture, as brief as it is, suggests that Wuellner's assessment of Pauline discourse in 1 Corinthians is easily misleading. Pauline discourse is not simply deeply embedded in Jewish culture and countercultural to Greco-Roman culture. Pauline discourse is embedded both in Greco-Roman culture and in Jewish culture. It is deeply embedded in the Mediterranean system of social patronage and locates itself in that system in a particular subcultural way. In contrast, Pauline discourse appears to have a contracultural relationship with the Greco-Roman system of self-esteem – deeply embedded in it, but inverting some of its social aspects. With regard to the Mediterranean system of adult education, Pauline discourse may well be described as nurturing a significant countercultural system in Mediterranean society. Concerning Jewish culture, Pauline discourse appears to have a significant *contra*cultural relation with it – deeply embedded in it, but inverting key aspects of it. Thus, the relationship of Pauline discourse to Jewish and Greco-Roman culture begins to emerge as intricate and complex. To the extent that any cultural phenomenon has any real vibrancy, any 'thickness', we should not expect anything different. There are still many more cultural characteristics of Pauline discourse. We shall explore only one more before turning to ideological texture.

Our analysis needs to be refined with insights from Jeremy Boissevain's *Friends of Friends* (1974). Using Boissevain's typology, the discourse in 1 Corinthians is 'faction culture' discourse. What characterizes a faction is the relation of people to each other on the basis of their allegiance to a leader. In other words, the people in a faction have gathered together as the result of the attractiveness of a leader, not on the basis of a natural affinity to one another. What they share with each other is a willingness, for one reason or another, to listen to this leader.

1 Corinthians embodies its discourse personally in Paul, whom it calls an apostle. The judgment of scholarship is that the attribution of the discourse to the historical person Paul has integrity, even though portions of multiple letters may have been gathered together to make the particular form of the letter that exists in the New

Testament. In the discourse of the letter, there are references to people who are interacting with one another on the basis of a relation to different leaders associated with the Christian movement (Paul, Cephas, Apollos, Christ: 1 Cor. 1.12), and there is an assertion that they gather together at certain times as an 'ecclesia', an assembly or congregation (1 Cor. 11.18). There appears, then, to be some kind of 'community' structure. But the discourse also claims there are 'divisions' (1 Cor. 1.10–13; 11.18), and these divisions are the result of loyalty to these different people (1 Cor. 1.12).

The guidelines of socio-rhetorical analysis call for an interpreter to distinguish between the assertions in discourse addressed to a situation and the social situation that may actually have existed there. In other words, one of the purposes of argumentative discourse is to 'create a particular kind of culture', and defining a situation in a particular way is an important technique in moving the discursive practices in a situation toward one's own goals. We should entertain the possibility, for example, that the Corinthian community actually was an 'action-set culture' (Boissevain 1974: 186) rather than a factionalized culture at the time this letter was written. In this case, the people themselves were functioning together over a common cause, and most of them did not consider their differences to be a problem. This common cause could be a basic identity as 'Christian'. As a result of the activity of various people, various households of 'Christians' had formed, and these households were gathering together on certain occasions as an 'assembly' because of this common identity. Such a situation would have certain analogies with the function of a synagogue, although the place of meeting would be in someone's house rather than in a separate building that functioned entirely for the purposes of the group. If this was the situation, the Pauline letter was introducing 'faction culture' discourse into an 'action-set culture'. The discourse uses a report by 'Chloe's people' (1 Cor. 1.11) to open the discussion. Either a 'clique' (Boissevain 1974: 174, 179) or a number of 'sub action-sets', or both interacting with each other, began for some reason to function in a manner that was problematic for some of the people in the coalition (Boissevain 1974: 171). Perhaps the difficulties in the group arose primarily from its success – it had attracted too many people to continue to function smoothly as an action-set. Perhaps a Pauline 'clique' had successfully formed in the Corinthian community and it seemed possible now to 'pull things together' in a manner that had not been possible previously. In other words, perhaps the time was now right to 'bring things around', that is, to 'unify the community' around Pauline ideology. One of the techniques to move toward this 'unity' was to describe the coalition as 'factionalized', to evaluate that factionalization as unacceptable, and to introduce a solution with Paul at the center – namely, one single faction. In order to analyse this further, we must move to ideological texture.

CONCLUSION

Analysis of specific social topics, common social and cultural topics and final cultural categories in New Testament texts takes us into analysis and interpretation of the social and cultural texture of texts. The most productive tool at present for sociological analysis of specific, material topics in the discourse is Bryan Wilson's typology of social responses to the world by religious sects. In contrast, as a result of the energetic efforts of social-scientific critics for two decades there are myriads of strategies available for analysis and interpretation of common social and cultural topics in New Testament discourse. To analyze final social and cultural categories, the strategies are just beginning to appear. The discussion in this chapter has combined the list of final categories in the *Rhetoric of Alexander* with a typology of cultures that various social scientists have been producing during the last two decades.

Rhetorical analysis of social and cultural topics and categories in New Testament literature can provide data to write a new account of first-century Christianity. This story will tell about early followers of Jesus who attended Jewish synagogues during the first decades after the death of Jesus. It will explore how these people argued about daily practices including the sabbath, food laws and ritual purity but continued to be active in those synagogues. It will explore followers who did not experience the resistance of other Jews during a period of about forty years after the death of Jesus, but lived in a world informed by colorful stories about the mighty deeds of God that occur through the leadership of the mighty men whom God appoints to carry out his tasks. This story will tell about people who lost out in addition to those who won out. This story will include feelings and experiences as well as thoughts and actions. This story will include bodies as well as minds, messy versions of the story as well as cleaned-up versions.

189

Paul's public emphasis on the crucifixion of Christ appears to have brought a new dimension to 'missionary' discourse toward the end of the second decade after the death of Jesus. Those who had developed the creed of Christ's death and resurrection in the context of scriptural interpretation (1 Cor. 15.3–5) seem not to have made a practice of proclaiming this in public. The evidence comes from Pauline discourse itself and Christian discourse after Paul. Those Christians who focused on Christ crucified during the first decade appear to have been strongly 'introversionist'. This may, in turn, have encouraged a 'gnostic manipulationist' environment in the Jesus movement. In other words, those Christians who pored over the scriptures to work out the meaning of Christ's death and resurrection may have formed communities that were significantly 'inner' directed. Unfortunately, we do not know how Saul conceptualized Christian beliefs and practices when he began to persecute members of the movement. After Paul became a member of this movement, he became an advocate of a conversionist 'Christian' culture that was an alternative to the Q conversionist version. By the middle 50s, Paul was supporting his conversionist presuppositions with assertions of 'not being publicly ashamed' of the crucified Christ. Other apostles may have seen Paul's 'public' flaunting of Christ's crucifixion to be quite objectionable. The Q material certainly does not contain this emphasis. Paul's emphasis probably created a distinctive place for him within the early Christian movement. According to other apostles, it was appropriate to announce the coming of the kingdom and the day of the Son of Man and to emphasize signs, miracles and wonders. Public proclamation of Christ's crucifixion, on the other hand, could only bring trouble – public dishonor – to the movement. This was a message for cultic assembly, not for public proclamation. In other words, where those who focused on the crucified Christ used discourse that intermingled introversionist and gnostic manipulationist responses to the world, Paul transformed the introversionist dimension into public conversionist discourse. Within time, Paul's merger of utopian, gnostic manipulationist and revolutionist discourse with conversionist discourse that focused on the crucifixion and resurrection of Jesus played a central, formative role in Christian belief and practice during the last three decades of the first century.

The story as it is told in the Acts of the Apostles is an alternative version to the one we see in New Testament discourse itself. Acts is an ideologically driven account that appeared near the end of the first century and that now stands alongside the account that emerges from all the voices available to us in the discourse of New Testament literature. Putting the material in the rest of the New Testament on an equal playing field with Acts can give us a fascinating and fuller understanding of the multiform face of Christianity during the first century.

This takes us to the issue of ideology. Would there be any good reasons to work carefully through each New Testament text available to us, plus other texts available to us, to try to ascertain the cultural relation of the multiple voices both to one another and to Jewish and Greco-Roman culture? The answer for me is a resounding yes. I would like to see an account of the first century that interrelates the people 'of importance', like Paul, with people 'on the fringes', like those who perpetuated Q discourse. This could present 'voices' of early followers of Jesus to the reading public that people have never listened to seriously in the story of first-century Christianity. This would present an important alternative to the 'great story' – the story of the victory of Christianity over both 'misguided Jews' (from the perspective of Acts) and followers of Jesus who did not yet have the 'full picture of Christian belief'. The story would intermingle 'great traditions' with 'little traditions' in a new account of the history of first-century Christianity. Let us move on to one more arena of issues in the analysis and interpretation of New Testament literature – ideological texture – before we attempt a fuller statement about this alternative version of the history of first-century Christianity.

6

IDEOLOGICAL TEXTURE
Every theology has a politics

In 1975, John Gager raised the issue of ideology in the interpretation of early Christian texts. Asserting that conflict reaches its most intense level when it involves competing ideologies or competing views of the same ideology, he presented three critical moments in the history of early Christianity:

(a) conflict with Judaism over the claim to represent the true Israel;
(b) conflict with paganism over the claim to possess true wisdom;
(c) conflict among Christian groups over the claim to embody the authentic faith of Jesus and the apostles.

(1975: 82)

In addition, he proposed that the intensity of the struggles was a function of two separate factors:

(a) the degree to which individuals considered themselves to be members of a group, so that any threat to the group became a threat to every individual;
(b) the role of intellectuals who transform personal motivations into eternal truths.

(1975: 82)

Gager uses the term 'ideology' alternatively with the phrase 'symbolic universe' (1975: 83). For an institution, an ideology integrates 'different provinces of meaning' and encompasses 'the institutional order in a symbolic totality'; for an individual, it 'puts everything in its right place' (1975: 82–3; using Berger and Luckmann 1966: 95, 98).

At present, the spectrum of ideology for socio-rhetorical criticism occurs in four special locations: (a) in texts; (b) in authoritative traditions of interpretation; (c) in intellectual discourse; and (d) in individuals and groups. We will discuss ideology in sections under these headings.

IDEOLOGY IN TEXTS

As mentioned in the previous chapter, John H. Elliott raised the issue of ideological analysis of New Testament texts with special force in his study of 1 Peter (1990a). Setting aside more specialized Marxian and Mannheimian concepts, he adopted a definition of ideology as 'an integrated system of beliefs, assumptions and values, not necessarily true or false, which reflects the needs and interests of a group or class at a particular time in history' (p. 268, quoting Davis 1975: 14). The ideological implications of a text, then, are more than its ideational or theological content or the constellation of its religious ideas. Rather, the task is to explore the manner in which the discourse of a text presents comprehensive patterns of cognitive and moral beliefs about humans, society and the universe that are intended to function in the social order. The investigation especially seeks to identify the intersection of ideas, ideals and social action and to detect the collective needs and interests the patterns represent (Elliott 1990a: 267).

For Elliott, the ideology of 1 Peter is manifested especially in its promotion of a view of Christianity as a Christian household throughout the world in which 'the stranger is no longer an isolated alien but a brother or sister' (p. 288). The ideological implications of this view, he suggests, are embedded in the special interests of a Petrine group that desired 'to stabilize and enhance its position in Rome as well as its influence and authority within the Christian movement abroad' (p. 280). The household ideology linked 'the symbols of the communal dimension of faith (brotherhood, family of God) with the experience of alienated (*paroikoi, paroikia* in society) and collective (household communities) social existence' (p. 283). This ideology provided the resources for distinctiveness, explaining the readiness of Christians to suffer, a radical sense of Christian community open to all and an emphasis on a community of care (pp. 284–5).

One of the central components of ideology is social location, since 'one's social location or rhetorical context is decisive of how one sees the world, constructs reality or interprets biblical texts' (Schüssler Fiorenza 1988: 5). Subsequent to Elliott's analysis, I developed a model for investigating the social location of the discourse in a text (Robbins 1991a), and Jerome Neyrey has applied this model to Jude and 2 Peter with excellent results (1993: 32–41, 128–41). The model correlates the rhetorical strategies of the implied author/reader, narrator/narratee and character/audiences (Chatman 1978) with the social arenas of previous events, natural environment and resources, population structure, technology, socialization and personality, culture, foreign affairs, belief systems and ideologies and political-military-legal system (Carney 1975). Since an implied reader personifies the discourse of a text in terms of its 'implied author', the essay explores the social location of the discourse in the mode of the implied author in the text. The exploration reveals a location of the thought of Luke-Acts among adult Jews and Romans who have power in cities and villages. The discourse speaks upwards toward Roman officials with political power but considers Jewish officials to be equal in social status and rank. The rhetoric of the discourse calls for distribution of wealth among the poor, but it does not argue for permitting the poor to become landowners or householders. The discourse claims that Christians are an authentic part of the heterogeneous population of the Roman empire and identifies some political-military-legal personnel as members of the Christian movement. Vigorous confrontation with Jewish people from whom it claims its heritage interweaves with direct but polite communication with Roman officials. Overall the discourse exhibits boldness of speech and action throughout the Mediterranean world, yet there is an ambivalence born of subordination: political-military-legal people both protect Christians and imprison them in an environment where conflict continually develops between Christians and Jews (Robbins 1991a: 331–2).

Elisabeth Schüssler Fiorenza has emphasized for some years that interpreters should investigate the 'ideological script' of a text (e.g. 1988: 15; 1989: 12). In 1991, Elisabeth A. Castelli's analysis of the discourse of power in Paul's statements concerning imitation of him appeared in print, and she exhibits how an interpreter may launch a programmatic analysis of ideology in a text. To establish a context for her analysis, she discusses traditional interpretation and briefly shows how most interpreters do not analyze the ideological aspect of Paul's discourse. Instead of investigating how a text has set up issues as a way of getting to certain kinds of 'answers' or goals, interpreters either spiritualize the text – removing it from any historical or social context that implies complex dynamics of conflict and competition – or they presuppose or assert continuity, authority and unity in tradition (Castelli 1991: 24–32). Castelli cites John Howard Schütz's investigation of the anatomy of apostolic authority in Paul (1975) and Benjamin Fiore's study of personal example in Socratic and Pastoral Epistles (1982) as two important exceptions to traditional approaches. Also, she once cites Graham Shaw's investigation of letters of Paul and the Gospel of Mark from the perspective of 'manipulation and freedom' (Castelli 1991: 114; Shaw 1983), but she might have used this study with greater benefit in her own investigation.

After establishing a context by exhibiting this absence in traditional interpretation, Castelli introduces Michel Foucault's 'analytic of power' (pp. 35–58) to position her own study. She describes her goal as describing 'how the text operates rather than what it means' (p. 18) and locates her interests between literary and sociological investigations (p. 38). Especially helpful for socio-rhetorical analysis of ideological texture, she presents a summary of Foucault's guidelines for analyzing power relations in a text (Castelli 1991: 50, 122), which appeared as an afterword in a major study of Foucault's work (Dreyfus and Rabinow 1983: 208–26). Her summary yields the following principles:

1 Define the *system of differentiations* that allows dominant people to act upon the actions of people in a subordinate position.
2 Articulate the *types of objectives* held by those who act upon the actions of others.
3 Identify the *means* for bringing these relationships into being.
4 Identify the *forms of institutionalization of power*.
5 Analyze the *degree of rationalization* of power relations.

Castelli does not attempt to follow these guidelines as actual steps in her investigation of texts (pp. 89–117), but after her analysis and interpretation she presents a paragraph for each principle, explaining what her investigation has revealed (pp. 122–4).

The centerpiece of Castelli's analysis is 1 Corinthians 1.10–4.21, and she personifies the discourse as 'Paul' in her interpretation. She observes repetition in the opening and closing of the unit, where Paul tells his readers 'I urge you' or 'I appeal to you' (*parakalo hymas*: 1 Cor. 1.10; 4.16; p. 102). The repetition of this appeal leads to analysis of 1.10–17 as the beginning and 4.14–21 as the ending of the unit. In the beginning unit, Paul fills the concept of 'difference' with negative meanings – difference 'must be erased in order to reestablish order' (p. 98). The discourse describes 'unity of mind' as the priority and unity within the community as the goal (1 Cor. 1.10–11). In this context, Paul describes his role simply as 'mediation' of the gospel: his own nature is 'contentless'; 'he is simply the conduit through which the gospel passes' (1 Cor. 1.17; p. 99). In this way Paul bestows on himself a privileged status in relation to the gospel. Paul has special authority to speak and also he has 'an emptiness which removes him from the fray' (p. 99).

In the ending, 1 Corinthians 4.14–21, Paul urges the Corinthians, 'Be imitators of me', calling himself their 'father in Christ Jesus through the Gospel' and indicating that he is sending Timothy to remind them of 'my ways in Christ, as I teach them everywhere in every church' (1 Cor. 4.17). The patriarchal image of Paul as father is, of course, striking. At this point she explores the 'cultural intertexture' of Paul's image of father by investigating the broader context of a passage about fatherhood in Epictetus' *Discourses* that Fiore cites. As the passage continues it sets the role of the father alongside the role of a military general who 'oversees and reviews and watches over his troops, and punishes those who are guilty of a breach of discipline' (Epict., *Discourses* 3.22.95–6; p. 100). Her point is that 'the image of the father must be read in cultural context' and that Paul has evoked 'a role of possessing total authority over children (p. 101). With this beginning and ending, '[s]ameness, unity, and harmony are to be achieved through imitation' of Paul, and 'difference is equated with diffusion, disorder, and discord' and 'placed outside the community'. To oppose Paul in any way, then, is not simply to express a different opinion. Rather, 'it sets one in opposition to the community, its gospel, and its savior' (p. 103). The beginning and the ending of the unit evoke a frame of understanding that Paul is simply a medium for a gospel of unity versus discord. The discourse implies that Paul is not imposing himself in any way; rather at the center of the gospel is an 'ideology of sameness, identity', and anyone who is somehow different is automatically against the gospel itself, against the community, against Christ and there-fore, of course, against Paul.

In the beginning and ending of the unit, then, the discourse 'articulates the types of objectives held by those who act upon the actions of others' and 'identifies the means for bringing these relations into being' (principles 2 and 3 above). The discourse describes the stated 'objective' as a 'removal of dissension, quarrel-ling, and discord' and the 'means' as argument for unity of mind and judgment aided by Timothy's 'reminding' them of Paul's ways. When an interpreter looks at this from the perspective of the 'con-struction of power', according to Castelli, this approach enacts an 'ideology of sameness' that invests total power in Paul's speech and action. The discourse removes any implication that Paul has motives for himself in the exchange. He is doing this simply because he was sent by Christ to perform this task, and it is natural – simply built into Christ's bringing of salvation – that anyone who differs in any way from what Paul says is against Christ, against Christ's gospel and against the community.

The middle of the unit contains three parts. The first two parts contain a series of oppositions that establish the framework for defining those who are 'inside' versus those who are 'outside' the benefits of Christ. In Foucault's terms, these oppositions are 'the system of differentiations that allows dominant people to act upon the actions of the subordinate people' (principle 1 above). The oppo-sitions are as follows:

(a) 1 Cor. 1.18–2.5
those who are perishing/those who are saved
word of the cross as folly/word of the cross as power of God
wisdom of the world/power of God
foolishness/wisdom
weakness/strength
(b) 1 Cor. 2.6–3.5
wisdom of this age/wisdom of God
spirit of the world/spirit which is from God
unspiritual person/spiritual person

This system of oppositions exhibits the matrix of a very high level of 'rationalization of power relations' (principle 5 above) in Paul's discourse. The mode of argumentation becomes progressively more ironic as it proceeds. The discourse introduces irony especially in the juxtaposition of strength and weakness in the first part, since 'Paul's self-ascribed weakness is itself a form of power (Castelli 1991: 104; Schütz 1975: 229). The second part builds on this irony as it makes clear that there is no 'reciprocal' relation – no give-and-take – between Paul and the community. Paul simply gives to the community what they need. They are 'babes in Christ' (3.1), 'not ready for solid food' (3.2). Therefore they, like Paul, are empty of content until they are filled. Paul presents them with 'the power of God' just as it came to him. In this he does not try to compete with 'the wisdom of men'. God's power itself is sufficient to deal with 'their wisdom'. The third part intensifies a 'hierarchical separation' between Paul and community by bringing another apostle, Apollos, into the discourse. This part of the argumentation asserts that Paul and Apollos are equal, since 'he who plants and he who waters are equal' (1 Cor. 3.8). This is simply a setup, however, since Paul supplants Apollos in the concluding section, becoming the singular model for imitation.

The beginning (1.10–17) and the middle (1.18–4.5) establish the context for the conclusion (4.16–21), which presents the final series of oppositions:

> we are fools for Christ's sake/you are wise in Christ
> we are weak/you are strong
> we are held in disrepute/you are held in honor.

In this set of oppositions, Paul's ironic discourse employs sarcasm. As the discourse sets 'our' sufferings against 'your' wisdom, strength and honor, it reaches a 'rhetorical crescendo' that prepares for an abrupt shift to first-person singular:

> *I* became your father in Christ through the gospel;
> *I* urge you, then, be imitators of *me*;
> *I* sent to you Timothy, *my* beloved and faithful child in the Lord, to remind you of *my* ways; as *I* teach them everywhere in every church;
> *I* will come to you soon;
> *I* will find out not the talk of these arrogant people but their power;
> Shall *I* come to you with a rod, or with love in a spirit of gentleness?

The conclusion invests Paul with total authority over the community. He is their father 'in Christ through the gospel', their 'model'. He is the example, the superior, filled person; they must lose their 'difference' from him in every way, becoming 'like' him as much as they can. Any way in which they are 'unlike' Paul is evil – against Christ, against the community and against God's ways of salvation.

Castelli's analysis of the manner in which Pauline discourse constructs power is a significant enactment of socio-rhetorical analysis and interpretation. She analyzes major rhetorical aspects of the inner texture of 1 Corinthians 1.10–4.21, though a more complete analysis would be possible to show the intricate manner in which the unit proceeds. She exhibits 'cultural intertexture' of the discourse, as mentioned above concerning the image of the father. In addition, she refers to the 'oral–scribal intertexture' of Paul's reference to 'my ways in Christ', by comparing this expression with expressions about 'God's ways' in the Hebrew Bible (p. 110). In her brief discussion of 1 Thessalonians 1.6, she observes 'historical intertexture': the discourse builds on the Thessalonians' imitation of Paul as a historical 'fact', through which they have become a model to others (p. 92). A person could perform a fuller socio-rhetorical analysis of these passages by exploring the nature of the social response to the world in them, which is strongly conversionist, with significant utopian and gnostic manipulationist aspects. Also, an interpreter could explore the cultural nature of the rhetoric. In these passages, the rhetoric is significantly countercultural in relation to other Christians. It would also be informative to explore the cultural nature of the rhetoric in relation to Jewish and Greco-Roman tradition (see Robbins 1993c). Castelli observes that 'the institutional location of Paul's pastoral power' is the 'weakest link in the use of Foucault's model' (p. 123). She could have used with great benefit, however, the social systems of honor and shame, kinship, purity and limited good (especially spiritual good) in her analysis. Castelli explores the ideological texture of the discourse in an exceptionally powerful manner, raising significant issues for further discussion. In her view, Paul's discourse in 1 Corinthians 1–4 constructs a 'special position', 'a privileged position from which to speak' (p. 108) which interpreters need to assess carefully in relation to other voices in New Testament literature.

IDEOLOGY IN AUTHORITATIVE TRADITIONS OF INTERPRETATION

Ideology resides not only in biblical texts; it also resides in interpretive traditions that have been granted positions of authority. One form of ideological challenge has come from Elisabeth Schüssler Fiorenza, the first woman president of the Society of Biblical Literature, who has called on the guild of American biblical scholars to identify and evaluate the political ideology that guides the interpretations it sanctions and the series of publications it nurtures (1988). Her call was based on a critical theory of rhetoric that considers discourse to generate reality, not merely be a reflection of it (1987: 387). In other words, discourse creates a world of pluriform meanings and a pluralism of symbolic universes, and this means that discourse is always implicated in power (1988: 14). The discourse of historical interpretation, therefore, has ideological texture:

> In the very language historians use to describe their projects they not only provide a certain amount of explanation or interpretation of what this information *means* but also give a more or less overt message about the attitude that the reader should take with respect to the historical 'data' and their interpretation.
>
> (Schüssler Fiorenza 1985b: 50)

The emphasis here lies on the ideology of a dominant tradition of interpretation, and her essay on 1 Corinthians will be used here to exhibit the manner in which a rhetorical interpretation can challenge the dominant ideology (Schüssler Fiorenza 1987). Working carefully in a mode of critical rhetorical analysis, Schüssler Fiorenza identifies an ideological feature in contemporary investigations where all interpreters 'follow Paul's dualistic rhetorical strategy without questioning or evaluating it'; namely, they presuppose that 'he is right and the "others" are wrong' (p. 390). Careful analysis of rhetorical arrangement and the rhetorical situation evoked by the discourse suggests that Paul countered the baptismal self-understanding of the Corinthians – whereby their community relationships overcame patriarchal divisions between Greeks and Jews, slave and free, men and women, rich and poor, wise and uneducated – with a patriarchal line of authority through himself (God, Christ, Paul, Apollos, Timothy, Stephanas and other local co-workers) which introduces patriarchal subordination of women to men (God–Christ–man–woman: 1 Cor. 11.2) (p. 397). I will build on these excellent analyses of 1 Corinthians by both Castelli and Schüssler Fiorenza in my analysis of ideological texture in 1 Corinthians 9 at the end of this chapter.

Another set of ideological challenges has come from Jonathan Z. Smith. His works, using 'critical anthropology', challenge New Testament interpreters to examine the innermost nature of the discipline itself, including the 'myth of origins' in which biblical interpreters embed their interpretive practices. For many interpreters this is embedded in a Protestant ideology, now even promulgated by some Roman Catholic scholars, in which earliest Christianity is a unique phenomenon – a phenomenon without analogy in the history of religions – which, of course, deteriorates rapidly into early Catholicism (J. Z. Smith 1990). Since one of the characteristics of scientific (*wissenschaftliche*) anlaysis is to hide its ideological foundations, it is natural that New Testament interpreters have been reluctant to evaluate their deepest commitments programmatically and to submit them to public scrutiny. Socio-rhetorical criticism calls for interpretive practices that include minute attention to the ideologies that guide interpreters' selection, analysis and interpretation of data.

Another challenge has recently been formulated by Amy L. Wordelman as she has identified 'orientalizing' in traditional interpretation. Her study focuses on Acts 14, which narrates a visit of Paul and Barnabas to Lystra in Lycaonia, where the people think Paul and Barnabas are Hermes and Zeus (1994). As she worked with traditional interpretations of the passage, she became conscious of an 'ideology of difference' that regarded the Lycaonians as backward, rustic, superstitious, barbarian people. Through a survey of literature on stereotyping, she concludes that the particular kind involved here was described well in Edward Said's well-known study entitled *Orientalism* (1979). Much of Western literature, Said reveals, contains an orientalizing ideology that caricatures people of the East as unintelligent, unrefined people, in contrast to people in the West, who are intellectually astute, democratically civilized and theologically sophisticated. The rhetoric of orientalism, Said proposes, communicates 'gross generalizations about "the Orient" as some kind of organic whole, completely opposite of and essentially inferior to "the Occident"' (Wordelman 1994: 17). The particular figures of speech vary within different authors, exhibiting a variety of stereotyping genres: 'a linguistic Orient, a Freudian Orient, a

Spenglerian Orient, a Darwinian Orient, a racist Orient – and so on' (Said 1979: 22). In each instance, the people of the Middle East and Asia are characterized as socially, culturally, morally and mentally inferior – sub-human, alien 'others' – to European people.

Equipped with a basic description and typology of orientalizing ideology, Wordelman analyzes traditional interpretations of Acts 14. Calvin, writing during the sixteenth century, stereotypes the Lycaonians as 'barbarous men', 'superstitious', 'infidels', 'unbelievers' and an 'unlearned multitude'. He uses this language especially for the priest of Zeus who prepares to make sacrifices in honor of the arrival of the gods in their midst, and he directs this language toward the Roman Catholicism of his day (Wordelman 1994: 31–2; Calvin 1844, II: 1–31). His virulent description is a launching pad for a wholesale attack on Catholicism in France, with an assertion that the superstition of the Greco-Roman world had lived on in the institutions of his day: 'the priests of France begat the single life of the great Cybele. Nuns came in place of the vestal virgins. The church of All Saints succeeded Pantheon' (Calvin 1844, II: 15, quoted by Wordelman 1994: 31–2). Thus, the stereotyping of the Lycaonians does not keep its focus on the people of Lystra; rather, this language is a medium for Calvin to describe the religious opponents against whom he sets himself as a reformer.

Sir William Mitchell Ramsay's use of terminology during the nineteenth century is not far behind. He characterized the Anatolian plateau in which Lycaonia is located as 'vast, immobile, monotonous, subdued, melancholy, and lending itself to tales of death' (Wordelman 1994: 73–4). The people who live in it in modern times (Turkey), he claimed, are '[s]impleminded, childish, monotonous, fickle, changeable, sluggish, obedient, peaceable, submissive' (p. 77). General Anatolian religion, in his view, was constituted by elaborate and minute ritual which was 'a highly artificial system of life' that perpetuated a 'primitive social condition' on a 'lower moral standard'. It glorified the 'female element in human life', which reflected its national character as 'receptive and passive, not self-assertive and active, and it emphasized rituals connected with graves (p. 87). For Ramsay, the goal was to authorize the Christian apostles as 'Hellenistic' in contrast to the Oriental spirit of the people whom they converted. Asia Minor, he proposed, was 'Greco-Asiatic', containing people with an oriental spirit and piety in a context of some Greek forms of culture and organization. Ramsay considers Paul's letter to the Galatians to exhibit the challenge for the apostles in an exemplary manner: formerly the people were enslaved to elemental spirits who were not God but cycles of nature; the apostles converted them to the true God and 'belief' rather than superstition (pp. 83–6). Ramsay does not use this analysis to attack Catholicism, as Calvin did, but to equate his form of European Protestant Christianity with enlightened Hellenistic belief and worship in contrast to the 'general Anatolian type', which was morally, spiritually and intellectually inferior.

After an extensive analysis of other commentators in addition, to exhibit the presence of an orientalizing ideology in traditional interpretation, Wordelman turns to ideology in the text of Acts. To what extent does the text itself exhibit an orientalizing ideology? To draw a conclusion about this, Wordelman investigates the 'geo-cultural map' manifest in the text, which extends from Jerusalem in the East to Rome in the West. Her conclusion is that Luke operates with a geo-cultural map in which the island of Malta is clearly a 'barbarian' culture but Lystra is not (p. 147). Lukan discourse refers to the people of Malta as barbarians (Acts 28.2, 28.4), and in this setting Paul heals but does not preach the gospel. This evokes a perception that the people are able to respond to religious belief on the level of miraculous cure but not on the level of understanding a system of belief. In turn, these friendly barbarians offer hospitality and bestow honor (pp. 144–5). The account at Lystra, on the other hand, has many parallels with the account of preaching and healing in Jerusalem (pp. 149–55). This suggests that Luke's geo-cultural map includes Lystra in the 'East' along with Jerusalem, and in the East, from the perspective of Lukan discourse, both wonderworking and preaching occur (pp. 150–61).

In contrast to both Malta and the East, however, in both Athens and Rome Paul speaks and argues with the people, but he does not heal anyone. This suggests to Wordelman that Luke imagines a religious and cultural ethos in Athens and Rome in which supernatural or wondrous deeds are problematic. For Athens, the challenge is philosophical, and for Rome the challenge is to convince Jewish leaders through explanation, argument and testimony. Paul's approach is somewhat different, but in neither locale does he attempt to convince the people through miraculous deed. In Wordelman's view, then, Lukan discourse presents a form of 'proto-orientalism': the West is 'the realm of rational thought', and the East is 'the realm of irrationality where exotic, wondrous, and supernatural things can happen' (pp. 172–3). Cultural-geographic location plays a greater role than religious location or identity. If Jews or Gentiles are in the East, miracles occur in their midst and early Christian leaders preach in the context of these exhibitions of God's power. If Jews or Gentiles are in Athens or Rome, Paul argues with them or teaches them, but no wonders occur in their midst. The only location for 'barbarians' on this geo-cultural map is the island of Malta. Here there is no attempt to preach, argue or give verbal testimony. Rather, communication between God and these generously hospitable people occurs only through miraculous escapes from danger and death and benevolent healings through the prayers and hands of people endowed with divine powers.

After this investigation of ideology in traditional interpretation and ideology in the text, Wordelman extends her analysis and interpretation toward a full socio-rhetorical project. This means that she does not limit her study to ideological texture but moves on to major aspects of the inner texture, intertexture and social and cultural texture of the text. She begins with 'historical' intertexture in the account. Observing a series of assertions that imply the presence of certain historical phenomena at Lystra, Wordelman makes an extensive exploration of archeological, inscriptional and literary data to ascertain the relation between assertions in the text and outside historical evidence about Lystra, both material and textual. The major questions are as follows. Is there any material or literary evidence that:

(a) people in Lystra spoke Lycaonian during the first century CE (Acts 14.11);

(b) a priest was appointed to Lystra to oversee a cult to Zeus (Acts 14.13);

(c) a temple dedicated to Zeus existed 'in front of the city' (Acts 14.13)?

Inscriptional evidence offers reasonably good support for worship of Zeus and Hermes in the region of Lycaonia and possible support for worship of them in Lystra (pp. 90–101). In Wordelman's words, 'it would not be unrealistic to suppose that Lystra had a temple to Zeus' (p. 211). No archeological evidence, however, has been found for a temple of Zeus at Lystra (p. 211), nor is there evidence of an appointment or selection of a priest for Zeus worship there. There is ample evidence for 'worship of Zeus – under various local designations – in Phrygia' (p. 212), and evidence that the local population in the mountainous regions directly south of Lycaonia in Cilicia

'Graecized the Hittite weather-god Tarhu(nt), calling him Zeus; and the divine protector of wildlife, Ru(nt), calling him Hermes' (pp. 212–13). By extension, then, a person may argue for the possibility of similar worship at Lystra, but again, there is no direct evidence for worship of either Zeus or Hermes there.

If Wordelman's study stopped at this point, it would not be a truly socio-rhetorical investigation of Acts 14. But her investigation continues. Given the plausibility but not the certainty of Zeus worship in Lystra, she returns to the inner texture of the account and performs a careful analysis of its 'cultural' intertexture in relation to the image of Lycaonia and the nature of mythical accounts of Zeus and Hermes in Greek and Roman literature. Her results are stunning. Her search takes her beyond Ovid's tale of Baucis and Philemon, which many commentators have cited in relation to the account in Acts. In this story, 'Zeus and Hermes appear in human form to ordinary people, and they do something miraculous' that exhibits their identity (p. 217). The problem is that the story occurs in Phrygia, and the Acts 14 story occurs in Lycaonia. The last story in Ovid's *Metamorphoses* features King Lycaon of Arcadia, and word-plays in literature show that Mediterranean people have fun with Lycaon as a person (King Lycaon), a place (Lycaonia) and being wolf-like (*lykon*) (pp. 231–8). The King Lycaon episode is 'the final straw which drives Jupiter and the other gods to destroy the world by flood' (p. 222). Jupiter, to test rumors that humans have become impious, descends from Mount Olympus and travels up and down the land as a god disguised in human form. Worrying most about King Lycaon, who is 'well known for his savagery', Jupiter travels to Arcadia, 'gives a sign that a god had come' into their midst, and the common people begin to worship him. King Lycaon does not believe the human-looking stranger is a god, so he puts him to a test. He makes a plot to kill him in his sleep, but serves him a meal of the flesh of a human hostage before sending him off to bed. Jupiter, knowing the flesh is human, destroys the house with a mighty thunderbolt, and when Lycaon tries to escape he gradually turns into a wolf, 'the same picture of beastly savagery' he had in his human form (p. 223). In Wordelman's words, 'Lycaon's new form as a wolf, reveals for all time his character as a human king' (p. 223).

Wordelman then reads the story in Acts 14 in relation to this myth of Zeus at the end of Ovid's *Metamorphoses*. Paul and Barnabas come into Lystra, and Paul heals a man who was crippled from birth. The local residents, seeing the deed and knowing the story of Zeus/Jupiter, are not fooled. They know that Paul is Hermes and Barnabas is Zeus, appearing to them in human form, so they cry this out 'in Lycaonian' (Acts 14.11). When the priest of Zeus begins to prepare sacrifices of oxen and garlands in honor of the visit of the gods, Paul and Barnabas are 'caught in this latest version of an ancient tale and largely unaware of their predicament. As Paul and Barnabas finally do catch on and object to the proceedings, the tone of the episode changes from one of entertainment to one of edification' (p. 240). But this is not the end of the story. Immediately after Paul and Barnabas clarify for the people who they really are and what they believe, 'Jews came there from Antioch and Iconium; and having persuaded the people, they stoned Paul and dragged him out of the city, supposing that he was dead' (Acts 14.19). Who, then, takes on the nature of a wolf-like creature? 'Wolf-friendship', Wordelman explains, is 'friendship characterized by an initial show of friendliness, which quickly turns to enmity or hostility' (p. 246). In Acts 14.18 the people 'are ready to serve a banquet to their guests', but 'the next minute they prefer to destroy them'. '[T]hrough the wolf analogy . . . the behavior of the Lycaonians becomes indicative of the larger persecution and rejection themes of Luke's narrative' (pp. 249–50). And then Wordelman expresses her shock:

> The analogies with primary themes in Luke's narrative jump out starkly from the page. 'The Jews' who rejected Jesus are responsible for his death, i.e., 'they' have tasted the flesh of a human victim. They have 'tasted kindred blood' with tongues and lips now unholy. The Lycaonians are that docile mob. Paul, the Roman citizen, is unjustly accused, dragged out of the city, and left for dead (14.19). Contact with 'ravenous wolves' has transformed the originally docile and worshipping Lycaonians into ravenous wolves themselves.
>
> (pp. 250–1)

Wordelman does not go on to analyze the social and cultural texture of this discourse in the socio-rhetorical manner recommended in the last chapter. I would suggest that Wordelman's analysis shows once again the dominant conversionist nature, in Wilson's terminology, of Lukan discourse. Paul and Barnabas take Christianity on the road to change people's attitudes to their worship. This conversionist argumentation is supported by thaumaturgic rhetoric about healing (Acts 14.8–10), which provides the occasion for the conversionist discourse but is also moderated by a general thesis about God's creating and nurturing of the universe and the people in it through the ages (Acts 14.15–17). Culturally, Lukan discourse presents Christianity as a Mediterranean subculture that understands and participates in Greek and Roman life. The narrator reveals that he knows Greek and Roman mythology and can use it to play with and persuade his reader/audience. Also, Christianity's belief system fulfills the highest values of Greek and Roman life: doing benevolent things that bring happiness to heart and body (Acts 14.17). This subcultural discourse, however, is embedded in *contra*cultural Jewish discourse. The fun the narrator has with his culturally informed audience occurs at the expense of Jewish tradition. Jews, whose overall behavior is 'wolflike', transform the hospitable Lycaonians into wolflike people, willingly stoning Paul and leaving him for dead after they had initially been hospitable. Despite all the 'Jewish' tradition that informs the Lukan story, what the reader hears again and again is rhetoric that suggests that Christianity is something quite distinct from, and quite opposed to, 'the Jews'.

Before leaving this section, I should mention a recent volume on ideological analysis containing a series of essays by biblical interpreters (Jobling and Pippin 1992). Some of the essays move toward socio-rhetorical analysis; others do not. Socio-rhetorical criticism, as a critical theory of rhetoric, calls for analysis of the ideological texture of authoritative traditions (cf. Clark 1994) in the context of careful analysis of biblical texts themselves.

IDEOLOGY IN INTELLECTUAL DISCOURSE

As mentioned at the beginning of this chapter, John Gager identified the role of intellectuals who transform personal motivations into eternal truths as an especially important issue in biblical interpretation (1975: 82). This issue, of course, involves this entire book: its presuppositions, its use of language, its format and its goals. Elisabeth Schüssler Fiorenza has raised this issue in the form of an ethics of historical reading (1988: 14), an ethics of accountability (1988: 15) and a critical theological hermeneutics (1992: 133–63). In this section, then, the entire issue of how one interprets, and how one interprets in intellectual modes, moves to the forefront.

Fortunately, the field of New Testament studies has a number of people who have been working on these issues.

The ideological issues at stake in intellectual discourse are being explored brilliantly at present by Stephen D. Moore. Two major literary figures lying behind the part of Moore's work I will discuss here are Jacques Derrida and Paul de Man. I will present Moore's analysis of them for biblical interpreters in this section, rather than go to the texts of these writers themselves. The interest in this chapter is to discuss biblical interpreters, among whom Moore is becoming a major figure. His distinctive contribution lies in the arena of the ideological analysis both of biblical texts and of interpretations of biblical texts. His first book focused entirely on biblical interpreters of the Gospels in the New Testament, exhibiting the nature and limitations of their work (Moore 1989). His second book explored Mark and Luke from poststructuralist perspectives (Moore 1992). His third book explains poststructuralism through extensive analysis and interpretation of the work of Jacques Derrida and Michel Foucault (Moore 1994). For the purposes in this section the reworked excerpts on Mark from his second book, which were printed as a separate essay in *Mark and Method: New Approaches in Biblical Studies* (Anderson and Moore 1992: 84–102), are most helpful for the investigation of ideology in intellectual discourse.

As Moore explains in the opening pages of his essay, a major problem with modern Western thought is the manner in which it is 'built on binary oppositions: soul/body, nature/culture, male/female, white/nonwhite, inside/outside, conscious/unconscious, object/representation, history/fiction, literal/metaphorical, content/form, primary/secondary, text/interpretation, speech/writing, presence/absence, and so on' (p. 84). I introduced this problem in the introduction to this work in the form of 'mind/body' dualism, and we have seen Castelli's analysis of such oppositions in Paul's discourse in 1 Corinthians 1–4. The practices of Western thinking introduce subordination in each pair rather than equality: the first term is superior to the second, so the relation between the two terms is hierarchical (superior/inferior), not reciprocal. One of the major ways this has influenced biblical interpretation is in the establishment of 'poetic boundaries', an issue discussed in chapter 3, where the interpreter sets up a strong opposition between the 'inside' and the 'outside' of the text. Another major influence has been the opposition of 'speech' and 'writing', also discussed in chapter 3. These traditional perspectives play into binary Western thinking where the first terms are the 'good' ones ('inside' and 'speech'), while the second terms are inferior, ordinary, lifeless or corrupted imitations of what is most true and real. Unfortunately but not surprisingly, these oppositions breathe through both biblical interpretation and Christian theology – since both are products of Western thought – establishing their agendas, goals and strategies. After addressing some of the oppositions in biblical interpretation, this section will turn to the problem of these oppositions in intellectual discourse, which includes not only biblical interpretation and Christian theology but also the disciplines of history, literary studies, linguistics, sociology, anthropology, philosophy and psychology. Instead of rehearsing specifically what Moore has done, I will use Moore's work as a medium to explain yet further the nature of socio-rhetorical criticism.

To confront the problem of binary oppositions in biblical interpretation, Moore uses the works of Derrida and de Man in the context of interpretation of aspects of the Gospel of Mark. One example he explores is the boundaries of a text. In contrast to clear boundaries that create an inside and an outside for texts, there are ways in which texts destroy their own boundaries. An excellent example is the end of the Gospel of Mark (pp. 86–7). Copyists wrote at least three different endings when they copied Mark in an attempt to establish a secure boundary at the end of the story. At the end, the text says that the women told no one what they had seen and heard at the empty tomb (Mark 16.8). But if they told no one, the narrative itself would not be able to contain the story: there would have been no means by which anyone could have known about the empty tomb. This contradiction breaks open the end of the text: somehow something had to happen, which the narrative does not tell about, which made it possible to include the story about the empty tomb. A major point with this is that 'inside' and 'outside' break down. Evidence that something 'outside' the text had to happen for the story to be in the text is actually 'inside' the text – namely the story of the empty tomb. Unless something happened outside the text besides the women's 'not telling' anyone, the author could not have included the story in the text (unless the author is one of those women, which Moore does not suggest!). At this point, then, opening–middle–closing texture breaks down the 'inside' and 'outside' of the text: the text contains inside–outside interaction 'in itself', as we would say.

A key example of a positive manifestation of this inside–outside interaction is the use of the term 'parable' in the narrative. At first the Twelve are told that only people 'on the inside', namely them, can understand the parables; people on the 'outside' are not able to understand them. Soon, however, those on the inside, namely the Twelve, are not able to understand what Jesus says and does, even though 'everything happens in parables' (Mark 4.11). The significance of this is that Markan narrative itself contains a term, namely 'parable', that deconstructs the 'inside/outside' opposition which it sets up near the beginning of the story. This is the kind of term both Derrida and de Man look for, namely a term that contains both sides of the opposition in itself and has no opposite in the language of the text itself. Parable is an 'inner–outer' phenomenon in the text itself that 'deconstructs' the opposition between inside and outside which a reader may wish to impose on the text.

Another issue is the opposition of speech and writing in biblical interpretation, which suggests that speech is superior to writing (pp. 89–93). In the text of Mark, Jesus speaks. According to the high evaluation of speaking in Western thought, speaking is superior to writing because the speaker is there to communicate directly. Communication is clear when it is embodied in the speaker himself; there should be no distortion because the speaker is there – everything should become clear through question and answer if it is not clear at first. In contrast, a written text cannot be clarified: it wanders around like an 'orphan', lost from its author/father. The author is not there to clarify the text, so its meanings have been 'lost'. The reader will anticipate me to know that when Jesus speaks in Mark, the disciples, who are supposed to be on the 'inside' of Jesus' 'speech', cannot understand the meaning of what Jesus says. It is as if they are trying to 'read' Jesus as though he were 'writing' and has gone away from his writing. That which is supposed to be true of writing, then, is present in the contexts where Jesus 'speaks' directly to the disciples. Alternatively, the 'reader' of the text of Mark 'understands' what the disciples should be able to understand. Modern biblical interpreters, especially, know what the disciples should have understood when Jesus spoke to them. In other words, those who read the 'written text' of Mark understand it as though it were 'direct speech' to them, while those who hear the spoken voice of Jesus cannot understand it. But is this really the case? The reader of my statements will again anticipate me, to know that Markan discourse deconstructs the traditional opposition between speech and writing in such a manner that the interpreter's belief that he or she can understand what is written is just as deceptive as thinking that the disciples had no understanding of Jesus' speech to them.

At this point, Moore moves to the opposition between text and reader, which has become another polarity in modern interpretation. Supposedly, either the reader 'imposes' meaning on the text or the text 'imposes' meaning on the reader. Some interpreters have it one way; others have it the other. For some modern interpreters, the reader is supposed to 'get out' from the text what is in it; for others, the reader 'constructs' what is in the text. But Moore shows that the situation is more complicated than this: we all act out something that is inscribed in the text; the question is 'what' aspect of it we act out. In Moore's words:

> The critic, while appearing to comprehend a literary text from a position outside or above it, is in fact being comprehended, being grasped, by the text. He or she is unwittingly acting out an interpretive role that the text has scripted, even dramatized, in advance. He or she is being enveloped in the folds of the texts even while attempting to sew it up.
>
> (p. 93; italics in original)

In other words, the reader is not completely outside or completely inside the text, nor is the text completely outside or inside the reader. Reader and text interact in ways that break down the traditional opposition between the two. This raises interesting issues not only about my own analyses but about Castelli's and Schüssler Fiorenza's analyses of Pauline discourse and Wordelman's analyses of Acts. In what ways are all of us acting out some interpretive role inscribed or dramatized by the text itself as we perform our analyses?

As Moore nears the end of his essay, he begins to play with the word 'cross'. The purpose is to show the fragility of language, to show how language is also not either one thing or another. Words are always in motion, meaning partly one thing here and partly another thing there, as well as partly one thing and partly another both here and there. Mark's theology is a theology of the cross, and the cross crisscrosses through other things said and done in the narrative. In other words, the cross 'crosses out' and 'crisscrosses' through the entire narrative, making Jesus absent where he seems to be present and present where he seems to be absent. Also, it makes the author absent where we might have thought he was present and present where we might have thought he was absent.

There is a moment in Moore's text that is especially important for socio-rhetorical criticism and its project. In the context of talking about 'cross' Moore introduces 'chiasmus'. 'A cross is also a chiasmus', he says, and he introduces Mark 8.35:

> 'whoever would *save* their life will *lose* it' is inverted ... to 'whoever *loses* their life ... will *save* it'.
>
> (p. 95)

This is an important moment for socio-rhetorical criticism, because chiasmus is another way to overcome binary oppositions, a way regularly used by 'new historicism'. Chiasmus represents a reciprocity rather than opposition between two things. Reciprocity between Jewish and Greco-Roman culture in the Gospel of Mark stands at the foundation of analysis and interpretation in *Jesus the Teacher* (Robbins 1982, 1984, 1992a, 1990: 47–72/1994a: 109–242). In Stephen Greenblatt's terms, there is reciprocal 'energy' exchanged by two phenomena, and the exchange is not simple but highly complex (Thomas 1991: 182–5, 193–6). To describe relations between texts and society, therefore, new historicists use a chiasmus like:

> the social dimension of an aesthetic strategy and the aesthetic dimension of a social strategy.
>
> (Thomas 1991: 193)

For socio-rhetorical criticism, this introduces four chiasmic statements which I have not tried to introduce to the reader prior to this section, but which are at work in each aspect of texture in a text. The four statements are as follows:

(a) inner texture: the textual culture of religion and the religious culture of text;

(b) intertexture: the intertextuality of biblical discourse and the discourse of biblical intertextuality;

(c) social and cultural texture: the sociological and anthropological culture of religion and the religious culture of sociology and anthropology;

(d) ideological texture: the ideological texture of intellectual discourse and the intellectual texture of ideological discourse.

Each chiasmus turns the initial formulation back on to itself in a manner that raises decisive issues about any mode of interpretation of a text. Every interpretation of a text requires an interpreter to use a mode of discourse. Every mode of interpretive discourse is ideological, but it is not 'just' ideological. All interpretive discourse both reinscribes some aspect of the discourse in the text and enacts an influential mode of discourse in its own time and place. To put it another way, every interpreter acts out both 'an interpretive role the text has scripted, even dramatized, in advance' (Anderson and Moore 1992: 93) and an interpretive role that influential discourse in his or her own time and place has authorized and dramatized. In still other words, the ideological nature of all interpretation manifests itself in the interplay between the choice of a mode of interpretive discourse and the choice of dimensions of the text the interpreter reinscribes. Let us explore this briefly in relation to each chiastic statement above.

Investigations of inner texture act out some configuration of repetition, progression, opening–middle–closing, narration, argumentation and/or aesthetic in the text itself. Yet every interpretation adopts an interpretive role that uses one or more currently available mode of intellectual discourse, such as literary, linguistic, narratological, rhetorical, philosophical, theological or aesthetic discourse. On the one hand, the challenge as stated in the chiasmus above is that Christianity is one of those religions that has created a textual culture that claims to present authentic discourse, perhaps *the only authentic* discourse, about God. On the other hand, it is the nature of text itself to create a religious culture about itself – texts both authorize their own view of the world and create the need for their own discourse. Analysis and interpretation of the inner texture of New Testament texts, then, occur in a space of interplay between Christianity as a religion that authorizes itself through the thought and action it advocates in its texts and biblical texts as a form of discourse in which narrational voices evoke religious authority for themselves and create a need for their own religious discourse. The ideological dimensions of inner textual analysis and interpretation play out some configuration of the authority and needs created by the text and the authority and needs in the discourse the interpreter chooses from his or her contemporary culture.

Investigations of intertexture play out, in one way or another, an interaction between the history, texts, cultures and social situations and institutions biblical texts evoke and the history, texts, cultures and social situations and institutions interpretations of biblical texts regularly evoke. In other words, individual biblical texts evoke canons, canons within canons and near-canons for their inter-textuality. In the context of this multiple display of intertextures, interpreters evoke canons, canons within canons and near-canons for their own interpretive discourse. The ideological nature of a particular intertextual interpretation, then, lies in the interplay between the intertextures of the biblical text it is reinscribing and the intertexture in the intellectual discourse the interpreter has chosen to analyze and interpret this intertexture.

Investigations of social and cultural texture configure together one or more social and cultural roles the religious text has scripted and one or more roles sociology and anthropology have authorized as important and/or definitive. The ideological nature of analyses and interpretation of social and cultural texture lies in the interplay between the selection of special, common and final social and cultural topics and categories in the discourse and the selection of models, typologies, theories and modes of analysis and explanation from the social sciences.

Investigations of the ideological texture of biblical texts configure an interplay between some mode of authority and creation of needs enacted by the discourse in the text and some mode of authority and creation of needs in modern or postmodern intellectual discourse. On the one hand, the discourse in texts evokes literary, historical, social, cultural, rhetorical, ideological, aesthetic and theo-logical modes of inquiry, discussion and interpretation. On the other hand, modern and postmodern intellectual discourse advances disciplinary, interdisciplinary, multidisciplinary, transdisciplinary, eclectic, empirical, theoretical, constructive and deconstructive modes of analysis and interpretation. Ideological interpretation features an interplay between the selection of a particular ideology to enact intellectual dimensions evoked by the biblical text and the selection of particular intellectual modes of discourse to enact the ideological dimensions of the interpretation. For example, the ideo-logical texture of anthropological discourse is regularly distinctive from the ideological texture of historical discourse. But a particular anthropological interpreter may choose an ideological position very close to a particular historical interpreter. The ideological texture of their respective interpretations exhibits itself both in the particular manner in which the interpreter enacts the discourse of the field of anthropology or history and in the particular manner in which the interpreter enacts an aspect of the anthropological or historical texture or intertexture of the text. Thus, in any ideological investigation there is a reciprocal interaction between the ideological texture of the particular mode of interpretation and the intellectual texture – be it anthropological, historical, literary, sociological, aesthetic or theological – of the ideological interpretation.

In conclusion, any investigation of inner texture must wrestle with the 'baptizing' of text by modern critics just as much as it must wrestle with texts' 'baptizing' of religion. Any investigation of intertexture must wrestle with biblical intertexualities' 'canonizing' of itself as much as it must wrestle with the Bible's 'canonizing' of its own intertextuality. Any investigation of social and cultural texture must wrestle with the 'adoption' by sociology and anthropology of a religious culture for themselves as much as religion's 'adoption' of sociological and anthropological culture for itself. Any investigation of ideological texture must wrestle with the 'ultimate' claim of any form of intellectual discourse for its own ideology just as much as ideological interpretation makes an 'ultimate' claim for its intellectual mode of discourse. Nothing we say, then, can escape the way we say it and the context in which we say it, and the way other people hear it in the context in which they hear it. But there is no cause for alarm. This is the way it always has been and always will be. And this is the context in which we encounter 'truth' as we know it.

IDEOLOGY IN INDIVIDUALS AND GROUPS

Not only every text but also every interpreter reflects presuppositions, interests, commitments, desires, privileges and constraints which are not simply different personal attitudes, dispositions, interests and convictions, but are part of a particular location in the 'historical web of power relationships' (Schüssler Fiorenza 1985b: 9). Groups find special portions of the Bible that function as paradigms for them, give prominence in analysis and interpretation to certain textures rather than others in these texts and select a particular configuration of intellectual modes of discourse to interpret them. Schüssler Fiorenza used the Markan account of the woman who anointed Jesus (Mark 14.3–9) to launch her book entitled *In Memory of Her* (1983). In a more recent book entitled *But She Said* (1992), the story of the Syro-Phoenician/ Canaanite woman in Mark 7.24–30/Matt. 15.21–8 provides the language, and the book uses a series of stories about women in the Bible to establish its discourse. She uses a combination of rhetorical, historical, ideological, feminist and theological discourse in her commentary on these biblical texts. In many ways, then, Schüssler Fiorenza has been articulating an ideology for women of belief for more than a decade.

This section will repeat an analysis of Clarice J. Martin's study of the conversion of the Ethiopian eunuch in Acts 8.26–40 which I presented in the introduction to the paperback edition of *Jesus the Teacher* (1992a: xxxiv–xxxvii). The essay is an excellent beginning place for a person who wants to explore in a socio-rhetorical manner the ideology of particular individuals or groups. Martin entitled her essay 'A Chamberlain's Journey and the Challenge of Interpretation for Liberation' (C. J. Martin 1989), and in it she interweaves back and forth through inner texture, intertexture, social and cultural texture and ideological texture. In the end, she displays a thickly interwoven matrix of meanings and ideologies in and around the text.

Martin begins with past studies of inner texture of the story in the Acts of the Apostles where an Ethiopian eunuch, riding back on his chariot after his visit to Jerusalem, converts to Christianity as a result of Philip's interpretation of a scriptural passage to him. The past studies Martin cites proceeded thematically. Many observed the role of the Holy Spirit in the preaching and evangelism in the story of the conversion of the Ethiopian eunuch itself (8.29, 8.39) and in the broader narrative of Luke-Acts (Luke 4.18; 24.44; Acts 1.8; 4.8–10; 7.55; 10.11–12; 13.4–10; 16.6–7). Others observed Philips' 'witness' to the death and resurrection of Jesus in the story and the theme of witness throughout Luke and Acts (Luke 1.1–4; 24.48; Acts 1.21–2; 4.33; 10.39–41; 22.14–15). Still others observed the 'joy' of the Ethiopian at the end of the story in (8.39) relation to the theme of joy throughout Luke and Acts (Luke 1.44; 2.10; 15.4–7; 19.6, 19.37; 24.41; Acts 2.47; 8.8; 11.18; 16.33) (pp. 106–7).

From these observations about the inner texture of the Ethiopian story and the overall narrative of Luke and Acts, Martin moves to an ideological phenomenon in the inner texture that provides a transition to intertextual analysis. In the story about the Ethiopian eunuch and throughout Luke and Acts, there is a presupposition that Old Testament prophecy is fulfilled in the experiences and activities recounted about Jesus and early Christianity. The Ethiopian eunuch is reading in the fifty-third chapter of the prophetic book of Isaiah about the lamb that does not open its mouth as it is led to slaughter. Philip, of course, uses the opportunities to tell the eunuch 'the good news of Jesus'. But for Martin, this moment in the story takes us to Isaiah 53. Going to the intertext that is explicitly recited in Acts 8, Martin observes that three chapters later in the book of Isaiah, Isaiah prophesied that eunuchs who keep the sabbath, who choose the things that please the Lord God and who hold fast to the Lord's covenant will go to God's holy mountain, be made joyful in God's house of prayer, and their burnt offerings and sacrifices will be accepted on the altar, because the Lord's house 'shall be called a house of prayer for all peoples' (Isaiah 56.4, 56.7–8). This prophecy reverses the prohibition in Deuteronomy 23.1 that forbids eunuchs from entering 'the assembly of the Lord'. With this move, Martin has extended her analysis beyond the oral–scribal intertexture of the story with Isaiah 53 to the broader social intertexture that Second and Third Isaiah nurture within biblical discourse.

Since the eunuch has, according to the story in Acts, gone up to Jerusalem to worship and is now returning home in his chariot (8.27–8), the story enacts the 'social reality' of the temple at Jerusalem becoming a 'house of prayer for all peoples' as Isaiah 56.4, 56.7–8 predicted, since the eunuch has just worshipped at the Temple and is now returning. But the intertextuality of the story with biblical social reality does not end here. The eunuch is not simply a eunuch; he is an Ethiopian. In Psalm 68.31 it says that Ethiopia will 'stretch out her hands to God'. This social reality also has been fulfilled in the story. Without saying that Psalms also are considered to be fulfilled in the activities in Luke and Acts, Martin has expanded the intertexture of the story beyond the specific issue of eunuchs in biblical culture. Her interest lies in an aspect of his identity that extends beyond his being a eunuch. He is an Ethiopian, an issue of special importance for an African-American interpreter of scripture. This story enacts the inclusion not only of eunuchs but also of Ethiopians in worship in the Jerusalem temple. But now we need to know who Ethiopians are. Thus, Martin has found a passageway through oral–scribal, social and cultural intertexture to a context for exploring the ethnographic identity of Ethiopians in Mediterranean antiquity (pp. 107–10).

In summary, adopting the modern mode of discourse regularly called liberation theology, Martin moved from analysis of inner texture to an ideological phenomenon within the text that provided a transition from traditional oral–scribal analysis of Isaiah 53 and 56 to analysis of Psalm 68.31 where Ethiopians worship the God of Israel. In the context of this intertextual analysis, she moves the issue in which she is most interested, the identity of the man as an Ethiopian, into the center. This opens a passageway into an ethnographic exploration of cultural intertexture of the story in relation to Hellenistic-Roman society and culture, which is a prominent aspect of the text of the Acts of the Apostles. Instead of going physically to a particular location as anthropologists do, Martin, like other researchers of Antiquity, does her 'fieldwork' in the literature, art and other cultural artifacts available in libraries, museums, etc.

Aided by Frank M. Snowden Jr.'s studies of blacks in antiquity (Snowden 1976a, 1976b, 1979), Martin brings to the reader's attention that 'Ethiopians were the yardstick by which antiquity measured colored peoples. The skin of the Ethiopian was black, in fact, blacker, it was noted, than that of any other people' (Snowden 1979: 23). In addition, Ethiopians were persistently characterized as having '"puffy" or "thick" lips, tightly curled or "wooly" hair, [and] a flat or "broad" nose' (C. J. Martin 1989: 111). Martin works through classical art to Homer, Herodotus and Seneca to thicken her description of Ethiopians in Mediterranean society and culture (pp. 110–14).

When Martin completes her ethnographic analysis and interpretation, she returns to Luke and Acts to exhibit a thicker texture for its ideology of promise and fulfillment. In Luke there is reference to 'all flesh' seeing the salvation of God (Luke 3.6), to repentance and forgiveness of sins being preached to 'all nations' (Luke 24.47) and to people coming from 'east, west, north and south' to sit at table with Abraham, Isaac and Jacob (Luke 13.29). At the beginning of Acts there is a proclamation that the mission in Acts will reach to the 'end of the earth' (Acts 1.8c). From this thicker picture of the ideology of Luke and Acts, Martin moves to Mediterranean cultural ideology about 'the end of the earth' and concludes, using Homer, Herodotus and Strabo, that Ethiopia lies on the edge of the 'Ocean' at the southernmost limit of the world. Her conclusion, in turn, suggests that the identification of the eunuch as Ethiopian should be significant, because in its context of culture this baptized Ethiopian is returning to his home at the end of the earth. In this context, then, Martin, much like Wordelman, moves to a discussion of the geo-cultural map the discourse in the book of Acts evokes.

From these observations about the cultural ideology and geo-cultural map of Acts, Martin returns once again to Luke and Acts and observes that these two volumes participate in a cultural ideology that focuses on Rome as the center of the Mediterranean world. As a result of this ideology, using the words of Cain Felder, 'the darker races outside the Roman orbit are circumstantially marginalized by New Testament authors' and the 'socio-political realities' of this 'tend to dilute the New Testament vision of racial inclusiveness and universalism' (Felder 1982: 22). When Martin turns to biblical maps for the New Testament to find Ethiopia, she discovers a 'politics of omission'. Only a map of the Roman world at the birth of Jesus in *The Westminster Historical Atlas to the Bible* includes Meroë (or Nubia). In all other cases, a person can find this area only in some maps for the Hebrew Bible. This 'politics of omission' is not only present in investigations of the New Testament, however. Quoting Snowden, Martin emphasizes that a similar omission has existed in classical scholarship, despite rich data of various kinds. But then, she observes, post-enlightenment culture itself has marginalized and omitted not only blacks but also women and other groups. It is necessary to activate a hermeneutics of suspicion, she therefore suggests, that can intercept ideologies that thrive on a 'politics of omission' (C. J. Martin 1989: 120–6).

The end of Martin's article addresses the issue of interpretation itself. Her words are as follows:

> If the ongoing process of interpreting biblical traditions is to be in any sense 'interpretation for liberation' – that is, interpretation which effects full humanity, empowerment, and justice in the church and society under God – interpreters must continue to critically discern ways in which a 'politics of omission' may be operative in perpetuating the marginalization and 'invisibility' of traditionally marginalized persons, groups, and ideologies in biblical narratives. It is only as we undertake such critical analyses that a potentially liberatory vision of biblical traditions can emerge and function as an empowering force in *all* contemporary communities of faith.
>
> (1989: 126)

In Martin's interpretation, then, there is concern about boundaries that nurture a 'politics of omission' and a plea for interpreters to bring to light the ways in which both the texts we interpret and the methods we use to interpret them marginalize, exclude and hide

219

persons, groups and ideologies. Her article is an excellent model of one way to proceed. Using the discursive power of liberation theology, she works carefully in the inner texture of both Luke-Acts and the Hebrew Bible, identifying ideological moments that expand intertextual exploration beyond a genetic mode to a broader literary mode that leads to social, cultural and ideological exploration of the meaning of the text.

Instead of functioning within tightly sealed boundaries, Martin finds passageways through boundaries into arenas of exploration that shed additional light on the story in Acts. As she moves through passageways to other arenas of exploration, Martin does not forget the text she is interpreting. She continually comes back to it to find the interwoven webs of significance within its inner, social, cultural and ideological texture. Moreover, she does not flee from environments of closure. She continually returns to them to look for passageways to other arenas of disciplinary investigation that have produced data that will help her explore additional webs of significance in the text.

Martin's investigation could have performed an even fuller socio-rhetorical analysis and interpretation if it had analyzed repetitive, progressive, narrational, argumentative and aesthetic features in the inner texture of the account of the conversion of the Ethiopian. Also, it could have explored the nature of the social response to the world in the discourse, which is dominantly conversionist, as we have seen in the previous chapter. The issue of the final categories at work in the narration would also be a highly interesting matter. Acts 8.33 specifically raises the issue of justice in a context of humiliation and Acts 8.39 suggests that a benefit that brings joy is a final category at work in the discourse. In addition, an important aspect of the story is the identification of the converted man as a eunuch, which is an aspect of the story Martin does not attempt to address at any length (cf. A. Smith 1995).

IDEOLOGICAL TEXTURE IN
1 CORINTHIANS 9

Let us move on, then, to analysis and interpretation of the ideological texture of 1 Corinthians 9. While analysis of social and cultural texture yields insights into dialogue among social and cultural systems in the discourse, analysis of ideological texture analyzes the nature of the power struggles in the context of these systems.

To facilitate analysis of ideological texture, socio-rhetorical criticism investigates a spectrum containing four subsets: (a) ideology in traditional interpretation; (b) ideology in the text; (c) ideology in intellectual discourse; and (d) ideology in individuals and groups.

Ideology in traditional interpretation

Most interpreters accept Pauline discourse in 1 Corinthians as an accurate account of the social situation at Corinth. In other words, interpreters begin with a presupposition of accurate historical intertexture for the discourse and use this presupposition as the point of view for analysis and interpretation of the text. This leads to three overarching practices for interpretation of 1 Corinthians 9:

(a) The interpreter submits to the narrational texture of the discourse. This means that the interpreter takes a point of view that the discourse represents the voice of 'authoritative Paul', true representative of the Gospel, of God and of Christ.

(b) The interpreter adopts the point of view that the discourse is 'representational' rather than 'generative'. The discourse reports the historical and social situation in Corinth rather than creating a particular view of 'historical and social reality' there. No other point of view would be 'God's view'. Paul's account is not biased or self-serving. It presents the appropriate way to understand the situation.

(c) The interpreter reconstructs the historical sequence of interaction at Corinth on the basis of Pauline discourse in the Corinthian correspondence available to us. Any other account that differs from the account in this discourse would be less reliable, because this is a 'first hand, inner account'. While the account is partial, it furnishes true, primary data for writing a history of the church at Corinth.

C. K. Barrett's commentary in 1968 is representative of this approach at a high standard of execution. Some people in Corinth had questioned Paul's apostolic status. Otherwise Paul would not 'have spent so long on the question of apostolic rights' (1968: 200). It is certain that there are real opponents of Paul at Corinth (p. 201) and they 'evidently wished to put the apostle to the test' (p. 202).

While this approach to 1 Corinthians 9 may appear to be 'self-evident', it is in fact an ideological approach to the discourse in the text. Traditional interpretations of 1 Corinthians 9 begin with a presupposition that Paul 'is right and the "others" are wrong' (Schüssler Fiorenza 1987: 390). It is time now to build further in a socio-rhetorical manner on the work of Schüssler Fiorenza and Castelli, which suggests that interpreters should exhibit the ideological texture of 1 Corinthians 9 rather than simply perpetuate its ideology.

Ideology in the text

Once interpreters start down the path of the traditional ideology of interpretation, they 'follow Paul's dualistic rhetorical strategy without questioning or evaluating it' (Schüssler Fiorenza 1987: 390). Interpreters accept the strategies of differentiation (or dissociation) and association throughout the chapter. In other words, these interpretations 'take Paul at his word', reinscribing the ideological texture of the text rather than showing the ideology of the discourse to the reader. What if Paul's way of talking about himself and the situation at Corinth 'creates' a particular view of the 'historical and social reality' there? After all, Paul does not claim to be living there at the time he is writing this discourse. What would an 'inside view' look like? Paul's view is from the outside, and it is clear that he has a personal agenda in mind as he speaks throughout his Epistle. Paul's view, in other words, is 'one view' of the situation. What if an interpreter gave some other voices in the situation 'equal play'? What would it look like if the interpreter gave some other voices in the situation 'the benefit of the doubt', as we say? Perhaps other people in the situation had good reasons for thinking and acting as they did. Reconstructing the points of view of other voices in the discourse can exhibit a fuller, thicker, more even-handed view of the situation at Corinth.

Once an interpreter encounters an ideological dimension in traditional interpretation that is based on one aspect of texture in the text, a search begins for a broader understanding of the ideological nature of the text itself. The analysis in the previous chapters of inner texture, intertexture and social and cultural texture in 1 Corinthians 9 provide data that contribute to ideological analysis. If we use the steps Elizabeth Castelli (1991) recommends for analyzing power relations, we can begin by defining the *system of differentiations* that allows the Pauline discourse in 1 Corinthians 9 to act upon the actions of members of the Corinthian community. These differentiations began to appear in our analysis of narrational

222

texture in 1 Corinthians 9. Some of the differentiations are as follows (statements in brackets are evoked as opposites rather than explicitly stated in the discourse):

(a) Paul is free/(some others must be enslaved in unacceptable ways);
(b) Paul is an apostle/(some others have not been sent by God and Christ to perform a special task in the world);
(c) Paul has seen Jesus our Lord/(others have not);
(d) The Corinthian Messianites are Paul's workmanship in the Lord/they are not the workmanship of someone else, like Apollos, Cephas, or Christ(!) (1.12);
(e) Paul is the apostle to the Corinthians/(no one else is the apostle sent to perform a special task with the Corinthians);
(f) Paul does not use the right to food and drink/other apostles do;
(g) Paul offers the gospel free of charge/others offer it for a price;
(h) Paul is in a position to win an imperishable crown/others receive a perishable crown;
(i) Paul does not run aimlessly/(others wander off the track of the gospel of Christ);
(j) Paul pommels his body and subdues it/others box in the air.

This system of differentiations establishes Paul as both an authoritative representative of God and Christ and the creator of the church at Corinth. The discourse differentiates Paul from other people by grounding its claims in the speech and activity of both God and Christ and by establishing Paul as a person who possesses the cognitive power in every situation to do what 'living by the gospel' (9.14) demands. In addition, it establishes Paul as a benevolent patron: one to whom the people at Corinth owe their very existence and identity but one who has never asked for any payment for his work among them. Paul lives a self-controlled life through which he embodies self-denial for the benefit of the wide variety of people in the communities he has founded. In contrast to Paul, there are apostles who 'live off' communities they or someone else has founded. The implication is that they probably do this because they do not embody the self-control and self-denial central to Paul's life.

The next step is to articulate the *types of objectives* held by Paul in his actions on the Corinthians. Castelli identified the major objective as 'removal of dissension, quarreling and discord'.

Socio-rhetorical analysis suggests a more far-reaching objective for Pauline discourse in 1 Corinthians – namely, the creation of a Pauline faction in the early Christian movement. A major objective of the discourse is to evoke a relation among all the members of the community that is based on an acceptance of Paul as their patron. He is 'their apostle' (9.2). They are 'his' workmanship, the seal of 'his' apostleship in the Lord (9.2–3). Paul and no one else occupies the position of authority in relation to the community. The object of the discourse is to make Paul the center of an early Christian faction culture, to make his close fellow workers a network that keeps channels of communication open between him and the community and to establish a clique in the community that uses his directives to guide the community's deliberations and actions so that the community follows the mind of Paul. According to the discourse, Paul wants people in the congregation at Corinth to identify him alone as the founder of the community in the name of God and Christ. Since Paul is absent from the community for long periods of time, this discourse invests representatives of Paul with the power to transmit authoritative decisions from Paul to them. For all matters of governance, then, they need to consult with Paul or one of his associates.

The third step is to identify the *means* for bringing these relationships into being. The initial means is to create a need for governance. The opening chapters do this by describing the community as divided, filled with dissension. In the context of creating the need the discourse offers the answer. The Corinthians need unified thought and action under the lordship of Jesus ('our' Lord). All need to 'think with the same mind and the same judgment' (1.10). All need to accept an 'ideology of sameness'. But what is the same and what is different? It is necessary to have one leader who authoritatively defines what 'the same' is and identifies 'that which is different'. In other words, this ideology creates a need for the very kind of thinking and clarification the discourse in the letter presents. It is necessary to have a person at the center who brings unity of thought and action rather than disparate voices saying different things.

Another means for placing Paul at the center is the recitation of quotations that show how the mind of both the Lord God and the Lord Jesus think (2.16; 9.9, 9.14). God has said that an oxen deserves his food (9.8) and Christ has said that those who proclaim the gospel should get their living from the gospel (9.14). Paul's thinking even transcends the speech of God and Christ! As a slave to all people and a noble athlete, he exercises self-denial and self-control that allows him to offer the gospel free of charge. The implication is that the speech of God and Christ is finally a concession to humans. The 'minds' of God and Christ surely prefer their apostles to offer the gospel free of charge! But, of course, only a few of those apostles will actually know the mind of God and Christ on this, since most will not have the cognitive powers to enact the life of the gospel in its fully authentic form. Recitation of statements from God and Christ, then, are an important means of moving toward the major objective at hand. Still another is to build confidence in certain people as 'fellow workers' (9.6). As Castelli keenly observes, the strategy is first to mention these people alongside Paul (e.g. Apollos: 3.9; 4.6–13), then to omit them with a shift to first-person singular 'I' (4.14–21). The same thing occurs in 1 Corinthians 9 when the discourse first places Paul alongside Barnabas in 9.6, 11–12, then omits Barnabas as it focuses totally on Paul in 9.15–27.

The fourth step is to identify the *forms of institutionalization of power*. One of the institutional forms of power in the discourse is apostleship. Here we can get a clearer view of Pauline discourse in 1 Corinthians 9 by contrasting it with the institutionalization of power in 1 Peter as John H. Elliott has analyzed it (1981, 1990a). We recall that Elliott identified the institutionalization of 'household' as a major form of enactment of the ideology of a family of God in which strangers are not aliens but brothers and sisters. In contrast, Pauline discourse invests apostleship with the status of an institutional office. In Corinthian discourse households are simply a basic social institution, like the social structure of the military that includes soldiers, the social structure of viticultural production that includes vineyard keepers and the social structure of herding culture that includes shepherds. The discourse uses 'family' language of brother and sister to advance its goals, but 'household' language refers quite straightforwardly to the conventional social institution of the household, not to the assembled congregation (1 Cor. 1.16; 11.34; 14.35; 16.19).

In this context institutional imagery for early Christian believers varies. The people in Corinth are 'an assembly of God' (11.18; 16.1, 16.19), 'sanctified in Christ Jesus, called to be holy' (1.2). They are God's temple, and God's temple is holy (3.16–17). On the other hand, their bodies individually are temples of the Holy Spirit (6.19). They are the body of Christ, both individually and as a group

(12.27). This varying imagery creates a framework for the institutionalization of the office of the apostle. God and Christ have called the people together through the one they have sent to them. When talking about the individual bodies of women and men, the order of hierarchy is God–Christ–man–woman (11.2). Since Paul is the representative of God and Christ, he knows the mind of God and Christ on matters concerning individual bodies. Concerning the entire community, the hierarchy is God, Christ, Paul, Apollos, Timothy, Stephanas and other local co-workers (Schüssler Fiorenza 1987: 397). The discourse in 1 Corinthians 9 institutionalizes the power of the apostle specially sent to a particular community of people. As we have seen before, this language stands at the opening of the chapter with the assertion that the people of Corinth are Paul's workmanship in the Lord, the seal of Pauls' apostleship in the Lord (9.1–2).

The fifth step is to analyze the *degree of rationalization* of the power relations. 1 Corinthians 9 exhibits a high degree of rationalization of the authoritative embodiment of Paul with power over the people in the Corinthian community. Castelli observes how the argumentation in 1.10–4.21 builds to a point where it becomes progressively more ironic: you are kings, we are sentenced to death; we are a spectacle to the world, fools, weak, in disrepute, the refuse of the world, the offscouring of all things (4.8–13). We have seen in the analysis of argumentative texture in chapter 3 how 1 Corinthians 9 presents a 'complete argument', a full rhetorical elaboration of the enthymematic formulations at the beginning of the chapter about freedom and apostleship. In this instance, as the argument proceeds it becomes progressively more hyperbolic. This becomes evident in the occurrences of 'all' and 'nothing' in the discourse. The first touch of hyperbole occurs in 9.10 where there is an assertion that God speaks 'entirely' (*pantos*) for our sake. This is something of an exaggeration, but its clarity alongside other analogies from social life recommends its insight into God's ways with the world. But this is a strategic setup. The discourse asserts that 'we' do not make use of this right that God provides 'entirely' for the sake of humans in the law of Moses (9.12). The reason is that we endure 'all things' (*panta*) in order not to put an obstacle in the way of the gospel. They endure some things, to be sure, but 'all' things? These are just the initial brushes of hyperbole in the discourse.

The fullest hyperbole emerges when the discourse moves into first-person singular:

226

I have not made use of 'any one' (*oudeni*) of these rights;
I would rather die;
'no one' (*oudeis*) may deprive me of my boast (9.15).

After this 9.19–23 contains reduplication (*anadiplosis*: Vickers 1988: 491) that forms an inclusio around Paul's being 'all things to all people':

Though I am free from all (*pantōn*), I enslave myself to all (*pasin*) (9.19);
To all (*pasin*) I have become all things (*panta*),
that I might by all means (*pantōs*) save some (9.22);
All things (*panta*) I do for the sake of the gospel (9.23).

The rationalization for 'everything' that the discourse claims is that everything Paul does he does for everyone! We became aware in the intertextual analysis that Epictetus presents the Cynic as one who is free in all things and one whom Zeus sends to all people as a herald and a servant. Pauline discourse adopts this mode of discourse and embeds it in discourse about the gospel of Christ. As Pauline discourse elaborates the topic of 'all', it becomes even more hyperbolic than the discourse of Epictetus. Paul is not only free from all but enslaved to all. He has 'become all things to all people'. The Cynic does not claim to do this. The Cynic is who he is and whether others learn from him or not is a matter that is finally left up to them. Pauline discourse moves beyond this, because it presupposes that God is at work in and through both Paul and the people to whom he goes. This supportive work by God and the spirit of God and Christ is not present in Epictetus' discourse about Cynics and the people to whom they go.

Embedded in the middle of the inclusio in 1 Corinthians 9.19–23 is an enumeration of all the people to whom Paul is all things: Jews (those under the law); those outside the law; and those who are weak (9.20–3). The existence of three groups breaks the polarity between those under and those outside the law in a manner that creates the impression of comprehensiveness. This discourse has forgotten no one! But there is still a problem. It is hard to break out of the polarities of freedom and slavery into an image that contains them both. In 9.14 this image emerges – the athlete. Paul embodies the attributes of the athlete, who is both free to compete and enslaved by rigorous discipline. Here the language changes:

All (*pantes*) run, but only one receives the prize (9.24);
Everyone (*pas*) who competes exercises self-control in all things
(*panta*);
they to receive a perishable wreath, but we an imperishable one
(9.25).

As 'all' and 'everyone' continue through the discourse, the image of
the athlete embodies both sides of the polarity of freedom and
slavery as 'parable' embodies both 'the inside' and 'the outside' in
the Gospel of Mark. Now the differentiations are:

(a) most do not receive a prize/one person does;
(b) athletes compete for a perishable wreath/we for an imperishable wreath.

The image of the athlete embodies all the polarities by shifting from
running to 'every' athlete back to those who run and then to those
who box. When the discourse shifts back to running, it shifts back
to first-person singular.

I do not run aimlessly;
I do not box as one beating the air;
but (*alla*) I pommel my body and enslave it,
lest after preaching to others,
I myself might be disqualified.

(9.26–7)

The negatives take us back to the very beginning of the chapter:
Am I not free? Am I not an apostle? Have I not seen Jesus our
Lord? Are not you my workmanship in the Lord? (9.1). Paul does
not run aimlessly; he does not box in the air. If he did he would not
be who he is and they would not be who they are. The 'but' (*alla*) in
the middle takes the reader back to 9.12:

But (*alla*) we do not exercise this right,
but (*alla*) all things we endure, in order that we not put some
obstacle in the way of the gospel of Christ.

By the conclusion, as we have noticed, the discourse has changed to
'I': 'But (*alla*) I pommel my body and enslave it' (9.27). Paul, the
apostle athlete, embodies the gospel in freedom and slavery,
strength and weakness, boast and self-control. He does it all for
others! He also does it lest he himself be disqualified. The rationality

of Paul's power over the community is intricate, elaborate and picturesque.

Ideology in the text itself, then, establishes a world around Paul. He has been authorized and sent by God and Christ to this community, and he personally embodies self-control and self-denial for the sake of the gospel, which is the Pauline term for the work of God and Christ. Embodiment of complete commitment to the gospel exists in Paul in the form of being all things to all people. The question now is what aspect of the ideology an interpreter will reinscribe. Moore has made the case that all of us inscribe 'some aspect' of the rhetoric of the text. Let us turn to ideology in intellectual discourse to take this ideological analysis yet a step further.

Ideology in intellectual discourse

Recalling our observation that every interpreter both reinscribes 'some aspect' of the rhetoric in the discourse of a text and enacts some aspect of current intellectual discourse, let us turn to the issue of the ideological texture of intellectual discourse in interpreting 1 Corinthians 9. Historical, social, literary, rhetorical, theological, anthropological, aesthetic and psychological interpretations are not 'just' ideological. One of the reasons is that each of these modes of interpretation reinscribes some aspect of the text it interprets. Yet every one of them has ideological texture. What is the ideological texture of my interpretive discourse?

I have chosen a mode of 'interdisciplinary' discourse. This, I suppose, enacts the Pauline rhetoric of being 'all things to all people'. I am trying to invite every aspect of New Testament discourse into my program of analysis and interpretation. Also, I am trying to invite them in a manner that meets the intellectual standards of people who specialize in analyzing all these kinds of data. This is, of course, too much for anyone to do. But it is an alternative to what many others do. Many others attempt to choose one discipline and to include everything in the text in the strategies of analysis and interpretation in that discipline. In contrast, I have chosen an inter-discipline. Rhetoric does not have a first disciplinary location in academia. I know of no departments of rhetoric in modern universities. Rhetoric is partially here and partially there, nowhere for certain but actually everywhere for certain. Rhetoric is a mode of intellectual discourse I am enacting in an interdisciplinary manner. To try to be all things to all people is too great a goal. I suppose that, instead, I am trying to be quite a few things to quite a few people. And how can this be? My presupposition is that discourse itself contains multiple modes of discourse. Let us briefly review some of the modes in 1 Corinthians 9.

'Am I not free?' at the opening of 1 Corinthians 9 introduces the possibility of adopting a mode of analysis that reinscribes philosophical dimensions of the discourse. 'Am I not an apostle?' introduces the possibility of adopting a mode of analysis that reinscribes social institutional dimensions of the discourse. 'Have I not seen Jesus our Lord?' introduces the possibility for a historical mode of analysis and interpretation. 'This is my defense to those who would examine me' (9.3) introduces the possibility of adopting a rhetorical mode of analysis. 'Is it only Barnabas and I who have no right to refrain from working for a living?' introduces the possibility of adopting an economic mode of analysis. Who 'serves as a soldier', 'plants a vineyard', 'tends a flock', is 'a plowman', is 'employed in the temple service', is a 'slave', is a 'steward' or is an 'athlete' introduces the possibility of adopting a mode of analysis that reinscribes social dimensions of the discourse. 'Do I say this on human authority?' (9.8) introduces the possibility of adopting a theological mode for interpreting the chapter. 'For it is written in the law of Moses' (9.9) introduces the possibility of adopting a literary mode for interpreting the entire chapter. 'For if I do this of my own will' (9.17) introduces the possibility of reinscribing psychological dimensions of Pauline discourse.

Ideology, then, concerns both the choice of mode a text somehow enacts or dramatizes and the manner of executing the mode in the context of other influential modes of interpretive discourse available to interpreters at a particular time and place in the world. I have adopted an interdisciplinary mode as a way of negotiating multiple modes of discourse in New Testament texts. The ideology of interpreters guides both the particular configuration of modes they reinscribe from the text and the intellectual discourse they use to interpret these modes. Regularly interpreters feel confident about both their choice and its execution because the interpretation is somehow reinscribing not only dimensions of the text itself but also some form of current intellectual discourse.

I began the analysis of the ideological texture of 1 Corinthians 9 with traditional interpretations that placed historical discourse in a position of prominence over other intellectual modes. For me, historical discourse encourages a disciplinary approach that establishes deeply entrenched boundaries and encourages hierarchical thinking that makes every other disciplinary approach a subdiscipline of historical discourse. If interpreters believe that firm boundaries and hierarchical structures are essential for keeping diversity from proliferating and for curbing unacceptable activity (like a man living with his father's wife, speaking in tongues, and people saying they are kings), then they are likely to perpetuate these aspects of Pauline discourse. The important feature of Pauline discourse, then, will be certain people's ability to exercise authority over others and certain people's willingness to live in accord with this authority. Leaders will need to articulate as clearly as possible the dangers of diversity, identify deviant activity, ground the authority of the leadership in transcendent divinity and characterize leadership as having the best interests of the community in mind.

There are others, however, who have strong suspicions about the integrity and benevolent interests of authoritative people and hierarchical structures. If an interpreter believes that hierarchical structures are inherently evil, he or she can find aspects of Pauline discourse that challenge structures of authority and hierarchy and they can find current modes of intellectual discourse that offer resources for analyzing them. Both Schüssler Fiorenza and Castelli have found ways of doing this. Also, Graham Shaw has found a way, reaching the following conclusion about Pauline discourse:

> The language of salvation acts as an effective disguise. Its emphasis on the benefit which Paul is conferring distracts attention from the obedience which he is demanding and for which he seeks consent.
>
> (1983: 83)

So far as he is concerned, Paul has subverted the freedom of the Corinthians. He finds resources both in Pauline discourse and in modern intellectual discourse to enact his analysis and interpretation.

Still another alternative may be to propose a variety of Christian communities based on the varieties of discourse in New Testament literature. Dale Martin appears to be suggesting this when he proposes that patriarchalism did not develop out of egalitarianism in early Christianity, but the two ideologies existed side by side in Christianity from the beginning. He seems to suggest that we should accept Paul as authoritative, emphasize that slavery as salvation is not benevolent patriarchalism and that egalitarianism and patriarchalism existed side by side throughout the first century in early Christianity, and work for a symbiosis between patriarchal and egalitarian modes of community within modern-day Christianity. In all of these cases, interpreters are adopting some intellectual mode of discourse to advance certain aspects of Pauline discourse their analytical strategies have enabled them to identify.

Ideology in individuals and groups

Socio-rhetorical analysis comes finally, then, to interpretations representative of certain individuals and groups. At this point I will engage only a few moments in some prominent interpretations from the perspective of socio-rhetorical criticism to argue that interdisciplinary interpretation is a better mode of current interpretation than eclectic or fragmentary modes. Underlying my approach is a presupposition that both fragmented and eclectic interpretations can be very misleading. In fact, I consider partial information, at certain levels of interpretation, to lead to false conclusions. I will explain.

At the beginning of one's work, partial information usually does not lead to false conclusions. At initial levels of interpretation, all partial information is true. A major reason is that an interpreter is working off basic aspects of texture and intertexture in the text without adopting a strong form of intellectual discourse for commentary. For example, as one begins to interpret assertions about freedom in 1 Corinthians 9, all data about freedom in New Testament texts and in literature of diaspora Judaism and Greco-Roman culture is true data. The reason is that all the data is true 'in its own context', and the interpreter's goal is to gather as much data as possible in the hopes of finding certain especially good data to aid in the interpretation of the concept of 'freedom' in 1 Corinthians 9.

At a certain point in the gathering stage, interpreters decide they have found enough relevant data to give a 'thick interpretation' of the text. This is the stage where they begin to enact some aspect of modern intellectual discourse. The tendency is to adopt a primary location in one influential current mode and to use other modes eclectically. Eclecticism creates an especially fertile context for ideological texture to dominate over other textures in the text. Socio-rhetorical criticism recommends an interdisciplinary rather than eclectic mode of analysis and interpretation. The reason is that an interpreter may investigate multiple textures of the text with fuller resources from various intellectual disciplines. This in turn can lead to fuller exploration of the textures of the text the interpreter has decided to explore.

Let us take an example concerning the interpretation of the statement 'Am I not free?' at the beginning of 1 Corinthians 9. In addition to comparing the assertions in 1 Corinthians 9 with the thirty-nine other occurrences of nouns, adjectives and verbs built on the stem *eleuther-* (free) in the New Testament, the interpreter will use other data. What will the data be? C. K. Barrett quotes Epictetus 3.22.48 because of its interrogative diatribe style, but there is no discussion of assertions about freedom in the Epictetus text. The quotation simply suggests that some other people were talking about freedom. This is either an eclectic or a subdisciplinary use of the Epictetus text. Barrett's interpretation of 1 Corinthians 9 asserts that Paul means that 'every Christian is free' and that a person is right to suspect that there was a special gnostic emphasis on freedom in Corinth (1968: 200). At the beginning, then, Barrett generalizes Paul's question about freedom so that it refers to 'every Christian', rather than keeping the question in the context of the succeeding question about being an apostle. Then Barrett writes: 'Do you suppose that because I limit my freedom out of love my freedom does not exist? If any Christian can claim to be free I can do so, for *am I not an apostle?*' (p. 200). Once an interpreter generalizes the issue to 'every Christian', there is no special reason to pursue the reasoning in the Epictetus text about the freedom of one who has been 'sent by God'. This is the moment the analysis and interpretation become eclectic or subdisciplinary rather than interdisciplinary. At this point the Epictetus text becomes subsidiary to the Pauline text. The interpretation does not return to the Epictetus text to see what it says 'on its own terms'. The problem is that another verse in 1 Corinthians 9 indicates that Paul's preaching of the gospel is 'a compulsion' (9.16). This raises the problem of how anyone who is being compelled to do something can be free, precisely an issue the Epictetus treatise discusses at length. When interpreting 9.19, Barrett asserts that Paul 'is free because, having been made free as a Christian, he cannot become the slave of men: 7.23' (p. 210). Barrett brings discourse from 1 Corinthians 7, which asserts that members of the community should not become slaves of men, into the discourse of chapter 9, which is concerned with the freedom of one who is an apostle. Either eclectic or subdisciplinary use of the Epictetus text creates an environment for 'Christianizing' the discourse in such a manner that any consideration of 'outside' discussions of freedom is superfluous.

Conzelmann, in contrast, perceives the issue not to be about the freedom of Christians or about apostleship 'in general' but about Paul's own particular freedom (1975: 152). In this context, he cites the Epictetus discussion of wandering Cynic preachers, but he directs interpretation away from it by asserting that the issue here is a concrete controversy. When Conzelmann comes to 9.19, he writes: 'the freedom which he [Paul] claims for himself takes the concrete form of service' (p. 159). This statement is fascinating indeed, since it is virtually exactly the assertion the Epictetus discourse makes. Either eclectic or subdisciplinary use of the Epictetus text, however, allows it to drop out of sight. There is no reference to Epictetus at this point in the commentary; the implication is that this is an especially 'Christian' understanding of things. Eclectic or subdisciplinary use, rather than interdisciplinary use, of the Epictetus text creates an open space for ideologically oriented implications in the commentary. Without stating more, the impression is left that surely no 'pagan' could ever have come up with such an idea.

If an implication of this commentary is that a distinctive contribution of Christian discourse to Mediterranean thought and belief was that a person could be both free and serve other people, this implication is false. As indicated above, commentators usually refrain from actually making such a statement. As a result, the particular selection of comparative data and the absence of certain kinds of statements encourage the implication, but the commentator makes no explicit comment one way or another. The commentator has covered himself. Or has he? He has covered himself only if we accept interpretations that reinscribe the power play of only one aspect of New Testament discourse through eclectic or subdisciplinary practices of analysis and interpretation. The goal, rather, should be to display the inner nature of multiple power plays at work in the discourse through interdisciplinary strategies of analysis and interpretation. In the end, these commentators encourage the reader to draw a false conclusion – a conclusion the discourse indeed may have been designed to evoke from its implied hearer/reader but which we need to see and understand rather than simply be submissive to. A closer look at the commentary suggests that the commentator has used eclectic or subdisciplinary strategies to enter into a personal dialogue with the text under the pretense of interpreting the dialogue for us. The problem is the interpreters' limited construal of the context of the dialogue. In the end, the commentators have limited the context of the dialogue by asserting 'a concrete controversy' for it. This limiting of the context of the voices results in a highly inadequate exhibition of the historical, social, cultural and ideological voices in dialogue in the text. Socio-rhetorical interpretation provides the opportunity to move beyond this kind of limited commentary to interpretation that seeks the multiple voices in the discourse itself.

CONCLUSION

Analysis and interpretation of ideological texture leads to socio-rhetorical analysis of modern commentaries as well as socio-rhetorical analysis of New Testament texts themselves. Thus, this chapter has featured programmatic socio-rhetorical analysis of statements by modern commentators while earlier chapters contained only partial analysis and interpretation of modern commentary.

One of the issues this chapter broaches is the underlying premise with which historical criticism begins its work. Historical criticism regularly begins with the presupposition that the narrator of a New Testament text is right and others in the historical context were wrong. In other words, it begins with a presupposition that 'those who were victorious were right'. Beginning with this presupposition, historical critics adopt a 'disciplinary approach' that subordinates other disciplines of analysis and interpretation to their historical strategies. Historical criticism is such a powerful tool that it consumes all strategies of interpretation within itself. In the end, socio-rhetorical criticism probably is not free from this all-consuming goal. It wrestles with historical criticism in a context where literary criticism and social science criticism have established considerable power and influence in biblical interpretation. Yet, as explained above, the goal is to invite multiple disciplines into analysis and interpretation 'on their own terms' rather than in subordinate modes.

As recently as a decade ago I wanted to think that my interest in socio-rhetorical criticism was less biased than many other interpretations of New Testament texts, since it was attempting to include both Jewish and Greco-Roman society and culture and multiple disciplines of study to analyze and interpret the dynamics of the text in this 'bi-cultural' setting. But the word is out that all interpretations of texts are ideologically located. This need not mean, however, that interpretations are 'just' ideological. Since interpretations reinscribe a combination of aspects of the discourse in a text and of modern modes of intellectual discourse, some approaches hold the potential for illuminating more aspects of a text than others. In the end, all interpreters will decide what strategies they want to use and how they will use them, and in many instances this will be related to strategies they think they are able to use 'successfully'. One of the goals of this book is to recommend strategies for analyzing aspects of texts that interpreters may not have thought they would be able to analyze. The reason is that, in my view, we are entering an era that calls for interpretive strategies that carry interpreters into dialogue with interpreters of scriptures in many other religious traditions without experiencing a loss of deep, rich analysis and interpretation of biblical literature on its own terms.

7

THE PROMISE OF
SOCIO-RHETORICAL
CRITICISM

The promise of socio-rhetorical criticism lies in three realms. First, the approach offers programmatic correlation of multiple textures of texts that invites resources from multiple disciplines of investigation into an integrated environment of analysis and interpretation. The emphasis on multiple disciplines discourages excessive claims for any one disciplinary approach and encourages the use of strategies that people in various fields of study have developed to analyze and interpret highly different phenomena. Second, the approach offers systematic attention to individual realms of texture in a text in a framework of awareness of multiple arenas of texture. Rather than celebrating highly limited and fragmented analyses, socio-rhetorical criticism calls either for programmatic analysis within the domain of one texture or for an interactive analysis with multiple arenas of texture if the investigation has a limited focus on textual data. Third, the approach offers resources for writing a new account of first-century Christianity in the context of the display, analysis and interpretation of discursive cultures in the literature available to us. In other words, socio-rhetorical criticism perceives texts to be located interactively between representing world and evoking world. Texts, then, display historical, social, cultural and ideological textures of discourse that are media both for transmission and for formation of culture. The multiple strategies of analysis and interpretation available to socio-rhetorical criticism provide the opportunity for interpreters to generate a new account of the formation and perpetuation of Christianity during the first century.

MULTIPLE TEXTURES IN TEXTS

Inner texture

Socio-rhetorical criticism uses the phrase 'inner texture' to refer to data that linguistic, literary, narratological, rhetorical and aesthetic interpreters gather when they emphasize the relation of signs in a text to one another. This approach yields six kinds of inner texture: (a) repetitive; (b) progressive; (c) opening–middle–closing; (d) narrational; (e) argumentative; and (f) sensory–aesthetic. Analysis and interpretation of these kinds of inner texture are one aspect of a thick description of discourse in a text.

Intertexture

Alongside analysis of inner texture, socio-rhetorical criticism sorts intertextuality into three arenas of texture: (a) intertexture; (b) social and cultural texture; and (c) ideological texture. In other words, when literary critics refer to intertextuality they may be referring or oral–scribal, historical, social, cultural or ideological data. Socio-rhetorical criticism establishes a framework for systematic exploration of intertextuality by distinguishing between arenas of analysis and interpretation that emphasize verbal signs (intertexture), voices (social and cultural texture) and points of view (ideological texture).

Limiting 'intertexture' to analysis that stays in close touch with verbal signs in a text, socio-rhetorical criticism offers a framework of four arenas to explore the spectrum of intertexture: (a) oral–scribal; (b) cultural; (c) social; and (d) historical. These arenas identify data in the wider world of the text that verbal signs in the text under investigation evoke. The verbal signs evoke words in other oral or scribal texts, various cultural concepts and configurations, multiple social modes of identity and practice or one or more historical events and circumstances.

In socio-rhetorical terminology, then, the intertexture of a text represents an environment of analysis and interpretation that focuses on the words in the text as verbal signs. As signs, the words not only evoke other signs in the same text (inner texture) but evoke data in the wider textual, cultural, social and historical world in which they participate and in which people live.

Social and cultural texture

Socio-rhetorical criticism organizes the resources of the social sciences in analysis and interpretation on the basis of three kinds of rhetorical topics in texts: (a) special, material topics; (b) common topics; and (c) final, strategic categories. Specific, material topics display the social response to the world in the discourse. Common social and cultural topics in the text display the social and cultural systems and institutions that are the media of exchange in the discourse. The final, strategic categories at work in the text display the cultural location and orientation of the discourse.

The resources of Bryan Wilson's typology of religious sects contribute significantly to analysis and interpretation of special, material topics in a text. This leads to a negotiation of seven types of religious discourse in religious texts: conversionist, revolutionist, introversionist, gnostic manipulationist, thaumaturgic, reformist and utopian. The configuration of these types of discourse in any one text sheds important light on the relation of the discourse in this text to the discourse in other early Christian texts.

The resources of social-scientific criticism as they have been nurtured in biblical studies contribute to analysis of common social and cultural topics in New Testament texts. Social-scientific interpreters have made available a long list of systems and institutions, like honor and shame, patronage, etc., with which to approach the common social and cultural topics in a text.

The resources of sociology of culture contribute significantly to analysis of final social and cultural categories in biblical literature. Here, major distinctions arise in the form of dominant culture, subculture, counterculture, contraculture and liminal culture. People argue in different ways depending on the kind of culture they are both representing and creating. This mode of analysis, which is only in its infancy, identifies the categories people are using in their arguments and the manner in which they do or do not use reasons to support their assertions.

Ideological texture

Every text and every interpretation of a text communicates a particular point of view. They present this view by selecting certain topics and categories for discussion and using a particular mode of discourse to advance the discussion. Socio-rhetorical analysis of ideological texture addresses four arenas: (a) ideology in traditional interpretation; (b) ideology in the text; (c) ideology in intellectual discourse; and (d) ideology in individuals and groups.

The particular ideological mode of socio-rhetorical criticism is interdisciplinary analysis and interpretation. Rather than selecting one major disciplinary mode of discourse, socio-rhetorical criticism invites multiple modes of discourse into analysis and interpretation of multiple aspects of the discourse of texts. The medium for this is rhetorical analysis and interpretation, which does not have a disciplinary home in modern and postmodern academia but is located hither and yon in various locations and areas of study. Socio-rhetorical criticism organizes rhetorical strategies into an interdisciplinary approach that invites multiple analytic and inter- pretive modes into the conversation in programmatic ways designed to place them in dialogue on equal terms with one another.

REWRITING THE HISTORIOGRAPHY OF FIRST-CENTURY CHRISTIANITY

In the context of its multiple uses of disciplines and modes of dis- course, socio-rhetorical criticism challenges the 'authorized version' of the history of first-century Christianity in the Acts of the Apostles and constructs an alternative account on the basis of data in all first-century Christian texts available to us. In other words, reconceptualizing 'history' as an interplay between 'perpetuation' and 'formation' of culture, the approach places all New Testament texts in a laboratory of data about first-century Christianity and negotiates the historical, social, cultural and ideological dimensions of the data in these texts. The ideological texture of each text, including the Acts of the Apostles, creates an environment where the interpreter puts 'great traditions' and 'little traditions' on as level a playing field as possible in the context of the data available to us. The interpreter places the 'little' thaumaturgic, gnostic manipu- lationist and conversionist traditions in an overall context that sheds light on the emergence of the 'great' conversionist, revolution- ist, and gnostic manipulationist traditions.

Socio-rhetorical criticism holds the promise, then, of taking inves- tigations of the Acts of the Apostles beyond comparison with the Pauline Epistles, comparison with historical, literary, social and cultural data in the Mediterranean world or literary analysis and interpretation – the three major activities of analysis and interpretation of Acts during the last half century. Using the data in Acts in the context of all the other data available in first-century Christian literature, the goal of socio-rhetorical criticism is to write an alternative account of first-century Christianity based on the panoply of little and great traditions in New Testament texts. This new account will use the ideological texture of the Acts of the Apostles as a primary datum of interest for understanding Christianity near the end of the first century, rather than allowing this ideology to drive the account.

The first two decades (30–50 CE)

This new account should focus decade by decade on the formation and perpetuation of early Christianity, using the data that programmatic socio-rhetorical analysis and interpretation yield. The first two decades (from 30 to 50 CE) are constituted by multiple points of view that neither individually nor together present the 'picture' of Christian belief a reader constructs on the basis of 'all' New Testament texts. Rather, 'Messianites' of various kinds thought and did various kinds of things with different kinds of discourse. Some Messianites perpetuated subcultural thaumaturgic responses to the world that built on the great traditions of Moses and Elijah. Some Messianites perpetuated subcultural gnostic manipulationist views of the world on the basis of parables and sayings about the 'mystery of the kingdom'. Some Messianites perpetuated a countercultural conversionist view of the world on the basis of short, pithy sayings that evoked a world related to the thought and activity of Cynics in the Mediterranean world. Still other Messianites evoked a contracultural reformist world in debate and conflict in synagogues over practices based on interpretations of the Torah and the prophets. Still other Messianites evoked a countercultural introversionist world on the basis of the death and resurrection of Jesus.

The third decade (50–60 CE)

The third decade (50–60 CE) represents a time when a significant 'Pauline faction' emerged, supported by a significant Pauline 'network' that supported Pauline 'cliques' in local settings. The emergence of a series of Epistles attributed to Paul, the self-proclaimed Pharisaic adherent to 'the crucified and resurrected Christ', played a formative role during this decade and the succeeding ones. During this decade thaumaturgic, gnostic manipulationist, conversionist and revolutionist groups within the Messianite movement began to engage more directly in conflict with one another. Still their existence in significantly 'localized' cultures allowed for distinctive discourses to continue with only limited intrusion or interruption.

The fourth decade (60–70 CE)

The fourth decade (60–70 CE) was highly traumatic, transitional and formative for the emergence of 'Christian' culture. During this decade, the death of Peter, Paul and James and the destructive Roman–Jewish Wars from 66 to 73 in Galilee and Judea created a context for special focus on death and on Jerusalem. By the end of the decade, at least one writer for the Messianite movement (the writer of the Gospel of Mark) was merging Pauline crucifixion-resurrection ideology with various kinds of thaumaturgic, gnostic manipulationist, revolutionist, conversionist and reformist Messianite discourses.

The fifth decade (70–80 CE)

The fifth decade (70–80 CE) displays the emergence of a significant 'coalition' culture in the Messianite movement. Crucifixion-resurrection ideology becomes the conceptual base both for identity among Messianites and for dialogue between Messianites and emerging 'Pharisaic culture'. By the end of the decade, a Messianite reconfiguration of the account of creation places the 'wisdom/logos Messiah' with God at the beginning of all things. This creates a correlation of the Messiah with God at the beginning and at the end of all things. This framework for Messianite belief provides the context for the development of 'fully configured' Christian belief.

The sixth decade (80–90 CE)

The sixth decade (80–90 CE) represents a time when some Messianite groups were excluded from some Jewish synagogues. In this context a richly textured, gnostic manipulationist and conversionist countercultural version of the life of Christ emerged (Gospel of John). Building on an ideology of the Messiah as logos/light at the beginning of creation, the Fourth Gospel supercharged thaumaturgically based conversionist discourse with a cosmological version of the Messiah's activity.

The seventh decade (90–100 CE)

The seventh decade (90–100 CE) exhibits the emergence of an account of first-century Christianity in the form of an extension of the biblical account of the history of Israel (Acts). During this same period of time, a highly pitched revolutionist countercultural version of Christian belief emerged in Asia Minor (Revelation).

SOCIO-RHETORICAL CRITICISM AND OTHER FIELDS OF STUDY

The question arises at the end of this book how people in other fields of study may use an approach to texts that has been advanced for the study of New Testament texts. The answer is to understand the approach as an 'interpretive analytics', an approach that attempts to find multiple kinds of data in texts and to use multiple modes of discourse to interpret them.

All interpreters use various strategies to find and exhibit to the reader certain words, phrases or emphases in a text. These are 'inner textual' strategies. Interpreters in any field of study may reflect on the strategies they use and develop a more programmatic approach to these strategies.

In addition to inner textual strategies, all interpreters compare the text they are interpreting with some kind of phenomenon that exists elsewhere. The phenomenon with which they compare the data in the text is an intertextual phenomenon. Reflection on the range of data with which the interpreter regularly compares data in the text can lead both to more programmatic use of this data and use of data in fields he or she had not previously used for comparison.

Beyond analysis of inner texture and intertexture, interpreters in any field may focus on the social and cultural texture of the texts they interpret. This is an area where interpreters may need to find more localized resources to open the social and cultural nature of the discourse in their texts. The literature under investigation in this book is all explicitly religious. Thus, a typology of religious sects serves as a natural way into the specific, material topics of the discourse. Perhaps modes more like Carney's (1975: 309–29; cf. Robbins 1991a) will be helpful to interpreters of other literature. The analysis of common social and cultural topics and final social and cultural categories, in contrast, should be directly suggestive to interpreters in other fields of study.

Analysis of ideological texture should also be quite accessible to interpreters in other fields of study. Interpreters in every field focus on particular kinds of data and use particular modes of discourse to interpret them. Reflection on and analysis of the data and modes of discourse to interpret the data should be a natural beginning place for analysis of the ideological texture of the data they analyze in modern commentary on this data.

In the end, socio-rhetorical criticism will never be all things to all people. This has never been my intention. If this approach helps some people some of the time to do some of the things they wish to do, then I shall rest content. It has, in any case, helped me to do some of the things I have wanted to do. Does a person have a right to ask for anything more?

BIBLIOGRAPHY

Abrams, M. H. (1953) *The Mirror and the Lamp: Romantic Theory and the Critical Tradition*, London: Oxford University Press.

Achtemeier, Paul J. (1970) 'Toward the Isolation of Pre-Markan Miracle Catenae', *JBL* 89: 265–91.

—— (1972) 'The Origin and Function of the Pre-Markan Miracle Catenae', *JBL* 91: 198–221.

Alter, Robert (1981) *The Art of Biblical Narrative*, New York: Basic Books.

Anderson, Janice Capel and Moore, Stephen D. (eds.) (1992) *Mark and Method: New Approaches in Biblical Studies*, Minneapolis: Fortress Press.

Bal, Mieke (1985) *Narratology: Introduction to the Theory of Narrative*, trans. Christine van Boheemen, Toronto: University of Toronto Press.

—— (1991) *On Story-Telling: Essays in Narratology*, Sonoma, CA: Polebridge Press.

Barclay, John M. G. (1992) 'Thessalonica and Corinth: Social Contrasts in Pauline Christianity', *JSNT* 47: 49–74.

—— (1995) 'Deviance and Apostasy: Some Applications of Deviance Theory to First Century Judaism and Christianity', in P. F. Esler (ed.) *Modelling Early Christianity*, London: Routledge.

Barrett, C. K. (1968) *A Commentary on the First Epistle to the Corinthians*, London: Adam & Charles Black.

Bartchy, S. Scott (1973) *[Malon chresai] First-century Slavery and the Interpretation of 1 Corinthians 7:21*, Missoula, MT: Scholars Press.

Barth, Fredrik (1969) 'Introduction', in F. Barth (ed.) *Ethnic Groups and Boundaries*, Boston: Little Brown & Co. = 'Ethnic Groups and Boundaries', in F. Barth, *Process and Form in Social Life*, London: Routledge & Kegan Paul, 1981, 198–227.

Barthes, Roland (1967) *Elements of Semiology*, trans. Annette Lavers and Colin Smith, New York: Hill & Wang.

—— (1972) *Mythologies*, trans. Annette Lavers, New York: Hill & Wang.

—— (1974) *S/Z*, trans. Richard Miller, New York: Hill & Wang.

—— (1977) *Image, Music, Text*, trans. Stephen Heath, New York: Hill & Wang.

—— (1981) 'Theory of the Text', in Robert Young (ed.) *Untying the Text: A Post-Structuralist Reader*, Boston: Routledge & Kegan Paul, 31–49.

Berger, Adolf (1953) *Encyclopedic Dictionary of Roman Law*, Transactions of the American Philosophical Society, new series 43: II, Philadelphia: American Philosophical Society.

Berger, Peter and Luckmann, Thomas (1966) *The Social Construction of Reality: A Treatise in the Sociology of Knowledge*, Garden City, NY: Doubleday.

Betz, Hans Dieter (1978) 'De Laude Ipsius (Moralia 539A–547F)', in H. D. Betz (ed.) *Plutarch's Ethical Writings and Early Christian Literature*, SCHNT 4, Leiden: Brill, 367–93.

Bhabha, Homi K. (1992) 'Postcolonial Criticism', in S. Greenblatt and G. Gunn (eds.) *Redrawing the Boundaries*, New York: Modern Language Association of America, 437–65.

Boers, Hendrikus (1979) *What is New Testament Theology? The Rise of Criticism and the Problem of a Theology of the New Testament*, Philadelphia: Fortress Press.

Boissevain, Jeremy (1974) *Friends of Friends: Networks, Manipulators and Coalitions*, Oxford: Basil Blackwell.

Booth, Wayne (1983) 'Rhetorical Critics Old and New: the Case of Gérard Genette', in Laurence Lerner (ed.) *Reconstructing Literature*, Oxford: Blackwell, 123–41.

Bouvard, Margarite (1975) *The Intentional Community Movement: Building a New Moral World*, Port Washington, NY: Kennikat.

Braun, Willi (1995) *Feasting and Social Rhetoric in Luke 14*, SNTSMS 85, Cambridge: Cambridge University Press.

Brown, Peter (1970) 'Sorcery, Demons and the Rise of Christianity from Late Antiquity into the Middle Ages', in Mary Douglas (ed.) *Witchcraft Accusations and Confessions*, London: Tavistock Publications.

Brown, Richard Harvey (1987) *Society as Text: Essays on Rhetoric, Reason, and Reality*, Chicago: University of Chicago Press.

Burke, Kenneth (1931) *Counter-Statement*, Berkeley, Los Angeles and London: University of California Press.

—— (1966) *Language as Symbolic Action*, Berkeley: University of California Press.

—— (1977) 'Bodies That Learn Language', Lecture at University of California, San Diego.

Calvin, John (1844) *Commentary upon the Acts of the Apostles*, two volumes, ed. Henry Beveridge and trans. Christopher Featherstone, Edinburgh: Calvin Translation Society.

Carney, Thomas F. (1975) *The Shape of the Past: Models and Antiquity*, Lawrence, KS: Coronado Press.

Castelli, Elizabeth A. (1991) *Imitating Paul: A Discourse of Power*, Louisville, KY: Westminster: John Knox Press.

Chatman, Seymour (1978) *Story and Discourse: Narrative Structure in Fiction and Film*, Ithaca, NY: Cornell University Press.

Chopp, Rebecca S. (1989) *The Power to Speak: Feminism, Language, God*, New York: Crossroad.

Clark, Elizabeth A. (1994) 'Ideology, History, and the Construction of "Women" in Late Ancient Christianity', *Journal of Early Christian Studies* 2: 155–84.

Colson, F. H. and Whitaker, G. H. (1958) *Philo*, ten volumes, Loeb edition, Cambridge, MA: Harvard University Press.

Conzelmann, Hans (1975) *1 Corinthians: A Commentary on the First Epistle to the Corinthians*, trans. James W. Leitch, Philadelphia: Fortress Press.

Crossan, John Dominic (1973) *In Parables: The Challenge of the Historical Jesus*, New York: Harper & Row.

—— (1976) *Raid on the Articulate: Cosmic Eschatology in Jesus and Borges*, New York: Harper & Row.

—— (1979) *Finding Is the First Act*, Semeia Supplements, Philadelphia: Fortress Press; Missoula, MT: Scholars Press.

—— (1980) *Cliffs of Fall*, New York: Seabury Press.

Culpepper, R. Alan (1983) *Anatomy of the Fourth Gospel: A Study in Literary Design*, Philadelphia: Fortress Press.

Daube, David (1956) *The New Testament and Rabbinic Judaism*, London: Athlone Press.

Davis, David Brion (1975) *The Problem of Slavery in the Age of Revolution 1770–1823*, Ithaca, NY: Cornell University Press.

de Beaugrande, Robert-Alain and Dressler, Wolfgang Ulrich (1981) *Introduction to Text Linguistics*, London: Longman.

Detweiler, Robert and Robbins, Vernon K. (1991) 'From New Criticism and the New Hermeneutic to Poststructuralism: Twentieth Century Hermeneutics', in Stephen Prickett (ed.) *Reading the Text: Biblical Criticism and Literary Theory*, Oxford: Basil Blackwell, 225–80.

Draisma, S. (ed.) (1989) *Intertextuality in Biblical Writings. Essays in Honour of Bas van Iersel*, Kampen, Neth.: Kok Press.

Dreyfus, Hubert L. and Rabinow, Paul (1983) *Michel Foucault: Beyond Structuralism and Hermeneutics*, Chicago: University of Chicago Press.

Duling, Dennis C. (1985) 'Insights from Sociology for New Testament Christology: A Test Case', *SBLSP*: 351–68.

—— (1992) 'Matthew's Plurisignificant "Son of David" in Social Science Perspective: Kinship, Kingship, Magic, and Miracle', *BTB* 22: 99–116.

—— (1993) 'Matthew and Marginality', *SBLSP*: 642–71.

Eagleton, T. (1983) *Literary Theory: An Introduction*, Minneapolis: University of Minnesota.

—— (1990) *The Ideology of the Aesthetic*, Oxford: Basil Blackwell.

—— (1991) *Ideology: An Introduction*, London/New York: Verso Press.

Eliot, T. S. (1920) 'Tradition and the Individual Talent', in T. S. Eliot, *The Sacred Wood: Essays on Poetry and Criticism*, London: Methuen, 47–59.

Ellens, G. F. S. (1971) 'The Ranting Ranters: Reflections on a Ranting Counter-culture', *Church History* 40: 91–107.

Elliott, John H. (1979) *1 Peter: Estrangement and Community*, Chicago: Franciscan Herald Press.

—— (1981) *A Home for the Homeless: A Sociological Exegesis of 1 Peter, Its Situation and Strategy*, Philadelphia: Fortress Press.

—— (1982) 'Salutation and Exhortation to Christian Behavior on the Basis of God's Blessings (1 [Peter] 1:1–2:10', *RevExp* 79/3: 415–25.

—— (1983) 'The Roman Provenance of 1 Peter and the Gospel of Mark: A Response to David Dungan', in Bruce Corely (ed.) *Colloquy on New Testament Studies: A Time for Reappraisal and Fresh Approaches*, Macon, GA: Mercer University Press, 182–94.

—— (1984) 'Review of E. Schüssler Fiorenza, *In Memory of Her*', *New Catholic World* 227/1361: 238–9.

—— (1985a) 'Review of W. A. Meeks, *The First Urban Christians*', *RelSRev* 11: 329–35.

—— (1985b) 'Backward and Forward "In His Steps": Following Jesus from Rome to Raymond and Beyond. The Tradition, Redaction, and Reception of 1 Peter 2:18–24', in Fernando F. Segovia (ed.) *Discipleship in the New Testament*, Philadelphia: Fortress Press, 184–209.

—— (ed.) (1986a) *Social-Scientific Criticism of the New Testament and Its Social World*, Semeia 35, Decatur, GA: Scholars Press.

—— (1986b) '1 Peter, Its Situation and Strategy: A Discussion with David Balch', in Charles H. Talbert (ed.) *Perspectives on First Peter*, National Association of Baptist Professors of Religion Special Studies Series 9, Macon, GA: Mercer University Press, 61–78.

—— (1987a) 'Patronage and Clientism in Early Christian Society: A Short Reading Guide', *Forum* 3/4: 39–48.

—— (1987b) 'Review of B. J. Malina (1986a) *Christian Origins and Cultural Anthropology*', *CBQ* 49: 512–13.

—— (1988) 'The Fear of the Leer: The Evil Eye from the Bible to Li'l Abner', *Forum* 4/4: 42–71.

—— (1990a) *A Home for the Homeless: A Social-Scientific Criticism of I Peter, Its Situation and Strategy*, Philadelphia: Fortress Press, reprint, paperback edition with new introduction.

—— (1990b) 'Paul, Galatians, and the Evil Eye', *Currents in Theology and Mission* 17: 262–73.

—— (1991a) 'The Evil Eye in the First Testament: The Ecology and Culture of a Pervasive Belief', in Jobling *et al.* (eds.) *The Bible and the Politics of Exegesis*, Cleveland, OH: Pilgrim Press, 147–59.

—— (1991b) 'Household and Meals vs. Temple Purity: Replication Patterns in Luke-Acts', *BTB* 21: 102–8 = *Hervormde Teologiese Studies* 47/2: 386–99.

—— (1991c) 'Temple versus Household in Luke-Acts: A Contrast in Social Institutions', in J. H. Neyrey (ed.) *The Social World of Luke-Acts*, Peabody, MA: Hendrickson Publishers: 211–40 = *Hervormde Teologiese Studies* 247/1: 88–120.

—— (1992a) 'Matthew 20:1–15: A Parable of Invidious Comparison and Evil Eye Accusation', *BTB* 22: 52–65.

—— (1992b) 'Peter, First Epistle of', in David Noel Freedman (ed.) *Anchor Bible Dictionary*, volume 6, New York: Doubleday, 89–99.

—— (1993) *What Is Social-Scientific Criticism?* Minneapolis: Fortress Press.

—— (1996) 'Phases in the Social Formation of Early Christianity: From Faction to Sect. A Social-Scientific Perspective', in Peder Borgen, Vernon K. Robbins, and David B. Gowler (eds.) *Recruitment, Conquest, and Conflict: Strategies in Judaism, Christianity, and the Greco-Roman World*, Emory Studies in Early Christianity, Atlanta: Scholars Press.

Elliott, John H. and Martin, R. A. (1982) *James, I–II Peter/Jude*, Minneapolis: Augsburg Publishing House.

Esler, Philip Francis (1987) *Community and Gospel in Luke-Acts: The Social and Political Motivations of Lucan Theology*, SNTS Monograph Series 57, Cambridge: Cambridge University Press.

—— (1992) 'Glossolalia and the Admission of Gentiles into the Early Christian Community', *BTB* 22: 136–42.

—— (1994a) *The First Christians in their Social Worlds: Social-Scientific Approaches to New Testament Interpretation*, London: Routledge.

—— (1994b) 'The Social Function of 4 Ezra', *JSNT* 53: 99–123.

—— (ed.) (1995) *Modelling Early Christianity: Social-Scientific Studies of the New Testament in its Context*, London: Routledge.

Felder, Cain (1982) 'Racial Ambiguities in the Biblical Narratives', in Gregory Baum and John Coleman (eds.) *The Church and Racism*, Concilium 151, New York: Seabury.

Fiore, Benjamin (1982) *The Function of Personal Example in the Socratic and Pastoral Epistles*, Ph.D. dissertation, New Haven, CT: Yale University Press.

Fishbane, Michael (1980) 'Revelation and Tradition: Aspects of Inner-Biblical Exegesis', *JBL* 99: 343–61.

—— (1985) *Biblical Interpretation in Ancient Israel*, Oxford: Clarendon Press.

—— (1986) 'Inner Biblical Exegesis: Types and Strategies of Interpretation in Ancient Israel', in Geoffrey H. Hartman and Sanford Budick (eds.) *Midrash and Literature*, New Haven, CT: Yale University Press, 19–37.

Fowler, Robert (1991) *Let the Reader Understand: Reader-Response Criticism and the Gospel of Mark*, Minneapolis: Fortress Press.

Fowler, Roger (1986) *Linguistic Criticism*, Oxford: Oxford University Press.

Frow, John (1986) *Marxism and Literary History*, Cambridge, MA: Harvard University Press.

Gager, John G. (1975) *Kingdom and Community: The Social World of Early Christianity*, Englewood Cliffs, NJ: Prentice-Hall.

—— (1982) 'Shall We Marry Our Enemies? Sociology and the New Testament', *Interpretation* 36: 256–65.

Garrett, Susan R. (1989) *The Demise of the Devil: Magic and the Demonic in Luke's Writings*, Minneapolis: Fortress Press.

Geertz, Clifford (1973) *The Interpretation of Cultures*, New York: Basic Books.

—— (1983) *Local Knowledge. Further Essays in Interpretive Anthropology*, New York: Basic Books.

Gordon, Milton M. (1970) 'The Subsociety and the Subculture', in D. Arnold (ed.) *Subcultures*, Berkeley: Glendessary Press, 150–63.

Goudriaan, Koen (1992) 'Ethnical Strategies in Graeco-Roman Egypt', in Per Bilde, Troels Engberg-Pedersen, Lisa Hannestad and Jan Zahle (eds.) *Ethnicity in Hellenistic Egypt*, Aarhus: Aarhus University Press, 74–99.

Gowler, David B. (1989) 'Characterization in Luke: A Socio-Narratological Approach', *BTB* 19: 54–62.

—— (1991) *Host, Guest, Enemy, and Friend: Portraits of the Pharisees in Luke and Acts*, Emory Studies in Early Christianity 1, New York: Peter Lang Press.

—— (1993) 'Hospitality and Characterization in Luke 11:37–54: A Socio-Narratological Approach', *Semeia* 64: 213–51.

Greenblatt, Stephen and Gunn, Giles (eds.) (1992) *Redrawing the Boundaries: The Transformation of English and American Literary Studies*, New York: Modern Language Association of America.

Grimes, Joseph E. (1975) *The Thread of Discourse*, The Hague: Mouton.

Hays, Richard B. (1989) *Echoes of Scripture in the Letters of Paul*, New Haven, CT: Yale University Press.

Held, Heinz Joachim (1963) 'Matthew as Interpreter of the Miracle Stories', in G. Bornkamm, G. Barth and H. J. Held (eds.) *Tradition and Interpretation in Matthew*, Philadelphia: Westminster, 165–299.

Hernadi, Paul (1976) 'Literary Theory: A Compass for Critics', *Critical Inquiry* 3: 369–86.

Hochman, Baruch (1985) *Character in Literature*, Ithaca, NY: Cornell University Press.

Hock, Ronald (1980) *The Social Context of Paul's Ministry*, Philadelphia: Fortress Press.

Hock, Ronald F. and O'Neil, Edward N. (1986) *The Chreia in Ancient Rhetoric. Volume I. The Progymnasmata*. Atlanta: Scholars Press.

Hollander, John (1981) *The Figure of Echo: A Mode of Allusion in Milton and After*, Berkeley: University of California Press.

Hollenbach, Paul W. (1981) 'Jesus, Demoniacs, and Public Authorities: A Socio-Historical Study', *JAAR* 49: 567–88.

—— (1983) 'Recent Historical Jesus Studies and the Social Sciences', *SBLSP*: 61–78.

—— (1985) 'Liberating Jesus for Social Involvement', *BTB* 15: 151–7.

—— (1986) 'From Parable to Gospel: A Response Using the Social Sciences', *Forum* 2: 67–75.

—— (1987) 'Defining Rich and Poor Using Social Sciences', *SBLSP*: 50–63.

—— (1989) 'The Historical Jesus Question in North America Today', *BTB* 19: 11–22.

—— (1993) 'Help for Interpreting Jesus' Exorcisms', *SBLSP*: 119–28.

Holmberg, Bengt (1990) *Sociology and the New Testament: An Appraisal*, Minneapolis: Fortress Press.

Horsley, Richard (1978) 'Consciousness and Freedom among the Corinthians: 1 Corinthians 8–10', *CBQ* 40: 574–89.

Hutcheon, Linda (1986) 'Literary Borrowing . . . and Stealing: Plagiarism, Sources, Influences, and Intertexts', *English Studies in Canada* 12/2: 229–39.

Jacobson, Arland (1992) *The First Gospel: An Introduction to Q*, Sonoma, CA: Polebridge Press.

Jameson, Frederic (1981) *The Political Unconscious: Narrative as a Socially Symbolic Act*, Ithaca, NY: Cornell University Press.

—— (1988) 'The Symbolic Inference; or, Kenneth Burke and Ideological Analysis', in Frederic Jameson (ed.) *The Ideologies of Theory. Essays 1971– 1986. Volume 1: Situations of Theory*, Theory and History of Literature 48, Minneapolis: University of Minnesota Press, 137–52.

Jewett, Robert (1986) *The Thessalonian Correspondence: Pauline Rhetoric and Millenarian Piety*, Philadelphia: Fortress Press.

Jobling, David, Day, Peggy L. and Sheppard, Gerald T. (eds.) *The Bible and the Politics of Exegesis: Essays in Honor of Norman K. Gottwald on His Sixty-fifth Birthday*, Cleveland, OH: Pilgrim Press.

Jobling, David and Pippin, Tina (eds.) (1992) *Ideological Criticism of Biblical Texts*, *Semeia* 59, Atlanta: Scholars Press.

Johnson, Luke Timothy (1986) *The Writings of the New Testament: An Interpretation*, Philadelphia: Fortress Press.

Johnson, Mark (1987) *Body in the Mind: The Bodily Basis of Meaning, Imagination, and Reason*, Chicago: University of Chicago Press.

Judge, Edwin A. (1983) 'The Reaction against Classical Education in the New Testament', *Journal of Christian Education*, Paper 77.

—— (1984) 'Cultural Conformity and Innovation in Paul: Some Clues from Contemporary Documents', *Tyndale Bulletin* 35.

Kennedy, George A. (1984) *New Testament Interpretation through Rhetorical Criticism*, Chapel Hill, NC: University of North Carolina Press.

—— (1991) *Aristotle, On Rhetoric: A Theory of Civic Discourse*, New York: Oxford University Press.

Kloppenborg, John S. (1986) 'Blessing and Marginality: The "Persecution Beatitude" in Q, Thomas and Early Christianity', *Forum* 2/3: 36–56.

—— (1987a) *The Formation of Q: Trajectories in Ancient Wisdom Collections*, Studies in Antiquity and Christianity, Philadelphia: Fortress Press.

—— (1987b) 'Symbolic Eschatology and the Apocalypticism of Q', *HTR* 30: 287–306.

—— (1988) *Q Parallels: Synopsis, Critical Notes & Concordance*, Sonoma, CA: Polebridge Press.

—— (1989) 'The Dishonoured Master (Luke 16.1–8a)', *Bib* 70: 474–95.

—— (1990a) 'Alms, Debt and Divorce: Jesus' Ethics in their Mediterranean Context', *Toronto Journal of Theology* 6: 182–200.

—— (1990b) '"Easter Faith" and the Sayings Gospel Q', *Semeia* 49: 71–99.

—— (1990c) 'City and Wasteland: Narrative World and the Beginning of the Sayings Gospel (Q)', *Semeia* 52: 145–60.

—— (1990d) 'Nomos and Ethos in Q', in J. E. Goehring, J. T. Sanders and C. W. Hedrick, in collaboration with H. D. Betz (eds.) *Gospel Origins and Christian Beginnings: In Honor of James M. Robinson*, Sonoma, CA: Polebridge Press, 35–48.

—— (1991) 'Literary Convention, Self-Evidence and the Social History of the Q People', *Semeia* 55: 77–102.

Krieger, Murray (1964) *A Window to Criticism*. Princeton, NJ: Princeton University Press.

Kristeva, Julia (1969) *Séméiotiké*. Paris: Seuil.

—— (1986) *The Kristeva Reader*, ed. Toril Moi, New York: Columbia University Press.

Krondorfer, Björn (1992) *Body and Bible: Interpreting and Experiencing Biblical Narratives*, Philadelphia: Trinity Press International.

Kuhn Thomas S. (1970) *The Structure of Scientific Revolutions*, Chicago: University of Chicago Press.

Lategan, Bernard C. and Vorster, Willem S. (1985) *Text and Reality: Aspects of Reference in Biblical Texts*, Philadelphia: Fortress Press; Atlanta: Scholars Press.

Lausberg, Heinrich (1990) *Handbuch der Literarischen Rhetorik*, Stuttgart: Franz Steiner.

Lawson, E. Thomas and McCauley, Robert N. (1990) *Rethinking Religion: Connecting Cognition and Culture*, Cambridge: Cambridge University Press.

Lentricchia, Frank and McLaughlin, Thomas (eds.) (1990) *Critical Terms for Literary Study*, Chicago/London: University of Chicago Press.

Mack, Burton L. (1987) *Anecdotes and Arguments: The Chreia in Antiquity and Early Christianity*, Occasional Papers 10, Claremount, CA: Institute for Antiquity and Christianity.

—— (1988) *A Myth of Innocence: Mark and Christian Origins*, Philadelphia: Fortress Press.

—— (1990) *Rhetoric and the New Testament*, Minneapolis: Fortress Press.

—— (1993) *The Lost Gospel: The Book of Q and Christian Origins*, San Francisco: Harper San Francisco Press.

Mack, Burton L. and Robbins, Vernon K. (1989) *Patterns of Persuasion in the Gospels*, Sonoma, CA: Polebridge Press.

McVann, Mark (1988) 'The Passion in Mark: Transformation Ritual', *BTB* 18: 96–101.

—— (1991) 'Rituals of Status Transformation in Luke-Acts: The Case of Jesus the Prophet', in J. H. Neyrey (ed.) *The Social World of Luke-Acts*, Peabody, MA: Hendrickson Publishers, 333–60.

Malbon, Elizabeth Struthers and Berlin, Adele (eds.) (1993) *Characterization in Biblical Literature, Semeia* 63, Atlanta: Scholars Press.

Malherbe, Abraham (1970) ' "Gentle as a Nurse": The Lyric Background to I Thess ii', *NovT* 12: 203–17.

—— (1986) *Moral Exhortation. A Greco-Roman Sourcebook*, Philadelphia: Westminster Press.

—— (1995) 'Determinism and Free Will in Paul: The Argument of 1 Corinthians 8 and 9', in Troels Engberg-Pedersen (ed.) *Paul in His Hellenistic Context*, Minneapolis: Fortress Press, 231–55.

Malina, Bruce J. (1978a) 'Limited Good and the Social World of Early Christianity', *BTB* 8: 862–76.

—— (1978b) 'The Social World Implied in the Letters of the Christian Bishop-Martyr (Named Ignatius of Antioch)', *SBLSP*, Vol. 2: Scholars Press, 71–119.

—— (1979) 'The Individual and the Community: Personality in the Social World of Early Christianity', *BTB* 8: 162–76.

—— (1981a) *The New Testament World: Insights from Cultural Anthropology*, Atlanta: John Knox Press.

—— (1981b) 'The Apostle Paul and Law: Prolegomena for an Hermeneutic', *Creighton Law Review* 14: 1305–39.

—— (1982) 'The Social Sciences and Biblical Interpretation', *Int* 37: 229–42.

—— (1983a) 'Why Interpret the Bible with the Social Sciences?', *American Baptist Quarterly* 2: 119–33.

—— (1983b) 'The Social Sciences and Biblical Interpretation', in Norman K. Gottwald (ed.) *The Bible and Liberation*, 11–25, expanded version of B. J. Malina (1982), 'The Social Sciences and Biblical Interpretation', *Int* 37: 229–42.

—— (1984a) 'Jesus as Charismatic Leader?', *BTB* 14: 55–62.

—— (1984b) 'Review of E. Schüssler Fiorenza, *In Memory of Her*', *RSR* 10: 179.

—— (1985a) *The Gospel of John in Sociolinguistic Perspective*, Protocol Series 48, Berkeley: Colloquy of the Center for Hermeneutical Studies in Hellenistic and Modern Culture.

—— (1985b) 'Hospitality', in Paul J. Achtemeier (ed.) *Harper's Dictionary of the Bible*, San Francisco: Harper & Row, 408–9.

(1985c) 'Review of W. A. Meeks, *The First Urban Christians*', *JBL* 104: 346–9.

—— (1986a) *Christian Origins and Cultural Anthropology: Practical Models for Biblical Interpretation*, Atlanta: John Knox Press.

—— (1986b) 'Interpreting the Bible with Anthropology: The Case of the Poor and the Rich', *Listening. Journal of Religion and Culture* 21: 148–59.

—— (1986c) 'Normative Dissonance and Christian Origins', in J. H. Elliott (ed.) *Social-Scientific Criticism of the New Testament and its Social World*, *Semeia* 35, Decatur, GA: Scholars Press, 35–59.

—— (1986d) 'The Received View and What It Cannot Do: III John and Hospitality', in J. H. Elliott (ed.) *Social-Scientific Criticism of the New Testament and its Social World*, *Semeia* 35, Decatur, GA: Scholars Press, 161–94.

—— (1986e) 'Religion in the World of Paul: A Preliminary Sketch', *BTB* 16: 92–101.

—— (1987) 'Wealth and Poverty in the New Testament and Its World', *Int* 41: 354–67.

—— (1988a) 'Patron and Client. The Analogy behind Synoptic Theology', *Forum* 4/1: 2–32.

—— (1988b) 'A Conflict Approach to Mark 7', *Forum* 4/3: 3–30.

—— (1989a) 'Dealing with Biblical (Mediterranean) Characters: A Guide for U.S. Consumers', *BTB* 19: 127–41.

—— (1989b) 'Christ and Time: Swiss or Mediterranean?', *CBQ* 51: 1–31.

—— (1990a) 'Does the Bible Mean What It Says?', *Window* (Creighton University) 6/2 (1989–90): 10–13.

—— (1990b) 'Mother and Son', *BTB* 20: 54–64.

—— (1991a) 'Interpretation: Reading, Abduction, Metaphor', in D. Jobling *et al.* (eds.) *The Bible and the Politics of Exegesis*, Cleveland, OH: Pilgrim Press, 253–66.

—— (1991b) 'Reading Theory Perspective: Reading Luke-Acts', in J. H. Neyrey (ed.) *The Social World of Luke-Acts*, Peabody, MA: Hendrickson Publishers, 3–23.

—— (1992) 'Is There a Circum-Mediterranean Person? Looking for Stereotypes', *BTB* 22: 66–87.

—— (1993) *The New Testament World: Insights from Cultural Anthropology*, Atlanta: John Knox Press, revised edition.

Malina, Bruce J. and Neyrey, Jerome H. (1988) *Calling Jesus Names: The Social Value of Labels in Matthew*, Sonoma, CA: Polebridge Press.

—— (1991a) 'Honor and Shame in Luke-Acts: Pivotal Values of the Mediterranean World', in J. H. Neyrey (ed.) *The Social World of Luke-Acts*, Peabody, MA: Hendrickson Publishers, 25–65.

—— (1991b) 'First-Century Personality: Dyadic, Not Individualistic', in J. H. Neyrey (ed.) *The Social World of Luke-Acts*, Peabody, MA: Hendrickson Publishers, 67–96.

—— (1991c) 'Conflict in Luke-Acts: Labelling and Deviance Theory', in J. H. Neyrey (ed.) *The Social World of Luke-Acts*, Peabody, MA: Hendrickson Publishers, 97–122.

Malina, Bruce J. and Rohrbaugh, Richard L. (1992) *Social Science Commentary on the Synoptic Gospels*, Minneapolis: Fortress Press.

Martin, Clarice J. (1989) 'A Chamberlain's Journey and the Challenge of Interpretation for Liberation', *Semeia* 47: 105–35; reprinted in Norman K. Gottward and Richard A. Horsley (eds.) (1993) *The Bible and Liberation:*

Political and Social Hermeneutics, Maryknoll, NY: Orbis Books, revised edition.

Martin, Dale (1990) *Slavery as Salvation*, New Haven, CT: Yale University Press.

Martyn, J. Louis (1968) *History and Theology in the Fourth Gospel*, New York: Harper & Row.

Meeks, Wayne A. (1972) 'The Man from Heaven in Johannine Sectarianism', *JBL* 91: 44–72.

—— (1975) 'The Social World of Early Christianity', *The Council on the Study of Religion Bulletin* 6/1: 1, 4–5.

—— (1977) 'The Unity of Humankind in Colossians and Ephesians', in Jacob Jervell and Wayne A. Meeks (eds.) *God's Christ and His People: Essays Presented to Nils Alstrup Dahl*, Oslo: Universitetsforlaget, 209–21.

—— (1979) '"Since Then You Would Need to Go Out of the World": Group Boundaries in Pauline Christianity', in T. J. Ryan (ed.) *Critical History and Biblical Faith*, Horizons, Villanova, PA: Villanova University/College Theology Society, 4–29.

—— (1983) 'Social Functions of Apocalyptic Language in Pauline Christianity', in David Hellholm (eds.) *Apocalypticism in the Mediterranean World and the Near East: Proceedings of the International Colloquium on Apocalypticism, Uppsala, August 12–17, (1979)*, Tübingen: J. C. B. Mohr (Paul Siebeck), 685–705.

—— (1985) 'Breaking Away: Three New Testament Pictures of Christianity's Separation from the Jewish Communities', in Jacob Neusner and E. S. Frerichs (eds.) *'To See Ourselves as Others See Us': Christians, Jews, 'Others' in Late Antiquity*, Chico, CA: Scholars Press, 93–115.

—— (1986a) 'A Hermeneutic of Social Embodiment', *HTR* 79: 176–86.

—— (1986b) *The Moral World of the First Christians*, Philadelphia: Westminster.

—— (1986c) 'Understanding Early Christian Ethics', *JBL* 105: 3–11.

—— (1987) 'Judgment and the Brother: Romans 14:1–15:13', in Gerald F. Hawthorne (ed.) *Tradition and Interpretation in the New Testament: Essays in Honor of E. Earle Ellis*, Grand Rapids: Eerdmans, 290–300.

—— (1988) 'The Polyphonic Ethics of the Apostle Paul', *Annual of the Society of Christian Ethics*: 17–29.

—— (1990a) 'Equal to God', in Robert T. Fortna and Beverly R. Gaventa (eds.) *The Conversation Continues: Studies in Paul and John in Honor of J. Louis Martyn*, Nashville: Abingdon, 309-21.

—— (1990b) 'The Circle of Reference in Pauline Morality', in David L. Balch, Everett Ferguson and Wayne A. Meeks (eds.) *Greeks, Romans, and Christians: Essays in Honor of Abraham J. Malherbe*, Minneapolis: Fortress Press, 305–17.

—— (1991) 'The Man from Heaven in Paul's Letter to the Philippians', in Birger A. Pearson (ed.) *The Future of Early Christianity: Essays in Honor of Helmut Koester*, Minneapolis: Fortress Press, 329–36.

—— (1993) *The Origins of Christian Morality: The First Two Centuries*, New Haven, CT: Yale University Press.

Mitchell, Margaret M. (1992) *Paul and the Rhetoric of Reconciliation. An Exegetical Investigation of the Language and Composition of 1 Corinthians*, Louisville, KY: Westminster/John Knox Press.

Montrose, Louis (1992) 'New Historicisms', in S. Greenblatt and G. Gunn (eds.) *Redrawing the Boundaries*, New York: Modern Language Association of America, 392–418.

Moore, Stephen D. (1989) *Literary Criticism and the Gospels: The Theoretical Challenge*, New Haven, CT: Yale University Press.

—— (1992) *Mark and Luke in Poststructuralist Perspectives: Jesus Begins to Write*, New Haven, CT: Yale University Press.

—— (1994) *Poststructuralism and the New Testament: Derrida and Foucault at the Foot of the Cross*, Minneapolis: Fortress Press.

Morgan, Thaïs (1989) 'The Space of Intertextuality', in P. O'Connell and R. Con Davis (eds.) *Intertextuality and Contemporary American Fiction*, Baltimore: Johns Hopkins University Press, 239–79.

Moxnes, Halvor (1983) 'Kropp som symbol: Bruk av socialantropologi i studiet av det Nye Testament', *Norsk Teologisk Tidsskrift* 84: 197–217.

—— (1985) 'Paulus og den norske vaerematen: "Skam" og "aere" i Romerbrevet', *Norsk Teologisk Tidsskrift* 86: 129–40.

—— (1987) 'Meals and the New Community in Luke', *Svensk Exegetisk Årsbok* 51–2: 158–67.

—— (1988a) *The Economy of the Kingdom: Social Conflict and Economic Relations in Luke's Gospel*, Philadelphia: Fortress Press.

—— (1988b) 'Honor and Righteousness in Romans', *JSNT* 32: 31–78.

—— (1988c) 'Honor, Shame, and the Outside World in Paul's Letter to the Romans', in Jacob Neusner et al. (eds.) *The Social World of Formative Christianity and Judaism*, Howard Clark Kee Festschrift, Philadelphia: Fortress Press, 207–18.

—— (1988d) 'Sociology and the New Testament', in Erik Karlsaune (ed.) *Religion as a Social Phenomenon: Theologians and Sociologists Sharing Research Interests*, Trondheim: Tapir, 143–59.

—— (1991a) 'Patron–Client Relations and the New Community in Luke-Acts', in J. H. Neyrey (ed.) *The Social World of Luke-Acts*, Peabody, MA: Hendrickson Publishers, 241–68.

—— (1991b) 'Social Relations and Economic Interaction in Luke's Gospel: A Research Report', in Petri Luomanen (ed.) *Luke-Acts: Scandinavian Perspectives*, Publications of the Finnish Exegetical Society 54, Helsinki: Finnish Exegetical Society, Göttingen: Vandenhoeck & Ruprecht, 58–75.

—— (1993) 'New Testament Ethics – Universal or Particular? Reflections on the Use of Social Anthropology in New Testament Studies', *Studia Theologica* 47: 153–68.

—— (1994) 'The Social Context of Luke's Community', *Int* 48: 379–89.

—— (1995) 'The Quest for Honor and the Unity of the Community in Romans 12 and in the Orations of Dio Chrysostom', in Troels Engberg-

Pedersen (ed.) *Paul in His Hellenistic Context*, Minneapolis: Fortress Press, 203–30.

Na, Kang-Yup (1995) 'The Meaning of Christ in Paul: An Exploration of the So-Called Pauline Christology in Light of Wilhelm Dilthey's *Lebensphilosophie*', unpublished dissertation proposal, Atlanta: Emory University.

Neirynck, Frans (1972) *Duality in Mark: Contributions to the Study of Markan Redaction*, BETL 31, Leuven: Leuven University Press (second edition 1988).

Neyrey, Jerome H. (1986a) 'Idea of Purity in Mark's Gospel', in J. H. Elliott (ed.) *Social-Scientific Criticism of the New Testament and Its Social World*, Semeia 35, Decatur, GA: Scholars Press, 91–128.

—— (1986b) 'Body Language in 1 Corinthians: The Use of Anthropological Models for Understanding Paul and His Opponents', in J. H. Elliott (ed.) *Social-Scientific Criticism of the New Testament and Its Social World*, Semeia 35, Decatur, GA: Scholars Press, 129–70.

—— (1986c) 'Witchcraft Accusations in 2 Cor. 10–13: Paul in Social Science Perspective', *Listening. Journal of Religion and Culture* 21: 160–70.

—— (1986d) 'Social Science Modeling and the New Testament' (review of B. J. Malina (1986) *Christian Origins and Cultural Anthropology*, Atlanta: John Knox Press), *BTB* 16: 107–10.

—— (1988a) *An Ideology of Revolt: John's Christology in Social-Science Perspective*, Philadelphia: Fortress Press.

—— (1988b) 'Bewitched in Galatia: Paul and Cultural Anthropology', *CBQ* 50: 72–100.

—— (1988c) 'A Symbolic Approach to Mark 7', *Forum* 4/3: 63–91.

—— (1988d) 'Unclean, Common, Polluted, and Taboo: A Short Reading Guide', *Forum* 4/4: 72–82.

—— (1990a) *Paul, In Other Words: A Cultural Reading of His Letters*, Louisville, KY: Westminster/John Knox Press.

—— (1990b) 'Mother and Maid in Art and Literature', *BTB* 20: 65–75.

—— (ed.) (1991) *The Social World of Luke-Acts: Models for Interpretation*, Peabody, MA: Hendrickson Publishers.

—— (1993) *2 Peter, Jude*, The Anchor Bible, volume 37C, New York: Doubleday.

Niebuhr, H. Richard (1951) *Christ and Culture*, New York: Harper & Row.

Oakman, Douglas E. (1985) 'Jesus and Agrarian Palestine: The Factor of Debt', *SBLSP*: 57–73.

—— (1986) *Jesus and the Economic Questions of His Day*, Lewiston, NY: Edwin Mellen Press.

—— (1987) 'The Buying Power of two Denarii', *Forum* 3/4: 33–8.

—— (1993) 'Cursing Fig Trees and Robbers' Dens: Pronouncement Stories Within Social-Systemic Perspective. Mark 11: 12–25 and Parallels', *Semeia* 64: 253–72.

O'Day, Gail R. (1990) 'Jeremiah 9: 22–23 and 1 Corinthians 1: 26–31: A Study in Intertextuality', *JBL* 109: 259–67.

Oldfather, W. A. (1979) *Epictetus*, 2 volumes, Loeb edition, Cambridge, MA: Harvard University Press.

Osiek, Carolyn (1984a) *What Are They Saying about the Social Setting of the New Testament?*, New York: Paulist Press.

—— (1984b) 'What Social Sciences Can Do to Scripture', *National Catholic Reporter*, October 19: 15–16.

—— (1992a) *What Are They Saying about the Social Setting of the New Testament?*, New York: Paulist Press, expanded and fully revised edition.

—— (1992b) 'The Social Sciences and the Second Testament: Problems and Challenges', *BTB* 22: 88–95.

Østergård, Uffe (1992) 'What is National and Ethnic Identity?', in Per Bilde, Troels Engberg-Pedersen, Lisa Hannestad and Jan Zahle (eds.) *Ethnicity in Hellenistic Egypt*, Aarhus: Aarhus University Press, 16–38.

Perelman, Chaim (1982) *The Realm of Rhetoric*, Notre Dame, IN/London: University of Notre Dame Press.

Perelman, Chaim and Olbrechts-Tyteca, L. (1969) *The New Rhetoric: A Treatise on Argumentation*, Notre Dame, IN: University of Notre Dame Press.

Petersen, Norman R. (1978) *Literary Criticism for New Testament Critics*, Philadelphia: Fortress Press.

—— (1980) 'When is the End not the End? Literary Reflections on the Ending of Mark's Narrative', *Int* 34: 151–66.

—— (1985) *Rediscovering Paul: Philemon and the Sociology of Paul's Narrative World*, Philadelphia: Fortress Press.

Pilch, John J. (1981) 'Biblical Leprosy and Body Symbolism', *BTB* 11: 108–13.

—— (1983) 'Community Foundation in the New Testament', *New Catholic World* 226/1352: 63–5.

—— (1984) *Galatians and Romans*, Collegeville Bible Commentary 6, Collegeville, MN: Liturgical Press.

—— (1985) 'Healing in Mark: A Social Science Analysis', *BTB* 15: 142–50.

—— (1986) 'The Health Care System in Matthew: A Social Science Analysis', *BTB* 16: 102–6.

—— (1988a) 'Interpreting Scripture: The Social Science Method', *The Bible Today* 26: 13–19.

—— (1988b) 'A Structural Functional Approach to Mark 7', *Forum* 4/3: 31–62.

—— (1988c) 'Understanding Biblical Healing: Selecting the Appropriate Model', *BTB* 18: 60–6.

—— (1989a) 'Sickness and Healing in Luke-Acts', *The Bible Today* 27: 21–8.

—— (1989b) 'Reading Matthew Anthropologically: Healing in Cultural Perspective', *Listening. Journal of Religion and Culture* 24: 278–89.

—— (1990) 'Marian Devotion and Wellness Spirituality: Bridging Cultures', *BTB* 20: 85–94.

—— (1991a) *Introducing the Cultural Context of the Old Testament*, Hear the Word, vol. 1, New York: Paulist Press.

—— (1991b) *Introducing the Cultural Context of the New Testament*, Hear the Word, vol. 2, New York: Paulist Press.

—— (1991c) 'Sickness and Healing in Luke-Acts', in J. H. Neyrey (ed.) *The Social World of Luke-Acts*, Peabody, MA: Hendrickson Publishers, 181–209.

—— (1991d) 'Health in the New Testament: Did Healings Happen?', *National Outlook* (Australia) 13 (June), no. 4: 12–14.

—— (1992a) '"Understanding Healing in the Social World of Early Christianity", BTB Readers Guide', *BTB* 22: 26–33.

—— (1992b) 'Lying and Deceit in the Letters to the Seven Churches. Perspectives from Cultural Anthropology', *BTB* 22: 126–35.

—— (1992c) 'Separating the Sheep from the Goats', *Professional Approaches for Christian Educators* 21 (April): 215–18.

—— (1992d) 'A Spirit Named Fever', *Professional Approaches for Christian Educators* 21 (May): 253–6.

—— (1993) 'Insights and Models for Understanding the Healing Activity of the Historical Jesus', *SBLSP:* 154–77.

Powell, Mark Allan (1990) *What Is Narrative Criticism?*, Minneapolis: Fortress Press.

Räisänen, Heikki (1990) *Beyond New Testament Theology: A Story and A Programme*, Philadelphia: Trinity Press International.

Reed, Walter L. (1993) *Dialogues of the Word: The Bible as Literature According to Bakhtin*, New York: Oxford University Press.

Rhoads, David and Michie, Donald (1982) *Mark As Story: An Introduction to the Narrative of a Gospel*, Philadelphia: Fortress Press.

Riches, John K. (1993) *A Century of New Testament Study*, Cambridge: Lutterworth Press.

Rimmon-Kenan, Shlomith (1983) *Narrative Fiction: Contemporary Poetics*, London/New York: Methuen.

Robbins, Vernon K. (1981) 'Summons and Outline in Mark: The Three-Step Progression', *NovT* 23: 97–114 = 1994a: 119–35.

—— (1982) 'Mark I.14–20: An Interpretation at the Intersection of Jewish and Graeco-Roman Traditions', *NTS* 28: 220–36 = 1994a: 137–54.

—— (1983) 'Pronouncement Stories and Jesus' Blessing of the Children: A Rhetorical Approach', *Semeia* 29: 43–74 = 1994a: 155–84.

—— (1984) *Jesus the Teacher: A Socio-Rhetorical Interpretation of Mark*, Philadelphia: Fortress Press; reprinted paperback with new introduction and additional indexes, Minneapolis: Fortress Press, 1992.

—— (1985a) 'Picking Up the Fragments: From Crossan's Analysis to Rhetorical Analysis', *Forum* 1/2: 31–64.

—— (1985b) 'Pragmatic Relations as a Criterion for Authentic Sayings', *Forum* 1/3: 35–63.

—— (1987) 'The Woman who Touched Jesus' Garment: Socio-Rhetorical Analysis of the Synoptic Accounts', *NTS* 33: 502–15 = 1994a: 185–200.

—— (1988a) 'The Chreia', in David E. Aune (ed.) *Greco-Roman Literature and the New Testament*, Atlanta: Scholars Press, 1–23.

—— (1988b) 'Pronouncement Stories from a Rhetorical Perspective', *Forum* 4/2: 3–32.

—— (1989) *Ancient Quotes and Anecdotes: From Crib to Crypt*, Sonoma, CA: Polebridge Press.

—— (1990) 'Interpreting the Gospel of Mark as a Jewish Document in a Graeco-Roman World', in Paul V. M. Flesher (ed.) *New Perspectives on Ancient Judaism*, Lanham, MD/New York/London: University Press of America, 47–72 = 1994a: 219–42.

—— (1991a) 'The Social Location of the Implied Author of Luke-Acts', in J. H. Neyrey (ed.) *The Social World of Luke-Acts*, Peabody, MA: Hendrickson Publishers, 305–32.

—— (1991b) 'Text and Context in Recent Studies of the Gospel of Mark', *RelSRev* 17: 16–23.

—— (1992a) *Jesus the Teacher: A Socio-Rhetorical Interpretation of Mark*, Minneapolis: Fortress Press, reprinted paperback with new introduction and additional indexes.

—— (1992b) 'The Reversed Contextualization of Psalm 22 in the Markan Crucifixion: A Socio-Rhetorical Analysis', in F. Van Segbroeck, C. M. Tuckett, G. Van Belle and J. Verheyden (eds.) *The Four Gospels 1992 Festschrift Frans Neirynck*, volume 2, BETL 100, Leuven: Leuven University Press, 1161–83.

—— (1992c) 'Using a Socio-Rhetorical Poetics to Develop a Unified Method: The Woman who Anointed Jesus as a Test Case', *SBLSP:* 302–19.

—— (ed.) (1993a) *The Rhetoric of Pronouncement*, Semeia 64, Atlanta: Scholars Press.

—— (1993b) 'Progymnastic Rhetorical Composition and Pre-Gospel Traditions: A New Approach', in Camille Focant (ed.) *The Synoptic Gospels: Source Criticism and the New Literary Criticism*, BETL 110, Leuven: Leuven University Press, 111–47.

—— (1993c) 'Rhetoric and Culture: Exploring Types of Cultural Rhetoric in a Text', in Stanley E. Porter and Thomas H. Olbricht (eds.) *Rhetoric and the New Testament: Essays from the 1992 Heidelberg Conference*, Sheffield: Sheffield Academic Press, 447–67.

—— (1994a) *New Boundaries in Old Territory: Forms and Social Rhetoric in Mark*, New York: Peter Lang Publishing.

—— (1994b) 'Socio-Rhetorical Criticism: Mary, Elizabeth, and the Magnificat as a Test Case', in Elizabeth Struthers Malbon and Edgar V. McKnight (eds.) *The New Literary Criticism and the New Testament*, Sheffield: Sheffield Academic Press, 164–209.

—— (1994c) 'The Ritual of Reading and Reading a Text as a Ritual: Observations on Mieke Bal's *Death & Dissymmetry*', in David Jasper and Mark Ledbetter (eds.) *In Good Company: Essays in Honor of Robert Detweiler*, Atlanta: Scholars Press, 385–401.

—— (1994d) 'Interpreting Miracle Culture and Parable Culture in Mark 4–11', *Svensk Exegetisk Årsbok* 59: 59–81.

—— (1994e) 'Oral, Rhetorical, and Literary Cultures: A Response', *Semeia* 65: 75–91.

—— (1995) 'Social-Scientific Criticism and Literary Studies: Prospects for Cooperation in Biblical Interpretation', in Philip F. Esler (ed.) *Modelling Early Christianity: Social-Scientific Studies of the New Testament in its Context*, London: Routledge, 274–89.

Roberts, Keith A. (1978) 'Toward A Generic Concept of Counter-Culture', *Sociological Focus* 11: 111–26.

Rohrbaugh, Richard L. (1978) *The Biblical Interpreter: An Agrarian Bible in an Industrial Age*, Philadelphia: Fortress Press.

—— (1984) 'Methodological Considerations in the Debate over the Social Class Status of Early Christians', *JAAR* 52: 519–46.

—— (1987a) 'Models and Muddles: Discussions of the Social Facets Seminar', *Forum* 3/2: 23–33.

—— (1987b) '"Social Location of Thought" as a Heuristic Construct in New Testament Study', *JSNT* 30: 103–19.

—— (1991a) '"The City in the Second Testament", BTB Readers Guide', *BTB* 21: 67–75.

—— (1991b) 'The Pre-Industrial City in Luke-Acts: Urban Social Relations', in J. H. Neyrey (ed.) *The Social World of Luke-Acts*, Peabody, MA: Hendrickson Publishers, 125–49.

Said, Edward (1979) *Orientalism*, New York: Vintage Books.

Schüssler Fiorenza, Elisabeth (1983) *In Memory of Her: A Feminist Theological Reconstruction of Christian Origins*, New York: Crossroad Press.

—— (1985a) *Bread Not Stone: The Challenge of Feminist Biblical Interpretation*, Boston: Beacon Press.

—— (1985b) 'Remembering the Past in Creating the Future: Historical-Critical Scholarship and Feminist Biblical Interpretation', in Adela Yarbro Collins (ed.) *Feminist Perspectives on Biblical Scholarship*, SBL Centennial Publications 10, Atlanta: Scholars Press, 43–63.

—— (1987) 'Rhetorical Situation and Historical Reconstruction in I Corinthians', *NTS* 33: 386–403.

—— (1988) 'The Ethics of Interpretation: De-Centering Biblical Scholarship', *JBL* 107: 3–17.

—— (1989) 'Biblical Interpretation and Critical Commitment', *Studia Theologica* 43: 1989.

—— (1992) *But She Said: Feminist Practices of Biblical Interpretation*, Boston: Beacon Press.

Schütz, John Howard (1975) *Paul and the Anatomy of Apostolic Authority*, SNTSMS 26, New York: Cambridge University Press.

Scott, Bernard Brandon (1989) *Hear Then the Parable: A Commentary on the Parables of Jesus*, Minneapolis: Fortress Press.

Scott, Bernard Brandon and Margaret E. Dean (1993) 'A Sound Map of the Sermon on the Mount', *SBLSP* 32: 726–39.

Shaw, Graham (1983) *The Cost of Authority: Manipulation and Freedom in the New Testament*, Philadelphia: Fortress Press.

Sisson, Russell B. (1994) *The Apostle as Athlete: A Socio-Rhetorical Interpretation of 1 Corinthians 9*, unpublished Ph.D. dissertation, Atlanta: Emory University.

Smelser, Neil J. (1992) 'Culture: Coherent or Incoherent', in Richard Münch and Neil J. Smelser (eds.) *Theory of Culture*, Berkeley: University of California Press, 3–28.

Smit, Joop F. M. (1994) '1 Cor 8, 1–6: A Rhetorical *Partitio*. A Contribution to the Coherence of 1 Cor 8, 1–1, 1', in R. Bieringer (ed.) *The Corinthian Correspondence*, BETL, Leuven: Leuven University Press.

Smith, Abraham (1995) 'A Second Step in African Biblical Interpretation: A Generic Reading Analysis of Acts 8: 26–40', in Fernando E. Segovia and Mary Ann Tolbert (eds.) *Reading from this Place (Volume One): Social Location and Biblical Interpretation in the United States*, Minneapolis: Fortress, 213–28.

Smith, Dennis E. (ed.) (1991) *How Gospels Begin*, Semeia 52, Atlanta: Scholars Press.

Smith, Jonathan Z. (1975) 'The Social Description of Early Christianity', *RelSRev* 1: 19–25.

—— (1978) *Map Is Not Territory: Studies in the History of Religions*, Leiden: Brill.

—— (1982) *Imaging Religion: From Babylon to Jonestown*, Chicago/ London: University of Chicago Press.

—— (1987) *To Take Place: Toward Theory in Ritual*, Chicago/London: University of Chicago Press.

—— (1990) *Drudgery Divine: On the Comparison of Early Christianities and the Religions of Late Antiquity*, Chicago: University of Chicago Press.

Snowden Jr., Frank M. (1976a) 'Ethiopians in the Greco-Roman World', in Martin L. Kilson and Robert I. Rottbert (eds.) *The African Diaspora: Interpretive Essays*, Cambridge, MA: Harvard University Press, 11–36.

—— (1976b) 'Iconographical Evidence on the Black Populations in Greco-Roman Antiquity', in Ladislas Bugner (ed.) *The Image of the Black in Western Art. From the Pharoah to the Fall of the Roman Empire*, vol. 1, New York: William Morrow, 133–245.

—— (1979) *Blacks in Antiquity: Ethiopians in the Greco-Roman Experience*, Cambridge, MA: Harvard University Press.

Staley, Jeffrey Lloyd (1988) *The Print's First Kiss: A Rhetorical Investigation of the Implied Reader in the Fourth Gospel*, SBLDS 82, Atlanta: Scholars Press.

—— (1995) *Reading with a Passion: Rhetoric, Autobiography, and the American West in the Gospel of John*, New York: Continuum.

Stark, Werner (1967) *Sectarian Religion*, New York: Fordham University Press.

Stock, Augustine (1989) *The Method and Message of Mark*, Wilmington, DE: Michael Glazier.

Stowers, Stanley K. (1991) 'Friends and Enemies in the Politics of Heaven: Reading Theology in Philippians', in Jouette M. Bassler (ed.) *Pauline Theology, volume 1: Thessalonians, Philippians, Galatians, Philemon*, Minneapolis: Fortress Press, 105–21.

—— (1995) 'Romans 7.7–25 as a Speech-In-Character (προσωποποιία)', in Troels Engberg-Pedersen (ed.) *Paul in His Hellenistic Context*, Minneapolis: Fortress Press, 180–202.

Tannehill, Robert C. (1975) *The Sword of His Mouth*, Philadelphia: Fortress Press; Missoula, MT: Scholars Press.

—— (1986/9) *The Narrative Unity of Luke-Acts: A Literary Interpretation*, two volumes, Philadelphia: Fortress Press.

Theissen, Gerd (1982) *The Social Setting of Pauline Christianity: Essays on Corinth*, ed. and trans. John H. Schütz, Philadelphia: Fortress Press.

—— (1987) *Psychological Aspects of Pauline Theology*, Philadelphia: Fortress Press.

Thomas Brook (1991) *The New Historicism and Other Old-Fashioned Topics*, Princeton, NJ: Princeton University Press.

Tompkins, Jane P. (1980) 'The Reader in History', in J. P. Tompkins (ed.) *Reader-Response Criticism: From Formalism to Post-Structuralism*, Baltimore/London: Johns Hopkins University Press, 201–32.

Trible, Phyllis (1978) *God and the Rhetoric of Sexuality*, Philadelphia: Fortress Press.

—— (1984) *Texts of Terror: Literary-Feminist Readings of Biblical Narratives*, Philadelphia: Fortress Press.

Tyler, Stephen A. (1987) *The Unspeakable: Discourse, Dialogue, and Rhetoric in the Postmodern World*, Madison, WI: University of Wisconsin Press.

Van Iersel, Bas (1989) *Reading Mark*, trans. W. H. Bisscheroux, Edinburgh: T. & T. Clark.

Van Tilborg, Sjef (1993) *Imaginative Love in John*, Biblical Interpretation Series 2, Leiden: Brill.

Via Jr., Dan O. (1967) *The Parables: Their Literary and Existential Dimension*, Philadelphia: Fortress Press.

Vickers, Brian (1988) *In Defence of Rhetoric*, Oxford: Clarendon Press.

Vorster, Willem (1989) 'The Reader in the Text: Narrative Material', *Semeia* 48: 21–39.

Wachob, Wesley H. (1994) *The Rich in Faith and the Poor in Spirit: The Socio-Rhetorical Function of a Saying of Jesus in the Epistle of James*, unpublished Ph.D. dissertation, Atlanta: Emory University.

Watson, Duane F. and Hauser, Alan J. (1994) *Rhetorical Criticism of the Bible. A Comprehensive Bibliography with Notes on History and Method*, Biblical Interpretation Series 4, Leiden: Brill.

Wevers, John William (ed.) (1977) *Deuteronomium*, Septuaginta III, 2, Göttingen: Vandenhoeck & Ruprecht.

Wilde, James A. (1974) *A Social Description of the Community Reflected in the Gospel of Mark*, Ann Arbor, MI: Xerox University Microfilms.

—— (1978) 'The Social World of Mark's Gospel: A Word about Method', *SBLSP*, vol. 2: 47–67.

Wilder, Amos N. (1956) 'Scholars, Theologians, and Ancient Rhetoric', *JBL* 75: 1–11.

—— (1964) *Early Christian Rhetoric: The Language of the Gospel*, New York: Harper & Row, reprinted Cambridge, MA: Harvard University Press, 1971.

Wilson, Bryan R. (1969) 'A Typology of Sects', in Roland Robertson (ed.) *Sociology of Religion*, Baltimore: Penguin Books, 361–83.

—— (1973) *Magic and the Millenium: A Sociological Study of Religious Movements of Protest Among Tribal and Third-World Peoples*, New York: Harper & Row.

Wordelman, Amy L. (1994) 'The Gods Have Come Down: Images of Historical Lycaonia and the Literary Construction of Acts 14', unpublished Ph.D. dissertation, Princeton, NJ: Princeton University.

Wuellner, Wilhelm H. (1973) 'The Sociological Implications of I Corinthians 1: 26–28 Reconsidered', in E. A. Livingstone (ed.) *Studia Evangelica VI*, *TU* 112, Berlin: Akademie Verlag.

—— (1976) 'Paul's Rhetoric of Argumentation in Romans: An Alternative to the Donfried–Karris Debate over Romans', *CBQ* 38: 330–51 = in K. P. Donfried (ed.) *The Romans Debate*, Minneapolis: Augsburg, 1977, 152–74.

—— (1978) 'Der Jakobusbrief im Licht der Rhetorik und Textpragmatik', *Linguistica Biblica* 43: 5–6.

—— (1979) 'Greek Rhetoric and Pauline Argumentation', in W. R. Schoedel and R. L. Wilken (eds.) *Early Christian Literature and the Classical Intellectual Tradition*, R. M. Grant Festschrift, Paris: Beauchesne, 177–88.

—— (1986) 'Paul as Pastor. The Function of Rhetorical Questions in First Corinthians', in A. Vanhoye (ed.) *L'Apôtre Paul. Personalité, Style et Conception du Ministère*, *BETL* 73, Leuven: Leuven University Press, 49–77.

—— (1987) 'Where Is Rhetorical Criticism Taking Us?', *CBQ* 49: 448–63.

—— (1988) 'The Rhetorical Structure of Luke 12 in its Wider Context', *Neot* 22: 283–310.

—— (1991) 'Rhetorical Criticism: Rhetorical Criticism and its Theory in Culture-Critical Perspective: The Narrative Rhetoric of John 11', in P. J. Martin and J. H. Petzer (eds.) *Text and Interpretation: New Approaches in the Criticism of the New Testament*, New Testament Tools and Studies 15, Leiden: Brill, 171–85.

—— (1993) 'Biblical Exegesis in the Light of the History and Historicity of Rhetoric and the Nature of the Rhetoric of Religion', in Stanley E. Porter and Thomas H. Olbricht (eds.) *Rhetoric and the New Testament: Essays from the 1992 Heidelberg Conference*, Sheffield: Sheffield Academic Press, 492–513.

Wuthnow, Robert (1992) 'Infrastructure and Superstructure: Revisions in Marxist Sociology of Culture', in Richard Münch and Neil J. Smelser (eds.) *Theory of Culture*, Berkeley/Los Angeles/Oxford: University of California Press, 145–70.

Yinger, J. Milton (1960) 'Contraculture and Subculture', *American Sociological Review* 25: 625–35.

—— (1982) *Countercultures: The Promise and the Peril of a World Turned Upside Down*, New York: Free Press.

INDEX OF SCRIPTURES AND ANCIENT TEXTS

Old Testament

Genesis
  6.1–24 106
  6.2 106
  6.4 106
  7.1 106
  7.7 106
Exodus
  3.2–6 105
  3.6 105
  34.28 107
Leviticus
  19.18 138
Deuteronomy
  1–34 122
  6.4 138
  6.13 104
  8.3 103
  12.1–25.3 83
  23.1 217
  25.4 121, 124, 129
  25.5–19 83
1 Samuel
  2.10 101
  21.3 105
  21.1–6 105
2 Samuel
  6.6–7 60
1 Kings 17–2 Kings 2 110
1 Kings 19.8 107
Psalm
  34.8 107
  68.31 217
  91.11 103
  91.11–12 103
Isaiah
  29.28–9 140
  35.5–6 140
  42.18 140
  53 108, 217, 218
  56.4 217
  56.7–8 217
  61.1 140
Jeremiah
  9.22–3 97–100
  9.24 104

New Testament

Matthew
  1–28 56, 59
  3.16 59
  4.9–10 104
  5.43–5 138
  5.48 138
  7.17–27 138
  8.9 180
  9.20–2 59
  10.7 123
  10.9–10 122
  10.10 123
  11.4 139, 140
  11.19 106
  15.21–8 215
  19.21 138
  22.3–4 180
  22.37–9 138
  24.46–51 180
  25.14–29 180
Mark
  1–16 3, 48, 52, 56, 57, 59, 109, 113,
    147, 150, 153, 166, 209, 210;
    abrupt ending 52
  1.10 59

1.13 52
1.14–15 52
1.15 151
1.16 52
1.31 52
1.45 153
2.25–6 105
3.17 175
4 113, 114, 152, 171
4.1–9 114
4.1–20 171
4.4–6 114
4.6 114
4.7 115
4.8 114
4.11 210
4.13–20 114
4.14 114, 115
4.14–17 114
4.15–20 114
4.18–19 115
4.17 171
4.19 172
4.18–20 115
4.20 114, 115, 171
4.21–22 171
4.24–25 171
4.26–32 171
4.30–2 115
5.20 153
6.15 110
7.24–30 215
9.18 94
9.21 94
10.17 94
10.17a 94
10.17b 94
10.17–22 94
10.17b–19, 20–1 94
10.18 95
10.18–19 94
10.20 94
10.21 52
10.21a 94
10.21–2 94
10.22 94
10.45 52
10.52 153
11.23 151

13 109
13.24–5 151
14.3–9 215
16.8 209
Luke
1–24 59
1.1–4 216
1.26–38 51
1.26–56 49, 51, 158
1.36–41 51
1.43–56 51
1.44 216
2.10 216
3.6 218
3.22 59
4.1–2 107
4.4 103
4.7 104
4.8 104
4.9–11 103
4.18 216
6.27–8 138
6.37–8 46, 47, 51
7.8 180
7.22 139, 140
7.33 106
7.36–50 162
7.37 162
7.39 162, 163
7.40 162
7.47 162
8.29 216
8.39 216
8.46 60
10.7 123
10.7–8 122
10.9 123
11–19 162
11.39 166
12.41 180
12.43–6 180
13.24 180
13.29 218
14 166
14.1–24 165
14.17 180
14.21–4 180
15.4–7 216
17.26–7 106

19.6 216
19.12–23 180
19.37 216
24.41 216
24.47 218
24.48 216
John
1–21 54, 118, 144, 153
1.19–3.36 54
3.8 153
4–21 54
4.7–30 153
4.39–42 153
4.14 153
5 119
7 119
7.50–2 153
9 118, 119, 152
9.1–41 153
9.22 118
9.28 118
11 152
12.42 118
16.2a 118
20.24–9 153
Acts
1–28 174, 175
1 216
1.8c 218
1.18 216
1.21–2 216
2.47 216
4.8–10 216
4.33 216
5 162
7.30–2 104, 107
7.55 216
8 216, 217
8.8 216
8.9–13 157
8.18–24 157
8.27–8 217
8.33 220
8.39 220
10.11–12 216
10.39–41 216
13.4–10 216
13.6–12 157
14 201, 205

14.8–10 207
14.11 204, 206
14.12 110, 162
14.13 204
14.15–17 207
14.17 207
14.18 206
14.19 206
16.6–7 216
16.33 216
19.19 157
22.14–15 216
23 162
26 162
28.2 203
28.4 203
Romans
7.7–25 63
13.9 138
1 Corinthians
1–16 66, 81, 98, 100, 104
1.2 225
1.10 224
1.10–13 187
1.10–17 196
1.10–4.21 196, 199, 226
1.11 188
1.12 187
1.16 225
1.17 196
1.18–2.5 197
1.18–4.5 198
1.21–5 179
1.23 137, 177
1.26 97, 100
1.26–31 98, 99, 104
1.31 104, 183
2.2–3 179
2.6–3.5 197
2.16 224
3 226
3.1 198
3.2 198
3.5–9 177
3.8 198
3.9 225
3.16–17 225
4.6–13 225
4.8–13 226

4.14–21 196, 225
4.16 196
4.16–21 198
6.9–20 140
6.19 225
7 233
7.20–4 179
7.23 233
8.1–11.1 93
8.13 93
9 3, 24, 43, 65, 66, 692–71, 77, 80,
   81, 89, 93, 120, 122–4, 126–30,
   137, 139, 142, 176, 178, 182, 220,
   221, 222, 223, 229, 230, 231, 232,
   233
9.1 67, 73, 86, 89, 228
9.1–2 67, 71, 226
9.2 74, 224
9.2–3 224
9.3 69, 70, 88, 90, 230
9.3–6 84, 87
9.3–13 93
9.3–14 176
9.4 90, 123
9.4–6 67, 74, 86, 139
9.4–10 71
9.4–12 86
9.6 125, 225
9.7 67, 75, 87, 90, 123, 127
9.8 224, 230
9.8–10 75, 86, 90, 129, 130
9.8–12 82
9.8–12a 87
9.8a 82
9.9 67, 76, 86, 121, 224, 230
9.9–10 121
9.9a 83
9.9b–10 75, 83
9.10 67, 76, 127, 226
9.10–11 69
9.11 71, 125
9.11–12 67, 76, 225
9.11–12a 83
9.11–13 67
9.11–18 71
9.12 76, 125, 141, 226, 228
9.12a 84
9.12b 84, 86, 87
9.12b–18 84, 87, 88

9.13 76, 90, 123, 127
9.13–14 84
9.14 67, 69, 76, 86, 90, 122, 123,
   137, 139, 177, 181, 223, 224
9.15 76, 85, 125, 226
9.15–16 90
9.15–17 85
9.15–23 67
9.15–27 225
9.15a 85
9.15b 85
9.16 140, 233
9.16–17 85
9.17 69, 86, 90, 123, 127, 230
9.18 76, 86, 123, 124, 128
9.19 69, 71, 86, 90, 127, 133, 177,
   227, 233
9.19–22 125, 176
9.19–23 79, 86, 87, 227
9.20 71, 86, 127, 128
9.20–23 227
9.20–25 71
9.21 86
9.22 69, 86, 227
9.22b–23 86
9.23 69, 227
9.24 67, 71, 87, 88, 91, 130, 228
9.24–7 79, 87, 88, 126, 131, 180
9.25 67, 69, 87, 131, 228
9.26 71, 131
9.26–27 228
9.27 131, 228
11 127
11.2 226
11.17–34 118
11.18 225
11.20–21a 116
11.34 225
12.9–10 176
12.27 226
13 177
14.35 225
15 127
15.42 131
15.5 75
15.50 140
15.51–2 177
15.53 131
16.1 225

16.19 225
2 Corinthians
  10.17 104
Galatians
  5.13–14 138
  5.14 138
1 Thessalonians
  1–5 157
  1.6 199
  2 111
  2.1 112
  2.2 111
  2.3 112
  2.5–6 112
  2.7 112
James
  1–5 137
  1.4 138
  1.8 138
  1.25 138
  2.5 140
  2.12 138
1 Peter
  1–5 154, 155, 193
  1.1 156
  2.3 107
  2.4–25 156
  2.11 156
  2.12 156
  2.13–17 156
  2.18–3.7 156
  2.22–25a 107
  3.1-2 156
  3.1–12 156
  3.13 156
  4.5 156
  4.7 156
  4.17 156
  5.1–5a 156

Apocrypha and Pseudepigrapha
4 Ezra 109, 158

Other Ancient Sources
Aristotle, *Rhetoric*
  1.2.8–22,2.22 59
  1.2.21–2 151
  1.3.7–9 159
  2.19–24 159

Epictetus, *Discourses*
  1.24.1–2 134
  2.18.28 135
  3.13.11 134
  3.20.9 135
  3.22.23–5 134
  3.22.40–2 135
  3.22.46–8 134
  3.22.48 233
  3.22.51–3 135
  3.22.81 134
  3.22.95 196
  3.24.51–2 135
  3.24.65 135
  3.24.71 135
  3.26.38–9 136
  3.26-27–31 135
  4.1.11 136
  4.1.35–6 136
  4.1.55 136
  4.1.6.3 136
  4.1.89 137
  4.3.9 134
  4.9.17 135
Hippocrates, *Law* III 113, 114
Homer, *Iliad and Odyssey* 110
Ovid, *Metamorphoses* 205
Philo, *Allegorical Interpretations*
  III.48 130
  III.201 132
  III.202 132
Change of Names 81–2 131
De Agricultura 180 130
Every Good Man Is Free
  23–4 132
  35–42 133
Migration of Abraham 133 130
On Dreams I.129–30 131
On Joseph 138 131
On Rewards and Punishments
  4–5 131
On the Virtues 130, 146
Worse Attacks the Better 41–2 131
Plutarch, *Lives* 63
Rhetorica ad Herrenium 82
Rhetorica ad Alexandrinus 166, 182, 189
Seneca, *Epistles* 38.2 114, 115

INDEX OF MODERN
AUTHORS

Abrams, M. H. 19
Achtemeier, Paul 19, 167, 170
Alter, Robert 46, 48
Anderson, Janice Capel 208, 213

Bakhtin, Mikhail, 33, 34, 143
Bal, Mieke 36
Barrett, C. K. 221
Barth, Fredrik 5, 6, 173
Barthes, Roland 33, 34, 36, 109
Berger, Adolf 154
Berger, Peter 4, 193
Berlin, Adele 63
Betz, Hans Dieter 184
Bhabha, Homi K. 170
Boers, Hendrikus 2, 15
Boissevain, Jeremy 187, 188
Booth, Wayne 54
Bouvard, Margarite 170
Braun, Willi 165, 166
Brown, Peter 146
Brown, Richard Harvey 8
Burke, Kenneth 33, 34, 36, 48, 59

Calvin, John 202, 203
Carney, Thomas F. 243
Castelli, Elisabeth O. 194, 196, 197,
    198, 199, 201, 208, 211, 222, 231
Chatman, Seymour 28, 54, 72, 194
Childs, Brevard S. 97
Chopp, Rebecca S. 11
Clark, Elizabeth A. 207
Conzelmann, Hans 234

Crossan, John Dominic 64
Culpepper, R. Alan 54, 55

Davis, David Brion 193
Daube, David 61
Dean, Margaret E. 48, 56
de Beaugrande, Robert-Alain 27
Delorme, Jean 109
de Man, Paul 208, 209, 210
Derrida, Jacques 208, 209, 210
Detweiler, Robert 1
Dilthey, Wilhelm 13
Draisma, S. 96, 108
Dressler, Wolfgang Ulrich 27
Dreyfus, Hubert L. 12, 36, 195

Eagleton, T. 7, 36
Eliot, T. S. 97
Elliott, John H. 5, 36, 154, 155, 159,
    166, 193, 225
Esler, Philip 157, 158

Felder, Cain 219
Fiore, Benjamin 195
Fishbane, Michael 97, 98
Foucault, Michel 36, 195, 197, 208
Fowler, Robert 56–8
Fowler, Roger 8
Frow, John 34

Gager, John G. 146, 147, 192, 193
Garrett, Susan 157
Geertz, Clifford 4, 5, 8, 35, 36, 129

Gordon, Milton M. 168
Gourdriaan, Koen 5, 173
Gowler, David B. 54, 55, 162, 163, 164
Greenblatt, Stephen 212
Grimes, Joseph E. 27

Hays, Richard B. 101, 102, 108
Held, Heinz Joachim 60
Hernadi, Paul 34
Hochman, Baruch 55
Hock, Ronald F. 59, 103, 105
Hockman, Baruch 55
Hollander, John 101, 102
Horsley, Richard 134
Hutcheon, Linda 30

Jacobson, Arland 139
Jameson, Frederic 36
Jewett, Robert 157
Jobling, David 207
Johnson, Luke Timothy 8
Johnson, Mark 8
Judge, E. A. 181, 184, 185

Kelber, Werner 56
Kennedy, George A. 50, 59, 151
Kloppenborg, John S. 123, 159, 180
Krieger, Murray 19
Kristeva, Julia 30, 143
Krondorfer, Björn 8
Kuhn, Thomas S. 1

Lategan, Bernard C. 6
Lausberg, Heinrich 167
Lawson, E. Thomas 13
Lentricchia, Frank 9
Luckmann, Thomas 193

McCauley, Robert N. 13
Mack, Burton L. 59, 61, 62, 77, 80, 100, 106, 113, 115, 116, 152, 164, 167, 170, 172, 173, 182
McLaughlin, Thomas 9
Malbon, Elizabeth Struthers 63

Malherbe, Abraham 110–13, 116, 134, 164, 178, 183
Malina, Bruce J. 36, 89, 159, 166
Martin, Clarice J. 216, 217, 218, 219, 220
Martin, Dale 127, 128, 133, 134, 182, 231
Martyn, J. Louis 118–120
Meeks, Wayne A. 8, 144, 145
Michie, Donald 54
Mitchell, Margaret M. 93, 100
Montrose, Louis 42
Moore, Stephen D. 208, 209, 211, 212, 213
Morgan, Thaïs 33, 109, 110
Moxnes, Halvor 166, 181

Na, Kang-Yup 13
Neirynck, Frans 48
Neyrey, Jerome H. 36, 159, 166, 194
Niebuhr, H. Richard 4

O'Day, Gail R. 97–101, 104, 108
Olbrechts-Tyteca, L. 61, 75, 86
O'Neil, Edward N. 59, 103, 105
Ong, Walter 56
Østergård, Uffe 5, 173

Perelman, Chaim 54, 75, 86
Petersen, Norman R. 19, 50, 179
Pippin, Tina 207
Powell, Mark Allan 21

Rabinow, Paul 12, 36, 195
Räisänen, Heikki 2, 15
Ramsey, William Mitchell 202, 203
Reed, Walter L. 34
Rhoads, David 54
Riches, John K. 2, 15
Rimmon-Kenan, Shlomith 28
Robbins, Vernon K. 1, 3, 6, 9, 12, 20, 35, 45, 56, 59–63, 77, 80, 100, 103, 106, 113, 115, 151, 152, 158, 160, 164, 167, 170, 171, 182, 194, 199, 212, 243
Roberts, Keith A. 151, 152, 166, 167, 169, 170, 185
Rohrbaugh, Richard L. 166

Said, Edward 201, 202
Sanders, James A. 97
Schüssler Fiorenza 194, 200, 201,
   207, 211, 215, 222, 231
Schütz, John Howard 195, 198
Scott, Bernard Brandon 48, 56, 160,
   161, 162, 166
Shaw, Graham 195, 231
Sisson, Russell B. 77, 80, 82, 128,
   130, 131, 134, 139, 181
Smelser, Neil J. 4, 5
Smit, Joop F. M. 93
Smith, Abraham 220
Smith, D. E. 50
Smith, Jonathan Z. 145, 146, 201
Snowden, Frank M., Jr. 218
Staley, Jeffrey 54
Stowers, Stanley K. 63, 164
Stark, Werner 170

Tannehill, Robert 46–8, 64, 65
Theissen, Gerd 12, 115–18
Thomas, Brook 212
Tompkins, Jane P. 57

Trible, Phyllis 46
Tyler, Stephen A. 18

Van Iersel, Bas 52
Van Tilborg, Sjef 54
Van Wolde, Ellen 109
Via, Dan O. 64
Vickers, Brian 34, 45
Voelz, James 109
Vorster, Willem S. 6, 27, 108, 109

Wachob, Wesley H, 139, 140
Wevers, John William 104
Wilde, James A. 147–52
Wilder, Amos N. 2, 4, 6, 7, 15, 16,
   64
Wilson, Bryan R. 35, 147, 153, 154,
   155, 157, 158
Wordelman, Amy L. 201–7, 211
Wuellner, Wilhelm H. 61, 73, 82, 85,
   97, 142, 182–8
Wuthnow, Robert 49

Yinger, Milton 170, 169

INDEX OF SUBJECTS

action-set culture: *see* culture
aesthetic texture: *see* inner texture,
    sensory-aesthetic
African-American interpretation 1,
    217
analogy 53,61, 76–8, 82, 84, 87–8,
    122, 131, 166
anthropology: critical 201; methods
    5; theory, *see* theory
archeology 204–5
argumentative texture: *see* inner
    texture
athlete 180, 185, 227
audience: implied 29; real 21–2,
    29–30
author(s) 23; as historical figures 39;
    implied 21–4, 28, 29, 58, 73; real
    21, 22, 29, 30
authoritative traditions 200–7, 221–2
axis: *see* rhetorical; mimetic axis

baptismal self-understanding 200
bi-cultural setting 236
binary oppositions: *see* oppositions
boasting: *see* self-esteem
body 90; and spirituality 91;
    concrete circumstances 7, 8, 19;
    narrator's 86–91, 123; reader's 89,
    90; social and historical aspects 7,
    8; social identity 90, 91
body–mind 7–8; dualism 208;
    interpretation 14, 26–8
border or boundary 9, 11, 18, 20, 22,
    66, 96, 98, 99, 109; around a text
    21; attitudinal 5, 6; author's 21;
    creating and dismantling 20;

disciplinary 98; in and around
    texts 20, 101; language 19, 20;
    poetic 19, 97, 208–9, rhetorical 46;
    to the world 21
broker: *see* patron/client/broker

canon criticism 15, 97
categories: *see* final cultural
    categories
challenge-riposte 162
characters 19, 22, 28, 29, 32
chiasmus 212
chreia 61–3, 94–5, 103–5, 166
city and countryside 159
client: *see* patron/client/broker
common topics: *see* topics
communication 23, 27, 28, 45
complete argument 80–8
conceptual subculture: *see* cultural
    texture
confirmation 77, 79–81
conflict 159
contexts, multiple 9
contraculture: *see* cultural texture
contrary 53, 84, 86–8
conversionist argumentation: *see*
    social texture
counterculture: *see* cultural texture
cultural: anthropology 2,4; definition
    110; dimensions 1–4, 7, 9, 11, 12,
    14, 81, 95; intertexture, *see*
    intertexture
cultural texture: contracultural
    170–4, 184; countercultural 147,
    158, 169–74, 183–7, 199, 241–2;
    dominant 168, 172, 185, 197;

liminal 170; subcultural 168–74, 183, 185–6, 241; subcultural conceptual 168; subcultural ethnic 168; subcultural network 168; see final cultural categories

culture: action-set 188; Christian 4–5, 63; coalition 5, 242; definition 4; extended 5, 6, 129; faction 187–8; Greco-Roman 141; Greek 134; Jewish diaspora 130, 133, 141; local 5, 6, 35, 129, 167; Mediterranean 129; New Testament 5; Palestinian Jesus 137–40; Pauline 138; primary 4,5; rhetorical 56, 57

Cynic discourse 110–13, 134–7, 142, 172, 227, 241

death 173, 180
deconstruction 33, 210
difference: ideology of 201
differentiations: strategies of 222; system of 195, 223
disciplinary: interpretation 98, 230–1, 235; methods 11, 97
discourse 112; as part power and practice 12; authoritative sphere 84; Christian, within Mediterranean society and culture 64; cultural 111; Greco-Roman 129, 133, 137; Jewish diaspora 129, 130, 142; marginal 11; moral philosophers 111, 112, 137; of emancipation 11; Palestinian Jesus 137, 140; Palestinian Jewish 129; Pauline 129, 130, 133, 137, 138, 141, 142; Philonic 132, 133; religious 14; richly textured 3; Stoic 110, 111; symbolic 2; that associates 76, 87; that authorizes 63, 74, 75, 83, 84, 87; that differentiates 76; that establishes rights 75
dissociation: see differentiations
dominant culture: see cultural texture
dropsy 165
dyadic personality 159

education: see paideia
echo 30, 31, 33, 35, 96–8, 101, 102, 108–18, 119, 129
eclectic interpretation 233–4
elaboration: see rhetorical
environment: complex 14; integrated 3; interactive 14, 30
epideictic 88–9
eschatology 2
ethics of accountability 207
ethnic identity 5, 216–20
ethnic subculture: see cultural texture
ethnographic analysis 218
example 53, 61, 75, 79, 82, 86–8, 166
exclusion from the synagogue 119
exegesis 8, 10

faction culture: see culture
feminist criticism 1, 194–201, 215–16, 222–9
final cultural categories 167–74, 182–8
folklore 2
form criticism 14, 32, 53
four arenas: see texture
freedom 185, 228, 230, 233

geo-cultural: location 203; map 218
gnostic manipulationist argumentation: see social texture
gospel 139; preaching the gospel 139, 140, 142

healing 36, 159
hermeneutics of suspicion 219
historical: and theological referents 8; criticism 8, 12–15, 29, 39, 42, 120; dimensions 3, 7, 11, 14, 95, 120; intertexture, see intertexture; method 8
historiography 240–3
history of religions 15, 146; see Religionsgeschichtliche Schule
honor and shame 36, 159, 162–4, 183, 199
hospitality 36, 159, 162–4
household 159, 193

ideological texture 3, 21, 24, 36–40, 192–236, 239–41, 244
ideology 1–3, 10–12, 14, 36, 81, 95, 99–101, 155, 193–4; methods 1
imitation 23, 24
implied author 194
information: implied 21–3
inner texture: 3, 21–4, 27–30, 32, 44–95, 98, 119, 123, 154, 162, 212–13, 216–17, 238, 243; argumentative 46, 53, 58–66, 71, 77–89, 92, 93, 158; narrational 46, 53–9, 63, 64, 66, 71, 72–7, 92–5, 158, 222–3; opening–middle–closing 46, 50–3, 59, 64, 66, 70–2, 76, 77, 81, 88, 92–4, 158, 160; progressive 69–70, 92, 158, 160; repetitive 66–9, 92, 154, 158, 160, 163; repetitive–progressive 46–50, 53, 58, 64, 66, 68–72, 77, 92, 160; sensory–aesthetic 46, 53, 64–6, 89–92
institutions 159, 192–3
intellectual discourse 10–13, 207–15, 229–32, 240
interdisciplinary: approach 13, 14, 41, 120; as ritual 20; interpretation 155, 229
interpretive analytics 11–13, 15, 97, 243
interrogatio 79, 82
intertextual investigation 33
intertexture 3, 21, 24, 30–3, 83, 92, 96–143, 212–14, 217, 238, 243; cultural 6, 8, 9, 20, 83, 92, 96, 102, 108–15, 126, 128, 129–43, 199; historical 6, 8, 9, 20, 96, 102, 118–20, 124–7, 158; oral–scribal 83, 92, 96, 97–108, 119–25, 154, 158, 199, 218; social 6, 8, 9, 20, 96, 102, 115–18, 119, 126–8, 158
intracultural phenomena 185
intrinsic approach 29
introversionist argumentation: see social texture
irony 198

judgments 166
judicial defense 88

kingdom of God 161
kinship 159, 162, 199

language 31, 32; as inner fabric of society 1, 2, 8, 9, 19, 39; as symbolic action 34, 46; implied 21, 23; patterns 144–6; social and historical aspects 19; textualized 113
liberation theology 1, 216–20
liminal culture: see cultural texture
limited good 159, 162, 199
linguistic: dimensions 2; methods 1, 14
literary: dimensions 1–3; methods 1, 10, 12, 14, 22, 23
logic 144

materialist methods 1
means 195
metaphor 160–1; of texts as windows and mirrors 18, 19
millenialist cults 147
mimesis 23, 24, 34
mimetic axis 23, 34
mind/body: see body–mind

narrational texture: see inner texture
narratology 55: narratological analysis 54, 62; narratorial texture 163
narrator 22, 28, 29, 58, 66, 73, 105
network subculture: see cultural texture
networks of meanings and effects 8, 9, 14, 18–20, 22, 30, 65, 66, 71
New Criticism 29, 58
New Hermeneutic 1

objectives 195, 223–4
objectivist argumentation 150
opening–middle–closing texture: see inner texture
oppositions 198; binary 208; inside/outside 210, 228
oral–scribal intertexture: see intertexture
orientalizing ideology 201–3

parables 160–3, 166, 175, 210
patron/client/broker 36, 159, 161–5,
    181, 183, 186
patterns: see language
paideia 152, 171, 181–2
personal pronouns 66–8, 72–4, 86–8
pharisee 164–6
polarity 86–8
poststructuralism 208
power 200; and practice 11–13;
    construction of 197;
    institutionalization of 195, 199,
    225; rationalization of 195, 197,
    226–9; relations 195, 197, 215
premises: unstated 59, 80–5
progressive texture: see inner texture
pronouncement stories 173
prosopopoiia 63
psychoanalysis 33
psychological texture 12, 13
purity 159, 162, 199

Q: discourse 172–3, 191; tradition
    123, 124, 139

rationale 51, 71, 77–81, 172, 185–6
reader: and ideology 38; implied
    22–4, 29, 73, 74, 76; real 21, 22,
    29, 30
reader response criticism 56
reciprocity 162, 198
recitation 102–7, 121–4
reconfiguration 102, 107–8, 111, 123,
    124, 127, 137, 141
recontextualization 102, 107, 108,
    111
redaction criticism 10, 14, 32, 53
reference 8, 108, 110, 111, 113,
    115–17
reformist argumentation: see social
    texture
relation: of Christianity to culture
    4
relationist argumentation 151–2
Religionsgeschichtliche Schule 2, 9,
    14, 15, 97, 101; see history of
    religions
repetitive texture: see inner texture

repetitive–progressive texture: see
    inner texture
revolutionist argumentation: see
    social texture
rhetorical 2, 3, 7, 8, 14; axis of
    communication 23, 29, 34;
    elaboration 62, 77, 165; methods 1,
    10, 12, 14; theory 164; topics 34
Russian formalism 29, 33

sameness: ideology of 196–7, 224
self-esteem/self-praise 181–4
semiotic methods 14
sensory–aesthetic texture: see inner
    texture
separation, hierarchical 198
sickness 159
slavery 179, 185, 228
social 1–3, 7, 9, 11, 12, 14, 81, 95, 120
social and cultural texture 3, 21, 24,
    33–6, 144–191, 206, 212, 214, 239,
    243–4; see cultural texture; final
    cultural categories; social texture;
    topics
social intertexture: see intertexture
social location 194
social-psychological studies 146
social-scientific criticism 55, 153, 159
social texture: conversionist 147,
    150–3, 155–7, 172–4, 176–8, 180,
    190, 206, 220, 241–2; gnostic
    manipulationist 148–9, 151–2,
    171–2, 178–9, 180, 189–90, 199,
    241–2; introversionist 148, 150,
    173, 176, 189–90, 241; reformist
    149–50, 152, 174, 176, 242;
    revolutionist 147–52, 156, 172–3,
    177–8, 190, 242–3; thaumaturgic
    149, 151–3, 157, 167, 170–2, 176,
    206, 241–2; utopian 149–52,
    177–8, 190
sociological 3; exegesis 153; methods
    1, 5, 12; theory, see theory
socio-rhetorical criticism 3, 10, 16;
    function of 11; goal of 3, 11–13,
    23; relationships 38
socio-rhetorical model 21
source criticism 14, 32, 53
specific social topics: see topics

steward 179, 181
strategies 1–3, 9, 13, 15, 16
structuralist: linguistics 33; methods 1, 10, 14
subculture: *see* cultural texture
subdisciplinary interpretation 231, 233–4
subject–object 28
subjectivist argumentation 150
subordinate people 197, 200
syllogism 59, 80–3, 85, 88
symbol 2
symbolic universe 200
systematic approach 2, 3, 9, 12, 19, 20

table fellowship 159
tapestry 14, 18
temple 159
text: as communication 21; as message 19; as performance of language 1; as work 96
text-immanent approach 8, 9, 29
textual criticism 14
textual form of reality 33
texture: aesthetic, *see* inner texture; argumentative, *see* inner texture; four arenas of 3, 16, 24; ideological, *see* ideological texture; inner, *see* inner texture; narrational, *see* inner texture; progressive, *see* inner texture; repetitive, *see* inner texture; repetitive–progressive, *see* inner texture; sensory–aesthetic, *see* inner texture; social and cultural, *see* social and cultural texture

thaumaturgic argumentation: *see* social texture
theological criticism 42
theology 3, 10–12, 15
theory: anthropological 144–6, 159; rhetorical 164; sociological 144–7, 154, 156, 159
thesis 77, 78, 80–2, 185
thick description 164, 179–80, 187, 232
topics: common social and cultural 159–66, 179–82; specific social 147–59; *see also* cultural texture; final cultural categories
tradition criticism 15
transformation 11

utopian argumentation: *see* social texture

verbal signs 21–3, 32
voice 35; as medium for consciousness 34; narrator's 72, 86, 92; narrator's questions 72–5, 77; social and ideological location 34

webs of signification 30, 65
world: ancient Mediterranean 21, 22, 38; historical 15; interpreter's 20–2, 24–7, narrative 118; New Testament textual 7, 161; represented 7, 21, 22, 24, 32, 34, 35; textual 6, 7, 22, 23
written testimony 53, 61, 78, 82–4, 88